What they're saying about *The Last Superstition*

"New Atheists Richard Dawkins, Christopher Hitchens, Daniel Dennett, and Sam Harris get their comeuppance from philosopher Feser in the spirit with which they abuse believers. 'Their books stand out for their manifest ignorance' of the Western religious tradition, he says, 'and for the breathtaking shallowness of their philosophical analysis of religious matters.' Far better than such no-quarters rhetoric, however, are the review of pre-Aristotelian philosophy and the summary of Aristotelian metaphysics and Thomas Aquinas' refinements of Aristotle that make up the heart, soul, and bulk of the book. Feser chooses to argue from Aristotle because he was not arguing from any religious perspective and because Aristotle's logic, his rationality, hasn't been improved upon or refuted by modern philosophy. Aristotle's proof that there is a prime mover or pure being – God – remains solid. Ignoramuses like the four horsemen of the apostasy, whose factual errors, half-truths, and mischaracterization Feser highlights with contemptuous glee, 'refute' Aristotle only by changing the playing field from metaphysics to science, from philosophical realism to materialism. With energy and humor as well as transparent exposition, Feser reestablishes the unassailable superiority of classical philosophy."
– Ray Olson, *ALA Booklist* starred review

"*The Last Superstition* should be assigned reading, and not only for those who think philosophical know-nothings like Richard Dawkins and Christopher Hitchens hot stuff. 'Secularism,' says author Edward Feser, 'is, necessarily and inherently, a deeply irrational and immoral view of the world, and the more thoroughly it is assimilated by its adherents, the more thoroughly do they cut themselves off from the very possibility of rational and moral understanding.' Feser gives the 'New Atheists' a dose of their own polemical medicine, but with a difference: Unlike them, he knows what he is doing. This rollicking counterattack is learned, carefully reasoned, and philosophically astute."
– J. Budziszewski, University of Texas at Austin, author of *What We Can't Not Know: A Guide*.

"Try to imagine the *Summa contra Gentiles* as written by Keith Olbermann, and you will have some idea of the tone and style of *The Last Superstition: A Refutation of the New Atheism*. The book's author, Edward Feser, is an immensely talented Aristotelico-Thomistic philosopher, and the pages he devotes to explaining the proofs for the existence of God are as clear, cogent, and convincing as any I've ever read (and I've read many)." – Michael Potemra, *National Review*

Other titles of interest from St. Augustine's Press

Aristotle, *Aristotle – On Poetics*; trans. S. Benardete & M. Davis
Aristotle, *Physics, Or Natural Hearing*
Joseph Owens, C.SS.R., *Aristotle's Gradations of of Being in* Metaphysics E–H
St. Augustine, *On Order [De Ordine]*
Plato, *The Symposium of Plato: The Shelley Translation*
Thomas Aquinas, *Commentary on Aristotle's* Metaphysics
Thomas Aquinas, *Commentary on Aristotle's* Nicomachean Ethics
Thomas Aquinas, *Commentary on Aristotle's* Posterior Analytics
Thomas Aquinas, *Commentary on Aristotle's* De Anima
Thomas Aquinas, *Commentary on Aristotle's* Physics
Thomas Aquinas, *Disputed Questions on Virtue*
John of St. Thomas, *Introduction to the* Summa Theologiae . . .
John Poinsot [John of St. Thomas], *Tractatus de Signis*
Roger Pouivet, *After Wittgenstein, St. Thomas*
Charles P. Nemeth, *Aquinas on Crime*
Francisco Suarez, S.J., *Metaphysical Demonstration to the Existence of God*
Gabriel Marcel, *The Mystery of Being* (in two volumes)
Gabriel Marcel, *Man against Mass Society*
Gabriel Marcel, *Homo Viator: Introduction to the Metaphysic of Hope*
Josef Pieper, *In Tune with the World*
Josef Pieper, *Happiness and Contemplation*
Josef Pieper, *Scholasticism*
Josef Pieper, *The Silence of St. Thomas*
Fulvio di Blasi, et al., *Ethics without God*
Fulvio di Blasi, *God and the Natural Law*
Jacques Maritain, *Natural Law: Reflections on Theory and Practice*
Germain Grisez, *God? A Philosophical Preface to Faith*
Rémi Brague, *Eccentric Culture: A History of Western Civilization*
Predrag Cicovacki, *Dostoevsky and the Affirmation of Life*
Peter Augustine Lawler, *Homeless and at Home in America*
John C. Calhoun, *A Disquisition on Government*
Peter Geach, *God and the Soul*
Leszek Kolakowski, *My Correct Views on Everything*
Leszek Kolakowski, *Religion: If There Is No God . . .*
Peter Kreeft, *The Philosophy of Jesus*
Peter Kreeft, *Jesus-Shock*
Roger Scruton, *The Meaning of Conservatism*
Nalin Ranasinghe, *Socrates in the Underworld: On Plato's* Gorgias
James V. Schall, *The Sum Total of Human Happiness*
Zbigniew Janowski, *Augustinian-Cartesian Index*
Zbigniew Janowski, *How to Read Descartes's Meditations*

THE LAST SUPERSTITION

A Refutation of the New Atheism

Edward Feser

ST. AUGUSTINE'S PRESS
South Bend, Indiana
2008

Manufactured in the United States of America.

2 3 4 5 6   14 13 12 11 10 09 08

Library of Congress Cataloging in Publication Data
Feser, Edward.
The last superstition: a refutation of the new atheism /
Edward Feser.
p. cm.
Includes bibliographical references and index.
ISBN-13: 978-1-58731-451-3 (hardcover: alk. paper)
ISBN-10: 1-58731-451-7 (hardcover: alk. paper)
1. God. 2. Atheism. I. Title.
BL473.F47 2008
211 – dc22   2008030859

∞ The paper used in this publication meets the minimum requirements of the American National Standard for Information Sciences - Permanence of Paper for Printed Materials, ANSI Z39.48-1984.

ST. AUGUSTINE'S PRESS
www.staugustine.net

Table of Contents

Preface and Acknowledgments

"And when the orator instead of putting an ass in the place of a horse puts good for evil being himself as ignorant of their true nature as the city on which he imposes is ignorant; and having studied the notions of the multitude, falsely persuades them not about 'the shadow of an ass,' which he confounds with a horse, but about good which he confounds with evil – what will be the harvest which rhetoric will be likely to gather after the sowing of that seed?"

Plato, *Phaedrus*[1]

"A small error in the beginning of something is a great one at the end."

St. Thomas Aquinas (paraphrasing Aristotle),
On Being and Essence[2]

At the time of this writing, exactly one week has passed since the Supreme Court of the State of California decreed that homosexuals have a "basic civil right" to marry someone of the same sex. Whether these Golden State solons will follow up their remarkable finding with a ruling to the effect that an ass is the same as a horse, it is too early to say; but they have already gone well beyond the sophistical orator of Plato's dialogue in "confounding good with evil," not to mention reason with insanity. Malcolm Muggeridge famously said that "without God we are left with a choice of succumbing to megalomania or erotomania."[3] The court's majority, in declaring by sheer judicial fiat the equal dignity under law of the family and sodomy, would appear to have gone Muggeridge one better by succumbing to both at once.

The reference to God is apropos. The successes of the movement to recognize "same-sex marriage" have been nothing if not sudden. Just over a decade ago the very idea would have been laughed off as crackpot or extreme; now it is those who oppose it who are frequently labeled crackpots and extremists. But equally sudden has been the rise of ostentatious unbelief as the de rigueur position of the smart set. Mainstream progressives and non-conformists of earlier generations would have found it necessary to profess belief in at least a "social gospel" and to hide their doubts about the metaphysical claims of religion behind a haze of pseudo-theological psychobabble. Yet atheist chic is now, out of the blue as it were, the stuff of best sellers, celebrity endorsements, and suburban reading groups. It is as if the urbane cocktail hour secularist liberalism of the twentieth century has, by way of the slow but sure inebriation produced by an unbroken series of social and judicial triumphs, now become in the twenty-first century fall-down-sloppy drunk and lost all inhibition, by turns blaspheming, whoring, and otherwise offending against all sane and decent sensibilities as the mood strikes it.

The confluence of these developments is no accident, though not for the reasons liberal secularists suppose. To their minds (or what is left of them) sexual libertinism and contempt for religion, as *public*, *mass* phenomena (rather than as the private eccentricities of a decadent elite, which of course have always been with us) constitute the final victory of reason, twin fruits of the modern scientific worldview whose full consequences are only now becoming widely perceived over four centuries after its birth. But in reality they are (to paraphrase Aquinas paraphrasing Aristotle) two very "great errors" that have followed gradually but inevitably, not upon any actual finding of modern science, but rather upon what might at first glance seem at most a relatively "small error" of a philosophical nature committed by the founders of modern science and modern philosophy.

This is a book about that error: about what the error is, why it is an error, what its consequences are, and how correcting it reveals that it is a (certain kind of) moral and religious traditionalist, and not the secular liberal, who is the true upholder of reason.

Disgust and distress over the New Atheism of Richard Dawkins and his ilk and at the near total collapse of traditional morality represented by "same-sex marriage" and related phenomena were only half of the motivation for my writing the essay that follows. The other half was disgust and distress over the largely inept and ineffective (as it seems to me) response to these developments put forward by many religious and political conservatives. Rather than counter the skeptic's false assertion that religion is necessarily based on "faith" (in the bastardized sense of the will to believe something in the absence of evidence), too many contemporary defenders of religion seem content to suggest that lots of what secularists believe is also based on faith, that religious belief is in any case here to stay and has certain social benefits, and so on. In the face of judicial decisions like the one recently made in California, too many conservatives natter on about whether it ought to be the courts or "the people" who get to "define" marriage, effectively conceding to their opponents the idiotic supposition that the question fundamentally concerns what meaning we ought arbitrarily to attach to a certain word.

But the most important thing to know about the belief that God exists is not that most citizens happen (for now anyway) to share it, that it tends to uphold public morality, and so forth. The most important thing to know about it is that it is *true*, and demonstrably so. Similarly, the most important thing to know about "same-sex marriage" is not that it has been lawlessly imposed by certain courts even though a majority of citizens happen (again, for now anyway) to oppose it. The most important thing to know about it is that the very idea is a metaphysical absurdity and a moral abomination, and (again) demonstrably so. It is no more up to the courts *or* "the people" to "define" marriage or to decide whether religion is a good thing than it is up to them to "define" whether the Pythagorean Theorem is true of right triangles, or whether water has the chemical structure H_2O. In each case, what is at issue is a matter of objective fact that it is the business of reason to discover rather than democratic procedure to stipulate.

What is needed to counteract the antireligious and libertine madness of the present time, then, is not crude populism or short-term political strategizing, but a rethinking of the relevant issues back to first principles. If you are someone who agrees that these developments constitute a kind of madness, and want to understand how we have reached such a low point in the history of our civilization, you will want to read this book. If you are someone who does not regard them as madness, you *need* to read it – to see (if I may say so) the error of your ways, or, if that is not likely, then at least to understand the point of view of those who disagree with you.

I want to thank my agent Giles Anderson for initiating this project, and my publisher Bruce Fingerhut for bringing it to fruition. During the many months on which I worked to complete the book, it often seemed as if I was doing little else. For this reason (and for so many others too) I owe my greatest debt to my beloved wife Rachel and to our dear children Benedict, Gemma, Kilian, and Helena, for their patience and love. It is to them that I dedicate this book, though I dedicate it also, and above all, *ad maiorem Dei gloriam*. These dedications are by no means pro forma. If this seems to be an angry book, that is because it is. But I hope that it is also, and more deeply, an expression of loyalty, gratitude, and love – for God and his many gifts, for family, and for a civilization that once defined itself in terms of these things, and which, even in its current depressing decadence, has managed to pass them on to me and to my loved ones.

In this connection I should make it clear at the outset that this is not a defense of an amorphous ecumenical something called "religion," but only and specifically of the classical theism and traditional morality of Western civilization, which, I maintain, are superior – rationally, morally, and socio-politically superior – to absolutely every alternative on offer. Nor am I suggesting merely that these founding elements of our civilization be permitted, hat in hand, to maintain a "place at the table" of some great multicultural smorgasbord alongside the secularist liberalism that seeks to abolish them. I hold instead that they ought to be restored to their rightful place as the guiding principles of Western thought, society, and politics, and that, accordingly, secularism ought to be driven back into the intellectual and political margins whence it came, and to which it would consign religion and traditional morality. For however well-meaning this or that individual liberal secularist may be, his *creed* is, I maintain (and to paraphrase Dawkins's infamous description of critics of evolution) "ignorant, stupid, insane, and wicked."[4] It is a clear and present danger to the stability of any society, and to the eternal destiny of any soul, that falls under its malign influence. For when the consequences of its philosophical foundations are worked out consistently, it can be seen to undermine the very possibility of rationality and morality themselves. As this book will show, reason itself testifies that against the pest of secularist progressivism, there can be only one remedy: *Écrasez l'infâme*.

1. Bad Religion

In 2004 the philosopher Antony Flew, who had been to that time perhaps the world's most prominent atheist, announced that he had changed his mind. While he had no intention of embracing Christianity or any of the other traditional monotheistic religions, he had, he revealed, been led by philosophical arguments to conclude that there really is a God after all – specifically, a First Cause of the universe of the sort described by Aristotle. The Aristotelian rationale for Flew's change of view might be as surprising as the conversion itself. Aristotle and his teacher Plato are almost universally regarded as the two greatest philosophers ever to have lived. Their arguments have been known and studied for over 2,300 years. Flew was 81 years old at the time, and had been for over fifty years one of the most influential and respected philosophers in the world. Surely, one would have thought, there were no arguments for the existence of God he hadn't already heard before. And yet at the end of his career, and in the face of the atheism he had for half a century made his reputation defending, Flew found himself admitting that the ancient Greek thinker the Medievals referred to simply as "The Philosopher" had been right all along. "I was not a specialist on Aristotle," Flew explained, "so I was reading parts of his philosophy for the first time."[1]

Outside the ranks of religious believers, the response to Flew's newfound philosophical theism seems to have been uniformly derisive. Comedian Jay Leno quipped, "Of course he believes in God now – he's 81 years old!" while another commentator speculated that "confronted by the end of life," Flew was simply "making one final desperate attempt at salvation" (though Flew had made it clear that he still did not believe in an afterlife).[2] One philosopher of a secular bent dismissed his conversion as "sad" and "an embarrassment," averring that "old age, as we know, takes its toll on people in many different ways" and that Flew's understanding of relevant scientific theory "is not, shall we say, robust."[3] Another accused Flew of "willfully sloppy scholarship."[4] Other than alleging that his views rested on a scientifically disreputable "Intelligent Design" theory, and peremptorily dismissing them on that basis, most of Flew's critics showed little interest in exploring in any detail what grounds he might have had for changing his mind. In particular, they studiously ignored the central role a reconsideration of Aristotle's philosophy evidently played in his change of view.[5] While Flew's conversion was still just a rumor, his secularist admirers had scrambled furiously to deny that it could be true of so intelligent a man; when he confirmed the rumors himself, he was treated as a heretic and dupe of the fundamentalist enemy, and his arguments dismissed as unworthy of serious attention. "I have been denounced by my fellow unbelievers for stupidity, betrayal, senility and everything you could think of," Flew complained, "and none of them have read a word that I have ever written."[6]

"The New Atheism"

This episode illustrates, in several respects, the main themes of this book. In their condescending assumption that belief in God could only be the product of wishful thinking, stupidity, ignorance, or intellectual dishonesty; in their corresponding refusal seriously to consider the possibility that that belief might be true and the arguments for it sound; and in their glib supposition that the only rational considerations relevant to the question are "scientific" ones, rather than philosophical; in all of these attitudes, Flew's critics manifest the quintessential mindset of modern secularism. And insofar as its self-satisfied *a priori* dismissal of outsiders as benighted, and of defectors as wicked or mad, insulates it from ever having to deal with serious criticism, it is a mindset that echoes the closed-minded prejudice and irrationality it typically attributes to religious believers themselves. Secularism is, in its way, a religion to itself, and it is a religion that cannot tolerate infidels or heretics. We shall see by the end of this book that this is by no means an accident, a mere byproduct of the passion and folly to which every human being succumbs from time to time. For secularism is, *necessarily and inherently*, a deeply irrational and immoral view of the world, and the more thoroughly it is assimilated by its adherents, the more thoroughly do they cut themselves off from the very possibility of rational and moral understanding. Moreover, and for this very reason, its adherents unavoidably find it difficult, indeed almost impossible, to perceive their true condition. The less they know, the less they know it.

These are, I realize, rather striking claims to make, not least because they are so utterly contrary to the self-understanding of secularists themselves. In the days and weeks following the 2004 U.S. presidential election – an election in which a concern for traditional moral and religious values is widely thought to have played a decisive part – secularists took to defining themselves as members of the "reality-based community," in contrast to the purportedly "faith-based community" of religious believers. As if in answer to Flew's abandonment of atheism, two secularist philosophers have, with much fanfare, recently published works purporting to demonstrate the moral and rational deficiencies of traditional religious belief: Sam Harris's *The End of Faith: Religion, Terror, and the Future of Reason* and Daniel Dennett's *Breaking the Spell: Religion as a Natural Phenomenon*. These books were soon followed by biologist Richard Dawkins's *The God Delusion* and journalist Christopher Hitchens's *God is Not Great: How Religion Poisons Everything*, and the press quickly took to pitting the "New Atheism" of Harris, Dennett, Dawkins, and Hitchens against a purportedly resurgent irrationalism and fundamentalism heralded by "Intelligent Design" advocates, "theocons," and other secularist bogeymen.[7] Several years ago, Dennett famously suggested in a *New York Times* piece that secularists adopt the label "brights" to distinguish them from religious believers.[8] His proposal doesn't seem to have caught on (perhaps because a grown man who goes around earnestly chirping "I'm a bright!" surely sounds rather like an idiot). But whatever the rhetorical deficiencies of "bright," it perfectly encapsulates the self-satisfaction of the secularist mentality: "We're intelligent, informed, and rational, while religious believers are stupid, ignorant, and irrational, not at all bright like us."

The irony is that to anyone who actually knows something about the history and theology of the Western religious tradition for which Harris, Dennett, Dawkins, and Hitchens show so much contempt, their books stand out for their manifest ignorance of that tradition and for the breathtaking shallowness of their philosophical analysis of religious matters. Indeed, as we will see, these authors do not even so much as understand what the word "faith" itself has actually meant, historically, within the mainstream of that tradition. One gets the impression that the bulk of their education in Christian theology consisted of reading *Elmer Gantry* while in college, supplemented with a viewing of *Inherit the Wind* and a Sunday morning spent channel-surfing televangelists. Nor do they evince the slightest awareness of the historical centrality of ideas deriving from classical philosophy – the tradition of thought deriving from Plato and Aristotle and whose greatest representatives within Christianity are Augustine and Thomas Aquinas – to the content and self-understanding of the mainstream Western religious tradition. This is perhaps not surprising in the case of either Dawkins – a writer of pop science books who evidently wouldn't know metaphysics from Metamucil – or *Vanity Fair* boy Hitchens, who probably thinks metaphysics is the sort of thing people like Shirley MacLaine start babbling about when they've lost their box office cachet. But such ignorance is simply disgraceful in the case of Dennett and Harris, who are trained philosophers. One would never guess from reading any of the "New Atheists" (not to mention the works of countless other secularist intellectuals) that the vast majority of the greatest philosophers and scientists in the history of Western civilization – not only the thinkers just mentioned but also many modern thinkers outside the classical tradition, including Descartes, Leibniz, Locke, Berkeley, Boyle, Newton, and on and on – have firmly believed in the existence of God, and on the basis of entirely rational arguments. And, needless to say, they offer their readers no account of the grave philosophical challenges to which the naturalism they are committed to – the view that the natural, material world is all that exists and that empirical science is the only rational source of knowledge – has consistently been subjected throughout the history of philosophy, and which many influential and sophisticated contemporary philosophers continue to press upon it.

Yet the fact is that, contrary to the standard caricature of philosophers as inveterate skeptics who have no truck with religion, among philosophers the view that the existence of God can be rationally demonstrated "enjoyed wide currency, if not hegemony . . . from classical antiquity until well after the dawn of modernity" (to quote the philosopher David Conway, writing in a book that had a major influence on Flew's conversion to philosophical theism)[9]; and the suggestion that human reason can be accounted for in purely materialistic terms has, historically speaking, been regarded by most philosophers as a logical absurdity, a demonstrable falsehood. Within the classical Western philosophical tradition, belief in the existence of God and the falsity of materialism has generally been thought to rest firmly and squarely on *reason*, not "faith."

The old philosophy

This brings us to another main theme of this book illustrated by the Flew episode, and indeed by Flew himself. When one seriously comes to understand the classical philosophical tradition represented by Plato, Aristotle, Augustine, and Aquinas – and not merely the potted caricatures of it that even many professional philosophers, to their shame, tend to rely on – one learns just how contingent and open to question are the various modern, and typically "naturalistic," philosophical assumptions that most contemporary thinkers (and certainly most secularists) simply take for granted without rational argument. And since the classical tradition is theistic and supernaturalist through and through, one also comes to see how powerful are the rational foundations of the Western religious tradition. Indeed, one comes to realize that the very possibility of reason and morality is deeply problematic at best on a modern naturalistic conception of the world, but perfectly intelligible on the classical philosophical worldview and the religious vision it sustains. More than that: One comes to see that it is very likely *only* on the classical Western philosophical-cum-religious worldview that we can make sense of reason and morality. The truth is precisely the opposite of what secularism claims: Only a (certain kind of) religious view of the world is rational, morally responsible, and sane; and an irreligious worldview is accordingly deeply irrational, immoral, and indeed insane. Secularism can never truly rest on reason, but only on "faith," as secularists themselves understand that term (or rather misunderstand it, as we shall see): an unshakable commitment grounded not in reason but rather in sheer willfulness, a deeply ingrained desire to *want* things to be a certain way regardless of whether the evidence shows they are that way.

Again, these are bold claims, and they will be defended at length in the pages to follow. Suffice it for now to note, for what it is worth – and since we have already been considering the individual case of one specific philosopher, Flew – that my own experience bears them out. I was myself for many years a convinced atheist and naturalist. This is not to begin some emotional Road to Damascus saga: I was never militantly hostile to religion (Dennett and his ilk, I am glad to be able to say, always struck me as tiresome blowhards); nor did I suddenly "find Jesus" at the bottom of a whiskey bottle or at the end of some sob story, after the manner of the treacly conversion tales popular in our therapeutic age. It is just that for many years I was firmly persuaded, on intellectual grounds, that atheism and naturalism must be true, and then very gradually came to realize, again on intellectual grounds, that they were not in fact true and could not be true. This change in view began with, of all things, a consideration of the work of Gottlob Frege and Bertrand Russell, the very founders of the modern "analytic" tradition in philosophy to which Dennett and Harris, like so many secularists, are adherents. Frege put forward a powerful defense of a kind of Platonism – the view that there exists, in addition to the material world and the "world" within the human mind, a "third realm" of abstract entities, in particular of meanings and of mathematical objects like numbers – as the only way to make sense of the very possibility of linguistic communication. Russell argued that the nature of perceptual experience and of scientific theorizing entails that we can actually know very little about the material world, and in particular only its abstract structure but not its intrinsic nature. Their work convinced me how naïve and unfounded is the assumption of materialists and naturalists that the material world is the touchstone of reality and that we have better knowledge of it than of anything else. This conclusion was reinforced, to my mind, by the work of contemporary philosophers like John

Searle and Thomas Nagel – purely secular thinkers like Frege and Russell, incidentally – who despite their own commitment to naturalism argued that no existing materialist attempt to explain the human mind has come anywhere close to succeeding.[10]

The work of other contemporary philosophers like Elizabeth Anscombe and Alasdair MacIntyre showed me how powerful and still relevant Aristotle's work was, particularly in the field of ethics. The writings of contemporary philosophers of religion like Alvin Plantinga and Richard Swinburne applied the most rigorous of modern philosophical methods to the defense of religious belief, and the scholarship of writers like William Lane Craig and John Haldane revealed that the arguments of classical thinkers like Thomas Aquinas had been very badly misunderstood by modern critics and commentators. All of this led me eventually to a serious reconsideration of the Aristotelian tradition in philosophy in general, and of Aquinas's adaptation of it in particular, and the end result was that I became convinced that the basic metaphysical assumptions which modern secular philosophers rather unreflectively take for granted, and which alone can make atheism seem at all plausible, were radically mistaken. The classical metaphysical picture of the world, which derives from Plato, was greatly modified first by Aristotle and later by Augustine, and was at last perfected by Aquinas and his followers, is, as I came to believe, essentially correct, and it effectively makes atheism and naturalism impossible.[11]

Now I don't expect these philosophical references to mean much, at this point anyway, to readers unfamiliar with philosophy. (We will be exploring many of them in detail before long.) My aim for now is merely to forestall the standard *ad hominem* dismissal of religious conversion as a purely subjective affair, a matter of feeling rather than reason. It was, in my own case, a matter of objective rational argument. Nor is my case unique. Contrary to the caricatures peddled in secularist literature (and which have crept into the popular culture at large), the mainstream tradition within Western religion has in fact always insisted that its basic claims must be and can be rationally justified, and indeed that they can be shown to be rationally superior to the claims of atheism and naturalism. If some religious believers nevertheless manifest an unfortunate tendency toward fideism – the view that religion rests on "faith" alone, understood as a kind of ungrounded will to believe – that is to a very great extent precisely because they have forgotten the history of their own tradition and bought into the secularist propaganda that has relentlessly been directed against it since the so-called "Enlightenment."

Secularists who indulge in such *ad hominem* criticism ought, in any case, to realize that it can often be applied to them with equal justice (and in fact with far greater justice, as we will see by the end of this book). This is certainly true of the accusation that their beliefs often rest on ignorance – a judgment shared even by some secularist thinkers themselves. The philosopher Quentin Smith, a far more serious and formidable defender of atheism than any of the so-called "New Atheists," has bemoaned the appalling lack of knowledge so many of his fellow secularist thinkers manifest when attempting to criticize religious belief. For they tend to show no awareness of the sophisticated arguments presented by philosophers of a religious bent, preferring instead to attack straw men and present simple-minded journalistic caricatures of religious belief. The upshot, in Smith's view, is that apart from those few secularist philosophers who, like himself, specialize in familiarizing themselves with and attempting to answer the arguments of serious religious thinkers, "the great majority of naturalist philosophers have an unjustified belief that naturalism is true and an unjustified belief that theism (or supernaturalism) is false."[12] Political philosopher Jeremy Waldron (by no means a member of the "religious right") makes a similar judgment about the attitudes secularists display toward religious arguments in politics:

> Secular theorists often assume they know what a religious argument is like: they present it as a crude prescription from God, backed up with threat of hellfire, derived from general or particular revelation, and they contrast it with the elegant complexity of a philosophical argument by Rawls (say) or Dworkin. With this image in mind, they think it obvious that religious argument should be excluded from public life. . . . But those who have bothered to make themselves familiar with existing religious-based arguments in modern political theory know that this is mostly a travesty . . [13]

Moreover, even when secular intellectuals do bother to consider the views of serious religious thinkers, they have a peculiar tendency to apply to them a standard they do not apply to other controversial arguments. A secularist can argue for the most offensive and intuitively preposterous conclusions – that there is nothing intrinsically wrong with bestiality, necrophilia, or infanticide, say, as Princeton ethicist Peter Singer suggests – and even philosophers who disagree with those conclusions are prepared to treat them with the very greatest seriousness, insisting that such views must, however prima facie implausible, at least get a respectful hearing. In every other area of controversy, virtually no argument is ever considered decisively refuted: The common attitude is that there is always some way a defender of a particular position might reply to the standard objections, so that the position must be considered "still on the table." Yet where, say, an argument for the existence of God is concerned, the mere fact that someone somewhere has raised an objection to it is treated as proof positive that the religious believer simply "hasn't made his case" and that his argument needn't be paid any further attention. Secular ideas are guaranteed consideration as long as the thinker presenting them possesses a minimum of argumentative and rhetorical ability. However speculative, intuitively implausible, or even crackpot, they are valued as ways of "making us think," of "advancing the discussion," and of "looking at things in a new way," and a place is made for them on the academic reading list and in the college curriculum. Religious ideas, by contrast, are treated as if only something as incontrovertible as a geometrical proof in their defense could make them worthy of a moment's notice.

That secularists, who pride themselves on their supposed greater knowledge and reasonableness, so often condemn religious believers in studied ignorance of what they really believe or without applying to them the standards by which they would judge their own ideas, indicates that another factor often attributed to such believers is at work here – namely wishful thinking, a desire for some claim to be true which is so powerful that it trumps a sober consideration of the evidence for it. For it is by no means the case that only those who believe in God could possibly have a vested interest in the question of His existence. Philosopher Thomas Nagel acknowledges that a "fear of religion" seems often to underlie the work of his fellow secularist intellectuals, and that it has had "large and often pernicious consequences for modern intellectual life." He writes:

> I speak from experience, being strongly subject to this fear myself: I want atheism to be true and am made uneasy by the fact that some of the most intelligent and well-informed people I know are religious believers. It isn't just that I don't believe in God and, naturally, hope that I'm right in my belief. It's that I hope there is no God! I don't want there to be a God; I don't want the universe to be like that. My guess is that this cosmic authority problem is not a rare condition and that it is responsible for much of the scientism and reductionism of our time. One of the tendencies it supports is the ludicrous overuse of evolutionary biology to explain everything about human life, including everything about the human mind.[14]

It is true that a fear of death, a craving for cosmic justice, and a desire to see our lives as meaningful can lead us to want to believe that we have immortal souls specially created by a God who will reward or punish us for our deeds in this life. But it is no less true that a desire to be free of traditional moral standards, and a fear of certain (real or imagined) political and social consequences of the truth of religious belief, can also lead us to want to believe that we are just clever animals with no purpose to our lives other than the purposes we choose to give them, and that there is no cosmic judge who will punish us for disobeying an objective moral law. Atheism, like religion, can often rest more on a will to believe than on dispassionate rational arguments. Indeed, as the philosopher C.F.J. Martin has pointed out, the element of divine punishment – traditionally understood in the monotheistic religions as a sentence of eternal damnation in Hell – shows that atheism is hardly less plausibly motivated by wishful thinking than theism is. For while it is hard to understand why someone would want to believe that he is in danger of everlasting hellfire, it is not at all hard to see why one would desperately want not to believe this.[15]

The abuse of science

Nagel's reference to evolutionary biology brings us to the third and final theme of this book illustrated by the Flew episode, namely the assumption that the question of whether religious belief is rationally justifiable is ultimately a scientific one, and that anyone who understands modern science will see that it favors the secularist answer. Nagel goes on to note that "Darwin enabled modern secular culture to heave a great collective sigh of relief, by apparently providing a way to eliminate purpose, meaning, and design as fundamental features of the world."[16] In fact the idea that science eliminates "purpose, meaning, and design as fundamental features of the world" goes back, as we will see, long before Darwin, to the very beginnings of modern science. And it informs the widespread perception that there has for centuries been a war between science and religion and that religion has been steadily losing.

Yet the idea in question is not itself a *scientific* one at all, but a *philosophical* one; and accordingly, the fabled "science versus religion" war is a myth – indeed, one might think of it as the founding myth of modern secularism, with Galileo and Newton taking the place of Romulus and Remus. For untold ages, modern secularists have told themselves (and everyone else), mankind lay in the darkness of religious bigotry, ignorance, and unreason; then came Science, and ever since the March of Progress has been relentless. The founding fathers of the scientific revolution got the ball rolling, Darwin accelerated it considerably, and now (so the story goes) a complete account of the universe in general and of human nature in particular in entirely materialistic terms – and in particular, without any reference whatsoever to "purpose, meaning, and design" – is within our grasp. Like most founding myths, this one is a mixture of oversimplification and falsehood. As historians of the period know, the Middle Ages were simply not in fact the benighted era of uniform superstition and barbarism portrayed in secular polemic and popular culture.[17] And the elimination of purpose and meaning from the modern conception of the material universe was not and is not a "result" or "discovery" of modern science, but rather a *philosophical interpretation* of the results of modern science which owes more to early modern secularist philosophers like Hobbes and Hume – as well as to non-atheistic but equally anti-medieval philosophers like Descartes, Locke, and Kant – than it does to the great scientists of the last few centuries (even if many of these scientists happened to accept this philosophical interpretation of their results). Finally, a complete account of the universe and of human nature in terms that make no reference whatsoever to purpose, meaning, and design is not within our grasp and never will be, for the simple reason that such an "account" is *in principle impossible*, and the hope for it based on nothing more than muddle-headedness mixed with wishful thinking. We can no more eliminate purpose and meaning from nature than we can square the circle.

Once again I am, I know, making large claims, but it is the point of the chapters that follow to justify them. Suffice it for now to say that the so-called "war between science and religion" is really a war between two rival *philosophical* worldviews, and not at bottom a scientific or theological dispute at all. Occasionally you'll find a secularist who admits as much. Nagel is one example. Another is biologist Richard Lewontin, who has written:

> Our willingness to accept scientific claims that are against common sense is the key to an understanding of the real struggle between science and the supernatural. We take the side of science in spite of the patent absurdity of some of its constructs, in spite of its failure to fulfill many of its extravagant promises of health and life, in spite of the tolerance of the scientific community for unsubstantiated just-so stories, because we have a prior commitment, a commitment to materialism. . . . It is not that the methods and institutions of science somehow compel us to accept a material explanation of the phenomenal world but, on the contrary, that we are forced by our a priori adherence to material causes to create an apparatus of investigation and a set of concepts that produce material explanations, no matter how counterintuitive, no matter how mystifying to the uninitiated. Moreover, that materialism is absolute, for we cannot allow a divine foot in the door.[18]

Similarly, physicist Paul Davies tells us that "science takes as its *starting point* the *assumption* that life wasn't made by a god or a supernatural being," and acknowledges that, partially out of fear of "open[ing] the door to religious fundamentalists . . . many investigators feel uneasy about stating in public that the origin of life is a mystery, even though behind closed doors they freely admit that they are baffled."[19] Among prominent contemporary philosophers, Tyler Burge opines that "materialism is not established, or even clearly supported, by science" and that its hold over his peers is analogous to that of a "political or religious ideology"[20]; John Searle tells us that "materialism is the religion of our time," that "like more traditional religions, it is accepted without question and . . . provides the framework within which other questions can be posed, addressed, and answered," and that "materialists are convinced, with a quasi-religious faith, that their view must be right"[21]; and William Lycan admits, in what he himself calls "an uncharacteristic exercise in intellectual honesty," that the arguments for materialism are no better than the arguments against it, that his "own faith in materialism is based on science-worship," and that "we also always hold our opponents to higher standards of argumentation than we obey ourselves."[22]

The conflict, then, is not over any actual results or discoveries of science, but rather over the more fundamental philosophical question of what sorts of results or discoveries will be allowed to *count* as "scientific" in the first place. In particular, it is a war between, on the one hand, what I have called the classical philosophical vision of Plato, Aristotle, Augustine, and Aquinas, and on the other hand, the naturalistic orthodoxy of contemporary secularism, whose premises derive from modern philosophers like the ones mentioned above. As we shall see, the radical differences between these worldviews with respect to what at first glance might seem fairly abstruse questions of metaphysics – the relationship between the universal and the particular, form and matter, substance and attributes, the nature of cause and effect, and so forth – in fact have dramatic repercussions for religion, morality, and even politics. It is only when the results of modern science are interpreted in naturalistic metaphysical terms that they can be made to seem incompatible with traditional religious belief, and it is only when modern naturalistic metaphysical assumptions are taken for granted, and the classical alternatives neglected, that the philosophical arguments for the traditional religious worldview (e.g. for the existence of God, the immortality of the soul, and the natural law conception of morality) can be made to seem problematic. By ignoring the challenge posed by the classical philosophical worldview, and distorting its key ideas and arguments on those rare occasions when it is taken account of at all, secularism maintains its illusory status as the rational default position. Prominent naturalists like the New Atheists are sure to "win" the public debate with their traditional religious critics every time, with the general public unaware that the game is being played with metaphysically loaded dice.

Religion and counter-religion

I have said that secularism is itself a kind of religion. Admittedly, this might seem odd considering that secularists think of themselves, of course, as rejecting all religion. So is there anything more to the charge than mere rhetorical turnabout, the flinging of an insult back at the person who first made it? There is – not least because I am very far from regarding "religion" and "religious" as *per se* insulting descriptions. Indeed, for reasons that will be clear by the end of this book – and they are *reasons*, not the ludicrous straw-man conception of "faith" at which the "New Atheists" (like all village atheists) like to take pot shots – I would say that a truly religious man is, all things being equal (and of course they are often very far from equal), for that reason and to that extent a sane and virtuous man; while a man who is irreligious, and especially a man who is positively hostile to religion, is (again, all things being equal) for that very reason and to that extent a bad man, and an irrational man. In short, a religious sensibility, properly understood, is a moral and intellectual virtue; and indifference or hostility to religion is a moral and intellectual vice. So, when I say that secularism is a religion, and imply that this is a bad thing, I am speaking very loosely, "speaking with the vulgar" as it were – in particular, speaking with secularists themselves (there are no greater vulgarians), insofar as I have claimed that secularists are "religious" in their own eccentric sense of that word as connoting dogmatism, ignorance, and intolerance.

But there is more to it than this. Many secularists like to assimilate religion to superstition, when in fact superstition is not religion *per se* but at most the corruption of true religion – just as tyranny is not government *per se* but merely the corruption of government, just as wage labor is comparable to slavery only very remotely and only under the very worst circumstances, and just as prostitution is not in any interesting sense even remotely comparable to marriage despite some extremely superficial analogies. Of course, there are people who deny that such obvious differences are real – Marxists, anarchists, radical feminists, and other denizens of the intellectual slums, who mistake an inability to make the simplest conceptual distinctions for deep insight. To these, it seems, we can add the ranks of secularist "thinkers." When "New Atheists" and their ilk assure us in all seriousness that believing in God is just like believing in the Easter bunny, or that teaching religion is tantamount to child abuse, they remind me of the freshman philosophy student who once proudly declared to me his "discovery" that taking a girl out on a date was really no different from hiring a call girl, since what it's "all about" is giving something in exchange for sex. In both cases, the analysis put forward is evidence not of profound philosophical understanding, but merely of being a shallow and sophomoric jackass.

Yet many secularists believe, or at least give every appearance of believing, things that are even more crassly stupid than this, things that merit *them* the label "superstitious" if anyone merits it. As the late David Stove has argued at length, Dawkins's famous claim that we are all "manipulated" by our "selfish genes" could only be both true and interesting if interpreted, absurdly, as a literal attribution of superhuman intelligence and cunning to what are quite obviously mindless tiny bits of biological matter – that is, as an ascription of godlike powers to genes.[23] (We shall see later why Dawkins and other "naturalistic" thinkers are, whether they intend this or not, necessarily pushed into such absurdities by the logic of their attempt to combine materialism with the biological fact that genes are carriers of information.) Dawkins also claims (as does his acolyte Dennett) that our minds are nothing more than congeries of "memes" – ideas, practices, and other cultural phenomena – that "compete" with one another the way genes do, and that the process of cultural evolution generated by this "competition" is what really determines our thoughts and behaviors. It is "natural selection" itself that is now treated as a pseudo-deity, guiding all our fates, with Dennett in particular constantly and shamelessly making reference to the "Good Design," etc., that evolution manifests, even though "evolution," as a purportedly blind and purposeless natural process, couldn't in any true and interesting sense manifest "design" or "guidance" without having godlike intelligence and will. (Again, there are reasons – which we will explore later on – why Dennett *has* to speak this way in order for his "naturalistic" worldview to come off as remotely plausible, but also why he nevertheless cannot possibly do so in a way that is ultimately consistent with his materialism and atheism.) And then there is, of course (and to go back to earlier generations of secularists), the quasi-divine status Marxists afforded the Laws of History and the quasi-ecclesiastical authority they invested in the Communist Party, Comte's "Religion of Humanity," and so forth.

G.K. Chesterton probably never actually said (as he is reputed to have said) that "he who does not believe in God will believe in anything." But he surely *would* have said it had he been acquainted with the lunacies one finds peddled by contemporary secularists. At the most extreme end of the spectrum, we find "eliminative materialist" philosophers who deny the very existence of the human mind – a minority view, to be sure, but one which is (as we will see) the logical outcome of the "naturalistic" trend of modern philosophical thinking. We have already mentioned Singer's obscene defense of infanticide, necrophilia, and bestiality. Or to take what is now, alas, a far less exotic example, there is the current push for "same-sex marriage," a metaphysical absurdity on all fours with round squares (as, again, we will see later on) that even the ancient pagans would have regarded as a contemptible mark of extreme societal decadence. And then there are the various moralistic causes – environmentalism, "animal rights," vegetarianism, veganism, and the like – not all inherently mad and not endorsed by all secularists, but often given a ridiculously exaggerated importance and fanatically pursued by them, each associated with its own obsessive-compulsive quasi-sacramental rituals (sorting one's garbage into various piles for recycling, driving only "hybrid vehicles," buying only "dolphin safe" tuna, etc.). Though he would scarcely have thought it possible, Chesterton would find that New Secularist Man circa 2008 is an even more absurd creature than the incarnation with which he had to deal: A copy of *Skeptic* magazine ostentatiously tucked under his arm, the Darwin fish on the bumper of his car proudly signals his group identification with other members of the herd of "independent thinkers." He "knows" that there is no God, and he isn't sure whether even the thoughts he thinks he's having are real or not. But he *is* pretty sure that his "selfish genes" and/or his "memes" in some way manipulate his every action, and quite certain that there's nothing questionable *per se* about "marrying" another man, strangling an unwanted disabled infant, or sodomizing a goat or a corpse (if that's "what you're into"). Despite his hatred of religion, he thinks global warming a greater danger than Islamic terrorism, and whether "meat is murder" is a proposition he thinks eminently worthy of consideration. Evidently, they don't make skeptics like they used to.

A second reason for characterizing secularism as a religious phenomenon, then, is that in some respects it resembles, if not religion per se, at least a corrupted form of religion: superstition, with all the irrationality and credulity that goes along with it. But both of the "religious" characteristics of secularism I've described so far – its bigotry and its superstition – stem from a third and deeper respect in which secularism can only properly be understood in religious terms, namely that the content of secularism as a philosophy and a sensibility is entirely parasitic on religion. It is not just that secularists happen to reject and oppose religion; it's that there is nothing more to their creed than rejecting and opposing religion. This point might seem obviously true, even banal, but it is not. For secularists often regard themselves as promoting a positive intellectual and moral vision of the world, not merely a critique of religion. They claim to have something new to put in its place. Hence they not only reject faith; they endorse reason and science. They not only reject traditional morality, especially in the area of sex; they affirm the value of free choice. They not only reject ecclesiastical authority; they promote democracy and tolerance. And so on. But look more closely and you'll find that this "positive vision" is really nothing more than a restatement of the negative one. As I have said already, and as will be blindingly obvious by the end of this book, the mainstream Western religious tradition itself very firmly rests on and embraces reason and science. That tradition also insists that religious conviction and moral virtue must be adopted of one's own free will, not imposed by force; and while it holds that some of the things people choose to do are morally unacceptable, secularists, who also profess to believe that there is a difference between right and wrong, hold the same thing. The Protestant John Locke and the Catholic Second Vatican Council (to take just two examples) endorsed religious toleration and democracy, and on theological grounds at that, while secularists are none too happy with democracy when, say, it results in school boards that mandate the teaching of "Intelligent Design" theory alongside evolution. So what, pray tell, is distinctively "secularist" about reason, science, free choice, toleration, democracy, and the like? Nothing at all, as it happens. The fact is that secularists are "for" reason and science only to the extent that they don't lead to religious conclusions; they celebrate free choice only insofar as one chooses against traditional or religiously oriented morality; and they are for democracy and toleration only to the extent that these might lead to a less religiously oriented social and political order. Again, the animus against religion is not merely *a* feature of the secularist mindset; it is the *only* feature.

In this connection we might take note of a curious fact about the practice of contemporary academic philosophers with respect to religion. Like Dennett and Harris, most of them are atheists. But unlike Dennett and Harris, most have very little if anything to say about religion in their published work. They are aware that some of their fellow philosophers are religious believers, and they regard the more obviously brilliant of these religious colleagues with a grudging and bemused respect. But the work of these religious philosophers, at least where it touches on religious matters, is mostly ignored. As John Searle has put it, with evident approval:

> Nowadays nobody bothers [to attack religion], and it is considered in slightly bad taste to even raise the question of God's existence. Matters of religion are like matters of sexual preference: they are not to be discussed in public, and even the abstract questions are discussed only by bores. . . . For us, the educated members of society, the world has become demystified. . . . The result of this demystification is that we have gone beyond atheism to a point where the issue no longer matters in the way it did to earlier generations.[24]

Yet anyone who reads very deeply in the work of contemporary analytic philosophers will find that one of their main obsessions, perhaps *the* main obsession, is the project of "naturalizing" this or that phenomenon – the mind, knowledge, ethics, and so forth – or showing, in other words, that it can be entirely accounted for in terms of "natural" properties and processes of the sort compatible with (their conception of) "natural science." And given what was said above, what this ultimately means is just accounting for it in terms that make no reference to God, the soul, or any other immaterial reality. Those "tough-minded" secularist philosophers who like to pretend, to themselves and others, that they are well beyond giving religion any thought whatsoever in their day-to-day work, thus reveal by the substance of that work that they are in fact and at bottom interested in little else. In particular, their mania for "naturalizing" every philosophically problematic phenomenon they can get their hands on evinces a desire to rationalize their atheism, however indirectly. Thomas Nagel (whose *mea culpa* was quoted above) is just the rare secularist philosopher willing momentarily to let the mask drop.

Now if the content of secularism derives entirely from its opposition to religion, this does not, of course, suffice to make secularism itself a religion, any more than opposition to communism, say, makes one a communist. But then, anti-communists were often accused by their critics (usually unjustly, but let that pass) of having become, in their overzealousness, the very thing they hated. So passionate was their hatred, and so obsessively focused were they on destroying the object of their hatred rather than promoting a positive alternative, that their cure became as bad as the disease, and even manifested some of its symptoms. (Again, so it was claimed – though if you really think Joe McCarthy, for all his faults, was *remotely* comparable to Stalin, Mao, or even Castro, I've got a bridge over the *Belomorkanal* to sell you.) Well, when we consider: (a) the fact that secularism is little more than an animus against religion, without any positive content; (b) the fact that its adherents are often committed to ideas as superstitious and/or mad as any that the most corrupt forms of religion exhibit (ideas which, though not essential to secularism *per se* and thus not accepted among all secularists, nevertheless usually tend to follow upon the rejection of religion as a substitute for it); and (c) the fact that they also typically manifest toward religion and religious believers exactly the sort of ignorance, intolerance, and dogmatism they attribute to religion itself; when we add all these factors together, it is surely plausible to regard secularism as something that is as much a "religion" – as much, that is to say, the very sort of thing it claims to oppose – as anti-communism can be said to have become the very thing that *it* opposed. Indeed, more so, since (as I have said) the charges against anti-communists are mostly unfair. And since secularists themselves were so often the loudest makers of those false charges against anti-communists (communism having been one of the sacred cows of an earlier generation of secularists), it is only fitting that they should be hoist with their own petard.

So, whereas Dennett proposes explaining "religion as a natural phenomenon," I propose interpreting naturalism and secularism as religious phenomena. Or rather, if secularism is not precisely a religion, it is what we might call a *counter*-religion. It has its counter-saints (Darwin, Clarence Darrow, Carl Sagan); its "Old Testament" counter-prophets, stern and forbidding, brimming with apocalyptic doom or at least pessimism (Marx, Nietzsche, Freud); and its kinder and gentler "New Testament" counter-apostles, hopeful for a realization of the Kingdom of Godlessness on earth via "progressive" educational policy and other schemes of social uplift (Dennett, Dawkins, Harris, and Hitchens – and into the bargain, each member of this foursome even has his own Gospel). It affords a sense of identity and meaning to those beholden to it, a metaphysics to interpret the world by and a value system to live by, even if all of this is little more than a negation of the sort of metaphysics and morality associated with religion: that is to say, a counter-metaphysics, a counter-morality.

And yet it is also a belief system that is, as I have said, deeply irrational and immoral, indeed the very negation of reason and morality. Thus do I call it the *last* superstition: not merely "last" in the sense of being the superstition that remains when all the others have purportedly been abolished by it, but also "last" in the sense of being the *ultimate* superstition, "the mother of all superstitions."

Things to come

The burden of the following chapters, then, will be to show that: 1. the so-called "war between science and religion" is in fact a war between rival philosophical or metaphysical systems, namely the classical worldview of Plato, Aristotle, Augustine, and Aquinas on the one hand, and modern naturalism on the other; 2. the naturalistic worldview, on which secularism rests, makes reason and morality impossible, though they are perfectly intelligible on (indeed only intelligible on) the classical view; and 3. secularism therefore cannot fail to manifest the irrationalism and immorality it falsely attributes to religion, while the religious vision enshrined in classical philosophical theism cannot fail to commend itself to every rational and morally decent human being who correctly understands it, free of the falsehoods and caricatures of it peddled by secularist critics.

Nothing that follows will require of the reader any prior acquaintance with philosophy or its history, but the discussion will in some places get a little abstract and technical – though never dull, I think, and the dramatic relevance of the occasional abstraction or technicality to issues in religion, morality, and science will amply reward the patient reader. Some abstraction and technicality is, in any case, unavoidable. The basic philosophical case for the existence of God, the immortality of the soul, and the natural law conception of morality is at one level fairly straightforward. But the issues have become ever more greatly obscured in the centuries since so-called "Enlightenment" thinkers and their predecessors first started darkening the understanding of Western man, and a nearly impenetrable philosophical smokescreen of unexamined assumptions, falsehoods, clichés, caricatures, prejudices, propaganda, and general muddle-headedness now surrounds the average person's (including the average intellectual's) thinking about religion. It takes considerable intellectual effort to dissipate this *Kultursmog* (to borrow R. Emmett Tyrrell's apt coinage).

The task is not unlike that which faces debunkers of popular but intellectually unsupportable conspiracy theories. As Vincent Bugliosi laments in *Reclaiming History*, his recent mammoth study of the JFK assassination, "it takes only one sentence to make the argument that organized crime had Kennedy killed to get his brother, Attorney General Robert Kennedy, off its back, but it takes a great many pages to demonstrate the invalidity of that charge."[25] One of the reasons for this is that certain fallacies and errors committed by conspiracy theorists can only be exposed via painstaking examination of eyewitness testimony, ballistic evidence, historical context, and other such minutiae. Another is the bias embodied in the vast number of things that people think they know about a particular case that just aren't so. To take only one example, everyone who has read a conspiracy theory book or seen Oliver Stone's *JFK* "knows" that a single bullet couldn't possibly have made the wounds in Kennedy's neck and in Governor Connally, since Connally was sitting directly in front of the President and the shot in question came diagonally from the rear – except that Connally was demonstrably *not* sitting directly in front of Kennedy, but to the front left and slightly below him on a jump seat, making his wounds perfectly in line with the one in Kennedy's neck.[26]

Similarly, everyone "knows" that the cosmological argument for God's existence says "Everything has a cause, so the universe has a cause, namely God" and that this argument is easily refuted by asking "Well, if everything has a cause, what caused God, then?" – except that that is *not* what the cosmological argument says, and none of the philosophers who have famously defended the argument – not Aristotle, not Aquinas, not Leibniz, not anyone else – ever committed such a stupid and obvious fallacy. Everyone "knows" that to say that morality depends on religion means that God arbitrarily decides to command something or other ("just 'cause He feels like it" apparently) and the only reason to obey is fear of hellfire – except that that is *not* what it means to say that morality depends on religion, certainly not in the thinking of the many serious philosophers who have defended that claim. And so on and on. To correct widespread and tiresome misconceptions like these requires an explanation of how the classical philosophical tradition understands what it is to be the "cause" of something, what it means to describe something as "good" or "bad," and a great many other philosophical issues our understanding of which modern philosophers and their successors have severely distorted. What began as bad philosophy and anti-religious propaganda in the writings of various early modern- and Enlightenment-era thinkers has congealed into a kind of pseudo-common sense, falsehoods and confusions so deeply enmeshed in contemporary thinking that few even realize there is any alternative to them.

This is as true of most contemporary philosophers and other intellectuals as it is of anyone else. Bugliosi relates how 85 to 90 percent of an audience of 600 lawyers he once polled said they rejected the findings of the Warren Commission.[27] Yet while about the same number said that they had seen Stone's movie *JFK* or read a conspiracy theory book, almost none of them – and these are lawyers, mind you, whom one would like to think would be sensitive to the need to hear both sides of a case – had actually read the Warren Report itself, presumably since they "already knew" that it's wrong. Similarly, a secularist colleague of mine once assured me that he didn't need to bother reading writers like Aquinas, since he "already knew" that they must be wrong – though judging from his grasp of what such writers *mean* by "God" (he confidently trotted out a few stupid anthropomorphisms, tiresome comparisons to the Easter bunny, etc.), it was obvious that he knew no such thing. It was like trying to discuss Titian with a three-year-old who thinks painting is something you do with your fingers. As we saw Quentin Smith and Jeremy Waldron complain above, apart from the few who make a professional specialty of arguing about religion, secularist thinkers are generally unacquainted with anything but absurd caricatures of traditional religious ideas and arguments, are utterly unaware that anything other than these caricatures exist, and thus don't bother to look for anything but straw men to attack. They simply don't know what they're talking about, and they don't know that they don't know it. If things are this bad with the people who are *supposed* to know these things – academics, writers, philosophers, scientists, and other intellectuals – it is hardly surprising if the average educated reader is no less ignorant. A detailed philosophical case of the sort I will be making in this book is thus unavoidable if the job is to be done adequately.

There is yet another hurdle anyone making such a case must face, and again it has a parallel in debates over conspiracy theories. Bugliosi notes that "people inevitably find conspiracies fascinating and intriguing, and hence subconsciously are more receptive to conspiratorial hypotheses"; those who debunk such hypotheses are thus seen as "taking the fun out of" things.[28] And as I have argued elsewhere, conspiracy theories also thrive on the widespread (but, as we will be seeing, quite false) modern assumption that science, philosophy, and "critical thinking" in general are all essentially in the business of undermining authority, debunking "official stories," and overthrowing received wisdom and common sense.[29] Similarly, given that even today most people have a religious upbringing of some sort and that a religious perspective inevitably has the status of being the traditional or received view of things, secularist views, however feebly defended, cannot fail to come across as new, exciting, and "intellectual," while the defender of religious belief, however powerful his arguments, is bound to seem an out-of-touch and tiresome killjoy. Rationally speaking, this is all quite juvenile and frivolous, of course, but it makes it that much more imperative for the defender of religious belief to rely on the sheer philosophical power of a detailed case, for he has precious little to offer in the way of "sex appeal." (All the same, I *can* promise that I will be saying some frank and offensive things about sex – though I suspect it is precisely those who most like to think of themselves as welcoming frank talk about sex who will be the most offended.)

Here, then, is the plan of the chapters to follow. Chapters 2 through 5 constitute a "crash course" in the history of Western philosophy, albeit a highly selective one, our focus being on those trends that led toward and led away from what I have called the "classical" philosophical picture of the world that underlies the Western religious tradition. Specifically, Chapter 2 surveys the key metaphysical ideas of Plato and Aristotle and their respective schools of thought; Chapters 3 and 4 explain how these ideas were developed and utilized by the medieval Scholastic thinkers, especially Aquinas, to articulate a comprehensive systematic account of the existence of God, the immateriality and immortality of the soul, and the natural moral law; and Chapter 5 examines the way in which "modern" philosophers, who broke radically with this Greek and medieval "classical" inheritance, set in motion a process that would gradually but relentlessly undermine not only the traditional Western moral and religious heritage, but also the foundations of reason, morality, and science itself.

Our story, then, is one of a steady ascent from sunny Greek valleys to the divine light of the medieval Gothic heights – followed by a nightmarish toboggan ride down into the dark bowels of modernity's version of Plato's cave. Chapter 6 shows us the way out and back up. Specifically, it shows that the classical metaphysical picture the modern one replaced is rationally unavoidable, and thus every bit as defensible today as it was in the days of Thomas Aquinas; and also that, since this picture is unavoidable, the traditional Western religious worldview it entails is rationally unavoidable as well.

As I have said, we will in the course of this book occasionally be addressing certain technical philosophical issues. (Some readers might find parts of Chapters 2 and 5 especially challenging.) But the technicalities are no more difficult than those one might find in a popular science book, and I am heartened by the example of Mortimer Adler, who devoted a career to expounding *Aristotle for Everybody* (to cite the title of one of his better-known books) and apparently made a gazillion dollars doing it. (OK, not really. Still, you've discovered my secret: I went into philosophy for the money. I'm starting to think my high school guidance counselor was something of a prankster.) As I have also said, the point of the technicalities will in any case be made evident when we see the many implications they have for religion, morality, and science. And I think I can guarantee this much: If you make the effort to work through the ideas I'll be setting out in this book, then even if you do not end up agreeing with me that the existence of God, the immortality of the soul, and the natural law conception of morality are rationally unavoidable, you *will* understand how reasonable people could be convinced of this.

As the reader has no doubt already figured out, this book will also be as polemical as it is philosophical, though hardly more so than the books written by the "New Atheists" to whom I am responding. I believe this tone is appropriate, indeed necessary, for the New Atheism derives whatever influence it has far more from its rhetorical force and "sex appeal" (as I have called it) than from its very thin intellectual content. It is essential, then, not only that its intellectual pretensions are exposed but that its rhetoric is met with equal and opposite force. In any event, as the argument of this book will show, it is the defenders of the traditional Western philosophical and religious worldview, and certainly not the "New Atheists," who have earned the intellectual right to indulge in polemics.

All the same, and notwithstanding what I have said in this chapter, I want to emphasize that I do not deny for a moment that there are secularists, atheists, and naturalists of good will, who are (apart from their rejection of religion) reasonable and morally admirable. What I deny is that they have or can have – whether they realize this or not – any *cogent rational grounds* for their trust in reason or morality given their atheism and naturalism, and I deny also that they can rationally remain secularists, atheists, or naturalists if they come to a proper understanding both of the religious views they reject and of the difficulties inherent in their own position. Of course, I am not so foolish as to think that no reasonable person could possibly fail to agree with me after reading this book. *No* single book on any subject, however well-argued and correct in its conclusions, can be expected to convince every reasonable person, certainly not all at once, all by itself, or after a single reading; the way in which we human beings come to believe things is, for good or ill, much more complicated than that. (There are no "magic bullets" in philosophy any more than in the JFK assassination.) Still, I urge secularist readers at least to consider that what I have to say in this book is merely the tip of an intellectual iceberg, and that if they explore more thoroughly the (no doubt far better) works of other writers in the tradition of thought my arguments represent, they will find that they have been far, *far* too glib in their dismissal of religious belief – and perhaps utterly mistaken in rejecting it.

I urge secular readers, then, to do what Dennett so tiresomely and condescendingly asks religious readers to do throughout his book *Breaking the Spell* – to consider that they have been wrong. I hope to show them that if they are, as they claim to be, truly rational and moral, they will come to see that they have hated what they should have loved. Not to put too fine a point on it, they ought – literally – to get down on their knees and worship the God who mercifully sustains them in being at every instant, even as they foolishly scoff at Him. This is not only an act of faith, rightly understood; it is the highest manifestation and fulfillment, in this life anyway, of human reason itself.

2. Greeks Bearing Gifts

It was said that he was born of a virgin, and that his father was a deity. He was worshipped by some as a god after his death, and he changed the course of Western civilization. No, it's not whom you think. I am speaking of Plato (429–347 b.c.), about whom all sorts of apocryphal stories grew up almost immediately after his death. Speusippus, his successor as head of the Academy, is one source of the claim that Plato's real father was the god Apollo. We are also told that he was born on Apollo's birthday, and that bees settled prophetically on his infant lips.[1]

Such idolatry is embarrassing, but it is at least somewhat understandable when we consider how profound Plato's impact has been on history, and was destined to be given the power of his ideas. Friedrich Nietzsche held that Christianity was nothing other than "Platonism for 'the people,'" which, while overstating things to the point of falsehood (standard procedure for Nietzsche) does hint at the profound influence Plato's philosophy has had on Christian theology.[2] Somewhat more soberly, Alfred North Whitehead famously remarked that the Western philosophical tradition "consists in a series of footnotes to Plato."[3] Even this is a little over-the-top, for two reasons. First, many philosophers would regard Plato's student Aristotle (384–322 B.C.) as a philosopher at least as great as Plato was, and more correct in his views to boot. Second, an important (if relatively brief) chunk of the history of Western philosophy *precedes* Plato, and thus can hardly be a "footnote" to him (even if one regards it as a mere prelude to him).

From Thales to Socrates

We will have plenty to say about Aristotle later on, but because one cannot properly understand either Plato or Aristotle without knowing at least a little bit about the Greek philosophers who came before them, let's begin by briefly saying something about some of those philosophers.[4] The first thing to note about them is that they were as much "scientists," as that term is understood today, as they were philosophers. Indeed, for most of the history of philosophy and science, there was no rigid distinction between these disciplines; "philosophy" was just that general "love of wisdom" – of coming to understand the world in all its variety and the causes that lay behind it – of which logic, physics, metaphysics, biology, ethics, and all the other branches of science and philosophy as we know them today were but a part. The "Pre-Socratic" philosophers, as they are known (since most of them came before Plato's famous teacher Socrates), were fascinated by the question of what the basic principle is that underlies all reality and unifies all the diverse phenomena of our experience. Thales of Miletus (6th century B.C.), who is the first Western philosopher and scientist known to us, famously thought that this basic principle – the one thing out of which everything else in our experience comes from – was *water*. (Don't ask. Given what was then known, this theory was not as weird as it sounds to us today; but you'll have to trust me on this, because we don't have time to go into the details.) Pythagoras (572–497 B.C.), by stark contrast and inspired by discoveries in mathematics, thought that everything was composed of *numbers*. (Again, and for the same reasons: Don't ask. Trust me.) Other thinkers proposed yet other first principles. But Thales and Pythagoras illustrate two divergent approaches to discovering the principles underlying the universe that would continue on and compete with one another for the entire history of Western philosophy and science: Thales, as evidenced by his focus on a particular observable phenomenon as the key to all reality, tended to emphasize the *senses* as the source of our knowledge; Pythagoras, given his focus on mathematics and the unobservable entities that seem to be its domain of study, emphasized instead the *intellect* or pure reason. And while Thales posits a *material* basis to all reality, Pythagoras posits something *immaterial*.

Part of what led to this interest in first principles among the Pre-Socratics was the notice they took of the phenomena of *change* and *permanence* in the world around them. A human being changes dramatically in both mind and body from conception through birth, childhood, adolescence, adulthood, old age, and on until death; and yet we say that it is the same human being who undergoes all these changes. Individual plants and animals constantly come and go, but the species carry on. Spring gives way to summer, which is followed by fall and then winter; and yet spring always returns, and the cycle begins again. And so on. How do we account for this relationship between change and permanence? Is one more basic than the other? There is also the question of the relationship between the *one* and the *many*. There are many individual human beings, and yet they are all nevertheless in some sense one thing: human. There are many individual trees, but they too all seem to be one insofar as they all have the nature of a tree rather than each having its own nature; there are many individual rocks but they are nevertheless all one in being rocks; and so on for everything in our experience. How do we account for this relationship? Again, is one of these things – the way in which things are "many" or the way in which they are "one" – more fundamental than the other? Pre-Socratic philosophers differed not only over whether to emphasize the senses or the intellect as the fundamental source of our knowledge, but also over whether to emphasize the oneness and permanence we observe in the world, or the diversity and change we also observe in it.

Heraclitus (c. 535–475 B.C.) and Parmenides (c. 515–450 B.C.) famously represent the absolute extreme positions on these questions. For Heraclitus, permanence is an illusion, and change is the universal feature of reality. By the time you finish this sentence you will be different from the person you were when you started it. "All things are in a state of flux," Heraclitus said; "You can never step in the same river twice." (Heraclitus might seem a veritable "king of the one-liners," but he is also notoriously obscure and is reputed to have been a rather ill-tempered misanthrope, another one of his quips being that "Most men are bad." Fun guy.) Parmenides took the diametrically opposite view. Change and diversity are the illusions, he tells us. For whatever exists is a being, and if something is not a being then it is a non-being, and thus nothing. Now a being could change only if caused to do so by something other than itself; and yet, as was just said, the only thing other than being is non-being, and non-being – since it is just nothing – cannot cause anything. Hence change is impossible. Furthermore, if every existing thing is a being – for example, an apple is a being, and an orange is a being – then they are really just the *same thing*, a being. Diversity is impossible too; there really is no difference between apples and oranges after all, or between anything else. For Parmenides there is really just one thing in existence: being itself, solitary, undifferentiated, and unchanging. That the senses lead us to think that there are innumerably many different things in the world – this apple, that orange, this book, that table, you, me, your dog, etc. – and that they are all constantly changing, simply shows that the senses aren't to be trusted.

Zeno (b. 490 B.C.), a disciple of Parmenides, developed similar arguments, such as the famous paradox of Achilles and the tortoise. Suppose Achilles and the tortoise are in a race, and the tortoise has a head start. Then Achilles, however fast he is, can never outrun the tortoise. For by the time Achilles reaches the point at which the tortoise had started, the tortoise will have reached a new position; by the time Achilles reaches that new position, the tortoise will have moved on, however slightly, to yet a new position; and so on ad infinitum. The very idea that Achilles, the tortoise, or anything else can move thus leads to paradox; hence motion is impossible. The senses may tell us otherwise, but they are refuted by reason. As all of this implies, the tendency to emphasize oneness and permanence as the fundamental features of reality tended to go hand in hand with an emphasis on the intellect and pure reason as the source of knowledge; while the tendency to emphasize the diversity and changeability of things was associated with an emphasis on the senses.

We are rushing through this – our aim is to get to Plato and Aristotle – and it is all pretty abstract. But as I have said, the dramatic relevance of such abstractions (which will be explained more carefully when we get to the two big names) to morality, religion, and other practical matters will be evident before long. In any case, some of the Pre-Socratics were concerned with practical affairs too. These were the Sophists, and their interest was in teaching the use of argumentative skills of the sort previous philosophers had exhibited, but as a means of attaining worldly success, for instance in politics. Unfortunately, they gained a reputation for being rather cynical and unscrupulous in their argumentative standards: any old argument would do as long as it persuaded one's listener, even if it was totally fallacious; what mattered was winning the debate, not arriving at the truth, and the line between logic and rhetoric was thus blurred. (The Sophists are still with us. Today we call them "lawyers," "professors of literary criticism," and "Michael Moore.") The Sophists also tended toward skepticism and relativism, thinking that no knowledge of objective truth is really possible and that every view is in principle as good as any other. As Protagoras (c. 485–414 B.C.) famously put it, "Man is the measure of all things" – man, that is to say, rather than objective reality.

Socrates (469–399 B.C.) vigorously opposed the Sophists and the moral corruption they had fostered within the Athens of his day.[5] He insisted that there is an objective difference between truth and falsity and good and bad, and that bad actions corrupt one's soul and thus harm the perpetrator whether or not they bring worldly success. He constantly challenged the people of the city with his questions – "What is justice?" "What is piety?" and so forth – exposing the inadequacy of their answers and seeking better ones, in the hope of finding the true *essences* of the things he was inquiring about. (Famously, he did not claim to have the answers himself.) The opinion of the majority was in his view not what mattered; rather, it was the opinion of the wise, those guided by reason, that counted. When put on trial by a jury of 500 of his fellow citizens for purportedly denying the gods of the city and replacing them with new ones, and in general corrupting the youth – the real motive may have been his associations with certain anti-democratic political figures of the day – he defended himself, Plato tells us, by claiming that he was divinely called to lead others to the improvement of their souls. Naturally, this democratic assembly had him executed. (Today they'd probably just denounce him as a "neo-con" or part of the "religious right" and haul him off for multicultural sensitivity training.)

Plato's Theory of Forms

This brings us at last to Socrates' student Plato, who gave us the first great attempt to combine all the various themes developed by his predecessors into a coherent comprehensive system. In particular, Plato provided a complete account of the relationships holding between the material and immaterial realms, the one and the many, and change and permanence, and the proper role of both the senses and the intellect in coming to know them; he wanted to show how the resulting metaphysical picture had implications for morality; and he sought to demonstrate that objective knowledge about all these things, and not mere opinion, was possible. All of this is enshrined in his famous Theory of Forms.[6]

What is a "Form"? It is, in the first place, an essence of the sort Socrates was so eager to discover. To know the essence of justice, for example – to know, that is to say, what the nature of justice is, what defines it and distinguishes it from everything that isn't justice – would for Plato just be to know the Form of Justice. But what *kind* of thing exactly is it that one knows when one knows this or any other Form? And how does one know it? Is it a kind of physical object, observable through one or more of the five senses? Is it something subjective, an idea in our minds, knowable via introspection? Is it something conventional, a mere way of speaking and acting that we pick up from other members of our community but which might change from place to place and time to time?

To the last three questions, Plato would answer with a very firm No, No, and No. To understand what he does have in mind, it will be useful to begin with a simpler example than justice. Consider a triangle; in fact, consider several triangles, as they might be drawn on paper, or on a chalkboard, in sand, or on a computer screen. Suppose some of them are small, some very large, some in between; some isosceles, some scalene, some obtuse, and so on; some drawn with thin lines, some with thick lines, some with a ruler and some more sketchily; some written in ink, others in chalk, others using pixels; some drawn with green lines, some with red, some with black, some with blue; some in fairly pristine shape, others partially erased, or with the lines not completely closed due to haste in drawing them. Now, a triangle is just a closed plane figure with three straight sides; that is its essence or nature. And it is by reference to this essence that we judge particular triangles of the sort we are taking as our examples to be triangles in the first place. But notice that all of these examples are inevitably going to have features that have nothing essentially to do with "triangularity" as such. They are all going to be either red, or green, or black, or whatever; but there is nothing in being a triangle which requires being any of these colors, or indeed any color at all. They are all going to be drawn either in ink, or chalk dust, or pixels, or some other medium; but there is nothing in triangularity as such that requires any of these things either. Nor is there anything in being a triangle which requires being large or small, or being drawn with thick lines or thin ones, or being drawn on this particular chalkboard or that particular book, this particular plot of sand or that particular computer screen. Notice too that all of our sample triangles are also going to *lack*, or at least not perfectly exemplify, features that *are* part of being a triangle. Due to damage or hasty drawing, some are going to have lines that are partially broken, or corners that are not perfectly closed. And no matter how carefully one has drawn them, every single one of them will have lines that are not perfectly straight, even if such imperfections might not always be visible to the naked eye.

In short, every particular physical or material triangle – the sort of triangle we know through the senses, and indeed the only sort we can know through the senses – is always going to have features that are simply not part of the essence or nature of trianglularity per se, and is always going to lack features that are part of the essence or nature of triangularity. What follows from this, Plato would say, is that when we grasp the essence or nature of being a triangle, what we grasp is *not* something material or physical, and not something we grasp or could grasp through the senses. This is even more evident when we consider that individual perceivable, material triangles come into existence and go out of existence and change in other ways as well, but the essence of triangularity stays the same. We also know many things about triangles – not only their essential features, but also that their angles necessarily add up to 180 degrees, that the Pythagorean theorem is true of right triangles, and so forth – that were true long before the first geometer drew his first triangle in the sand, and that would remain true even if every particular material triangle were erased tomorrow. What we know when we know the essence of triangularity is something *universal* rather than particular, something *immaterial* rather than material, and something we know through the *intellect* rather than the senses.

That does not mean, however, that in knowing the essence of triangularity we know something that is purely mental, a subjective "idea."[7] Nor is this essence a mere cultural artifact or convention of language. For what we know about triangles are *objective* facts, things we have *discovered* rather than invented. It is not up to us to decide that the angles of a triangle should add up to 38 degrees instead of 180, or that the Pythagorean theorem should be true of circles rather than right triangles. If the Canadian parliament, say, should declare that in light of evolving social mores, triangles should be regarded as sometimes having four sides, and decree also that anyone who expresses disagreement with this judgment shall be deemed guilty of discriminatory hate speech against four-sided triangles, none of this would change the geometrical facts in the least, but merely cast doubt on the sanity of Canadian parliamentarians. The Pythagorean theorem, etc., were true long before we discovered them and will remain true long after we're all dead, just as the sun and planets were here before we were and would remain even if we blasted ourselves out of existence in a nuclear conflagration.[8]

Now if the essence of triangularity is something neither material nor mental – that is to say, something that exists neither in the material world nor merely in the human mind – then it has a unique kind of existence all its own, that of an abstract object existing in what Platonists sometimes call a "third realm." And what is true of the essence of triangles is no less true, in Plato's view, of the essences of pretty much *everything*: of squares, circles, and other geometrical figures, but also (and more interestingly) of human beings, tables and chairs, dogs and cats, trees and rocks, justice, beauty, goodness, piety, and so on and on. When we grasp the essence of any of these things, we grasp something that is universal, immaterial, extra-mental, and known via the intellect rather than senses, and is thus a denizen of this "third realm." What we grasp, in short, is a Form.

Where, one might ask, *is* this "third realm" of the Forms? The question is a bad one. It assumes that Forms have a spatial location; but if they did, then they would exist somewhere in the material world, and we have just got done saying that they *aren't in* the material world. To understand Plato, we have to break free of the lazy assumption that everything real must have some location in time and space; indeed, his whole point is that the Theory of Forms, if correct, *proves* that there is more to reality than the world of time and space. We also have to break free of the lazy habit (as Plato sees it) of assuming that our senses are our only sources of knowledge of reality. For the highest level of reality is not knowable through the senses, but only via the intellect. The world of the senses – of particular geometrical objects, particular human beings, particular just or unjust actions, and the like – might serve at most as kind of a pointer to something beyond itself, to a realm that includes the Form of Triangularity, the Form of Humanness, and the Form of Justice. We can see, hear, taste, touch, and smell the former world, but not the latter, which we know instead through pure thought or unaided reason.

In general, the world of material things is merely a faint copy of the realm of the Forms. Particular things and events are what they are only by "participating in," or "exemplifying," or "instantiating" the Forms. Socrates, Aristotle, and George Bush, though distinct and separated by time and space, are all men because they all participate in the same one Form of Man. Fido, Rover, and Spot are all dogs because they all participate in the Form of Dog. Paying your phone bill, staying faithful to your wife, and voting to strike down *Roe v. Wade* are all just actions because they participate in the Form of Justice. These individual exemplars or instantiations are all imperfect in various ways; the Forms are perfect, being the archetypes or standards by reference to which we judge something to be a man, dog, just action, etc. Individual material things come and go; the Forms, being outside time and space, are eternal and unchanging. Indeed, the Forms are *more real* than the material things that exemplify them. For consider that shadows, reflections, images, and the like depend on physical objects for their reality, in a way that makes them "less real" than the objects themselves. There is a metaphysical asymmetry in their ways of existing: a shadow or reflection won't exist at all unless a physical object casts it, while the object will exist whether or not its shadow or image does. By the same token, the physical objects themselves exist only insofar as they participate in the Forms, while the Forms would exist whether or not the particular physical instantiations did.

Thus is Plato led to posit a hierarchical structure to reality, illustrated in his famous image of the "divided line." Supposing a line divided into four segments – labeled, from the top down (and from most real to least real), A to B, B to C, C to D, and D to E – the bottom segment (D to E) represents shadows, images, illusions, and the like, and the next one up (C to D) ordinary material objects. The second highest segment (B to C) represents mathematical reasoning and the sorts of incomplete abstractions that we entertain when we contemplate mathematical entities via sensory imagery. The highest segment (A to B) corresponds to pure Forms, abstractions known directly by the intellect and divorced from sensory imagery and the like altogether. Corresponding to these degrees of reality are degrees of knowledge, the lowest two segments (from C to E) – our sensory knowledge of the physical world – constituting mere "opinion," and the highest two (A to C) alone constituting knowledge in the strict sense.

Now as has been indicated, the Forms, as archetypes or perfect patterns, are the standards by reference to which particular things in the world of our experience count as being the kinds of things they are. A triangle is a triangle only because it participates in the Form of Triangularity; a squirrel is a squirrel only because it participates in the Form of Squirrel; and so forth. By the same token, something is going to count as a *better* triangle the more perfectly it participates in or instantiates triangularity, and a squirrel will be a *better* squirrel the more perfectly it participates in or instantiates the Form of Squirrel. Hence a triangle drawn slowly and carefully on paper with a Rapidograph and a straight edge is going to be a more perfect approximation than one hastily scrawled in crayon on the cracked plastic seat cover of a moving bus. Hence a squirrel who likes to scamper up trees and gather nuts for the winter (or whatever) is going to be a more perfect approximation of the squirrel essence than one which, through habituation or genetic defect, prefers to eat toothpaste spread on Ritz crackers and to lay out "spread eagled" on the freeway. This entails a standard of *goodness*, and a perfectly objective one. It is not a matter of *opinion* whether the carefully drawn triangle is a better triangle than the hastily drawn one, nor a matter of opinion whether the toothpaste-eating squirrel is deficient as a squirrel. That there might be habituation or a genetic factor in the latter case is irrelevant: behavioral and affective deviations from the essence are still deviations, whatever their cause and whether or not a creature which exhibits them has come to enjoy them. If a squirrel could be conditioned to want to eat nothing but toothpaste, it wouldn't follow that this is good for him. Nor, if there were a genetic factor behind this odd preference, would it follow that it is normal for him, any more than a genetic factor behind blindness or clubfeet shows that being blind or having a clubfoot is normal even for those people who are tragically afflicted with these ailments. In every case, the thing in question is still a triangle, or a squirrel, or a human being or whatever – not instantiating a Form perfectly doesn't mean that something doesn't instantiate it at all – but it is nevertheless the case, given such imperfections, that it instantiates it only more or less well.

This normative element in his theory of Forms led Plato to place special emphasis on the Form of the Good. For (Plato seems to think) if to know a thing requires knowing its Form, and to know any Form is just to know the perfect archetype of the thing – that which makes it a more or less good instance of the kind of thing it is – then to know any Form itself requires in turn knowing the Form of the Good by reference to which it counts as a perfect archetype. The Form of the Good is thus the highest of the Forms, their source, and indeed the source of all being. It is, accordingly, the highest object of contemplation, and knowledge of it is the supreme kind of knowledge. Does Plato think of it as God? Some have argued that he does, but it is only in later centuries, with the rise of Neo-Platonism (as it came to be known) that we see his followers clearly make this connection.[9] He is clear, however, that the soul, since it can know the Forms, must be like what it knows in being immaterial or non-physical, and also immortal. (Famously, he thought the soul existed prior to birth in direct contact with the Forms, and will return to this condition after death. We will wait, though, to get to Aristotle and Aquinas before saying much about the soul and its nature.)

As I have suggested, Plato's theory can be understood as an attempt to weave together in a systematic way what was of lasting value in the views of those philosophers who preceded him. With Parmenides, he identifies reality, at least in the fullest sense of the term, with what is eternal and unchanging, and insists that it is known through the intellect rather than the senses. But he also throws a bone to Heraclitus in acknowledging (as Parmenides did not) that the ceaselessly changing material world has at least an inferior and derivative kind of reality, and that the senses provide at least an inferior sort of knowledge. Like the Pre-Socratics in general, he holds that the world is ultimately to be explained in terms of a single unifying principle (in his case, the Form of the Good). Like Socrates, he is interested in discovering the essences of things, wants to show how knowledge of them is possible, and links this knowledge with an understanding of the good and thus with ethics. (I say "the good" rather than "moral values" – a very unfortunate expression common these days even among conservatives – because the word "values" implies something dependent on someone who is doing the valuing, and thus insinuates that morality is subjective. For Plato – and Aristotle, and the medieval philosophers who followed them – nothing could be further from the truth: the good for a thing, including for a human being, is entirely objective; it is determined by its essence or Form and has nothing necessarily to do with what we happen contingently to "value" or desire.)

Pointing forward in time, we see in Plato the first detailed formulation in Western thought of themes that would persist and be developed further in the classical philosophical tradition, from Aristotle to Augustine to the Scholastics: that the material world points beyond itself to an eternal source; that things have immutable forms or essences; that the foundation of morality is to be found in this source and in these essences; that human beings have immaterial souls; that all of this is knowable through reason, and that knowing it is the highest end of philosophy and science.

Plato sums up his overall vision of philosophy in his famous "allegory of the cave." Imagine a number of individuals chained deep inside a cave, their heads held fixed in such a way that they can look at nothing but the wall of the cave in front of them. Behind them is a fire, and there are people walking between them and the fire carrying statues of various ordinary objects. All the chained individuals ever see are the flickering shadows of these statues cast on the wall before them, and all they ever hear are whatever sounds are made by the people carrying the statues. Assuming they have been chained there all their lives, almost their entire conception of reality will be determined by their experience of such shadows and sounds, and they will form all sorts of false beliefs based on correlations they observe between shadows and other shadows, sounds and other sounds, and shadows and sounds. Now suppose that one of these individuals is freed, makes it out of the cave, and for the first time experiences the world of everyday physical objects illuminated in broad daylight. At first he will be wildly disoriented, and the sun will nearly blind him. But eventually he will come to realize that what he now sees in the outside world are the models of the crude images he knew before, and that the world he left was but a vastly inadequate copy of the world he has now discovered. He would also see that the sun, which he can perceive clearly once his eyes adjust, is the source of the visibility of the physical objects that occupy this new world. If he goes back down into the cave and reveals what he has discovered, the other cave dwellers will think he is mad, and indeed will be unable to understand him. Yet he alone will have achieved a true understanding of reality.

The cave, for Plato, represents the world of ordinary life, and the chained cave dwellers who know only fleeting and flickering images represent the ignorant masses living in thrall to their ever-changing passions and fancies. The statues correspond to the ordinary objects of everyday life, the things outside the cave to the Forms, and the sun to the Form of the Good. The man who makes it out of the cave is the philosopher, who, with his knowledge of the Forms, alone knows the real nature of things, yet is bound to be regarded as eccentric by those who prefer to be guided by emotion and by appearances, rather than by intellect and truth.

Realism, nominalism, and conceptualism

Pretty heady stuff. Yet even the most sympathetic reader might wonder if Plato has gone off the rails a bit; Aristotle certainly thought so. But it is important to understand that, certain details and rhetorical flourishes aside, the core of Plato's theory is admitted even by many who are unsympathetic to his overall worldview to be highly plausible and defensible, and has always had power-ful advocates down to the present day. The reason is that at least something *like* Plato's theory is notoriously very hard to avoid if we are to make sense of mathematics, language, science, and the very structure of the world of our experience.

To understand why, let's consider three sorts of things (though there are more than that) that give every appearance of being abstract objects of the sort Plato is committed to, viz. entities exist-ing outside time and space and outside the human mind. The first are *universals*, examples of which we've seen already. Over and above this or that particular triangle, we have the universal "trian-gularity"; over and above this or that particular human being, we have the universal "humanness"; over and above this or that partic-ular red thing, we have the universal "redness"; and in general, each particular thing seems to instantiate or exemplify various uni-versal features. The particular things are unique and non-repeatable – there is just one Socrates, one Aristotle, one George W. Bush, etc. – but the features they exemplify (e.g. "humanness") are repeatable and common to many things, hence "universal."

A second example would be *numbers* and other mathematical entities. Numbers are not physical objects: the numeral "2" isn't the *number* 2 any more than the name "George Bush" is the same thing as the man George Bush, and erasing every numeral 2 that anyone has ever written won't suddenly make $2 + 2 = 4$ false. Nor are num-bers purely mental: as with geometrical truths, the truths of mathe-matics in general are things we discover rather than invent; they are in some way already "out there" waiting for us to find them, and thus cannot depend for their truth on our thinking about them. They are also necessary truths rather than contingent ones. To know, say, that there are clouds on Venus is to know a contingent fact, that is, one that could have been otherwise. For example, it could have turned out that Venus never existed, or that its orbit took it so close to the sun that any atmosphere it had was long ago burned off; and at some point in the future the sun will in any case expand and engulf Venus and its cloud covering within it, inciner-ating them entirely. But to know even a simple mathematical fact like $2 + 2 = 4$ is to know a *necessary* truth, one that *could not* have been otherwise[10]; 2 and 2 were 4 long before anyone realized it, and would remain 4 forever even if we all forgot about it or died out. Indeed, 2 + 2 = 4 would remain true even if the entire universe collapsed in on itself. But if this mathematical truth is necessary in this way, then the things it is a truth about – numbers – must also exist in a necessary way, outside time and space and independently of any mind.

Then we have what philosophers call *propositions* – statements about the world, whether true or false, which are distinct from the sentences that express them. "John is a bachelor" and "John is an unmarried man" are different sentences, but they express the same proposition. "Snow is white" and "Schnee ist weiss" are also different sentences – indeed, one is a sentence of English, the other a sentence of German – but they too express exactly the same proposition, namely the proposition that snow is white. When the mind entertains any thought at all, whether true or false, it is ultimately a proposition that it is entertaining, and not a sentence. That is why we can all entertain the very same thoughts despite our being separated by different languages and different times and places: when Socrates and George Bush think that snow is white, they are thinking *exactly the same thing*, despite the fact that one of them expresses this thought in Greek in the Athens of the 5th century B.C., and the other in English in 21st-century Texas. Being different from any sentence, or indeed from any other sequence of physical sounds or shapes we might use to express them, propositions are in some sense distinct from the material world. But since a proposition is either true or false whether or not we happen to be entertaining it – again, 2 + 2 = 4 would be still be true even if we forgot this tomorrow, 2 + 2 = 5 would be false even if we all came to believe it, and snow was white long before anyone first saw it – it seems to follow that propositions are also independent of any mind.

The view that universals, numbers, and/or propositions exist objectively, apart from the human mind and distinct from any material or physical features of the world, is called *realism*, and Plato's Theory of Forms is perhaps the most famous version of the view (though not the only one, as we will see). The standard alternative views are *nominalism*, which denies that universals and the like are real, and *conceptualism*, which acknowledges that they are real but insists that they exist only in the mind; and like realism, each of these positions comes in several varieties. The debate between the three views is ancient, and extremely complicated.[11] It can also seem at first glance to be very dry, esoteric, and irrelevant to practical life. But nothing could be further from the truth. Indeed, it is not too much of an exaggeration to say that virtually every major religious, moral, and political controversy of the last several decades – of the last several centuries, in fact – in some way rests on a disagreement, even if implicit and unnoticed, over the "problem of universals" (as it is known). That includes the dispute between the "New Atheists" and their critics, ignorant though the former (though also often the latter) are of the true roots of this dispute. When Richard Weaver famously made the observation that "Ideas Have Consequences," he was not making the banal point that what we believe affects the way we act; he was referring to the radical social and moral implications that the abandonment of realism and the adoption of nominalism has had within modern Western civilization.[12]

We will be examining these consequences in due course. For now, let us briefly consider some of the reasons why realism, in some form or other, has seemed inescapable even to many thinkers viscerally inclined to reject it; and why the escapes attempted by other philosophers – namely nominalism and conceptualism – have seemed ultimately indefensible, however eagerly (or desperately) some have tried to defend them.

Some of these are arguments to which we have already alluded, but it will be useful to summarize them and make them more explicit. (A few are also slightly technical; I beg the reader's indulgence.) For simplicity's sake, some of the arguments will be stated in a "Platonic" way; realists of other stripes would modify them slightly.

1. The "one over many" argument: "Triangularity" "redness," "humanness," etc., are not reducible to any particular triangle, red thing, or human being, nor even to any collection of triangles, red things, or human beings. For any particular triangle, red thing, or human being, or even the whole collection of these things, could go out of existence, and yet triangularity, redness, and humanness could come to be exemplified once again. They also could be, and

often are, exemplified even when no human mind is aware of this fact. Hence triangularity, redness, humanness, and other universals are neither material things nor collections of material things, nor dependent on human minds for their existence.

2. The argument from geometry: In geometry we deal with perfect lines, perfect angles, perfect circles, and the like, and discover objective facts about them. Since these facts are objective – we didn't invent them and couldn't change them if we wanted to – they do not depend on our minds. Since they are necessary and unalterable facts (unlike facts about material things), and since no material thing has the perfection that geometrical objects have, they do not depend on the material world either. Hence they are facts about a "third realm" of abstract objects.

3. The argument from mathematics in general: Mathematical truths in general are necessary and unalterable, while the material world and the human mind are contingent and changing. These truths were true before the material world and our minds existed and would remain true if the latter went out of existence. Hence the objects these truths are truths about – numbers and the like – cannot be either material or mental, but abstract. Furthermore, the series of numbers is infinite, but there are only finitely many material things and only finitely many ideas within any human mind or collection of human minds; hence the series of numbers cannot be identified with anything either material or mental.

4. The argument from the nature of propositions: Propositions cannot be identified with anything either material or mental. For some propositions (e.g. truths of mathematics like 2 + 2 = 4) are necessarily true, and thus would remain true if neither the material world nor any human mind existed. Many contingently true propositions would also remain true in such a circumstance: "Caesar was assassinated on the Ides of March" would remain true even the entire world and every human mind went out of existence tomorrow. Even if neither the material world nor any human mind had ever existed in the first place, the proposition "There is neither a material world nor any human mind" would have been true, in which case it would not be something material or mental. And so forth.[13]

5. *The argument from science*: Scientific laws and classifications, being general or universal in their application, necessarily make reference to universals; and science is in the business of discovering objective, mind-independent facts. Hence to accept the results of science is to accept that there are mind-independent universals. Science also makes use of mathematical formulations, and since (as noted above) mathematics concerns a realm of abstract objects, to accept the results of science thus commits one to accept that there are such abstract objects.[14]

These are direct arguments for realism. There are also indirect arguments, i.e. arguments to the effect that the alternatives to realism cannot be right. Consider nominalism, which holds that there are no universals, numbers, or propositions.[15] Where we think there are universals, the nominalist says, there are really only general names, words we apply to many things. Hence, for example, there is the general term "red," which we apply to various objects, but no such thing as "redness." Of course, this raises the question *why* we apply the term "red" to just the things we do, and it is hard to see how there could be any plausible answer other than "Because they all have redness in common," which brings us back to affirming the existence of universals after all. The nominalist might seek to avoid this by saying that the reason we label different things "red" is that they resemble each other, without specifying the respect in which they resemble each other. This is implausible on its face – isn't it just obvious that they resemble each other with respect to their *redness*? – but there are other problems too:

6. *The vicious regress problem*: As Bertrand Russell noted, the "resemblance" to which the nominalist appeals is itself a universal.[16] A "Stop" sign resembles a fire truck, which is why we call them both "red." Grass resembles The Incredible Hulk's skin, which is why we call them both "green." And so on. What we have, then, are multiple instances of one and the same universal, "resemblance." Now the nominalist might seek to avoid this consequence by saying that we only call all of these examples cases of "resemblance" because *they* resemble each other, without specifying the respect in which

they resemble each other. But then the problem just crops up again at a higher level. These various cases of resemblance resemble other various cases of resemblance, so that we have a higher-order resemblance, which itself will be a universal. And if the nominalist tries to avoid *this* universal by once again applying his original strategy, he will be just faced with the same problem again at yet a higher level, *ad infinitum*.

7. *The "words are universals too" problem*: The nominalist claims that there are no universals like "redness," just general terms like "red." Yet this claim seems obviously self-contradictory, since the term "red" is itself a universal. You utter the word "red," I utter the word "red," Socrates utters the word "red," and they are all obviously particular utterances of the *same* one word, which exists over and above our various utterances of it. (As philosophers usually put it, each utterance is a different *token* of the same word *type*.) Indeed, this is the only reason the nominalist proposal has any plausibility at all (*if* it has any plausibility at all, that is): that the same one word applies to many things might seem sufficient to capture (if you don't think too carefully about it, anyway) our intuitive sense that there is something in common between them. But, again, if it is the same one word, then since there are different utterances of it, we have just the sort of "one over many" situation the nominalist wants to avoid. To evade this result, the nominalist might say that when you, me, and Socrates each say "red," we are *not* in fact uttering the same word at all, but only words that resemble each other. This would, of course, be just plain stupid on its face, and pathetically desperate. Into the bargain, it would entail that communication is impossible, since we would never be using the same words (indeed, you would never be using the same word more than once even when talking to *yourself*, but only words that resemble each other) – in which case, why is the nominalist talking to us? And the appeal to "resemblance" would open the door up again to the vicious regress problem.

In general, it is notoriously very difficult to defend nominalism in a way that doesn't surreptitiously bring in through the back door a commitment to universals or other abstract objects, in which case the view is self-undermining. For reasons such as this, conceptualism hopes to avoid realism not by denying that universals exist, but rather by denying only that they exist outside the mind. It is an attempt at a middle way between realism and nominalism. But it too faces what are widely regarded as insuperable difficulties:

8. *The argument from the objectivity of concepts and knowledge*: When you and I entertain any concept – the concept of a dog, say, or of redness, or of conceptualism itself for that matter – we are each entertaining *one and the same concept*; it is not that you are entertaining your private concept of red and I am entertaining mine, with nothing in common between them. Similarly, when we each consider various propositions and truths, we are entertaining the *same* propositions and truths. So, for example, when you think about the Pythagorean theorem and I think about the Pythagorean theorem, we are each thinking about *one and the same truth*; it is not that you are thinking about your own personal Pythagorean theorem and I am thinking about mine (whatever that would mean). So, concepts (and thus universals) and propositions do not exist only in the mind, subjectively, but independently of the mind, objectively. Related to this argument is another one:

9. *The argument from the possibility of communication*: Suppose that, as conceptualism implies, universals and propositions were not objective, but existed only in our minds. Then it would be impossible for us ever to communicate. For whenever you said something – "Snow is white," say – then the concepts and propositions that you expressed would be things that existed only in your own mind, and would thus be inaccessible to anybody else. Your idea of "snow" would be entirely different from my idea of "snow," and since your idea is the only one you'd have any access to, and my idea is the only one I'd have access to, we would never mean the same thing whenever we talked about snow, or about anything else for that matter. But this is absurd: we *are* able to communicate and grasp the same concepts and propositions. Hence these things are not subjective or mind-dependent, but objective, as realism claims.

Arguments like these last two are associated with the logician Gottlob Frege (1848–1925), who was concerned to uphold the scientific status of logic and mathematics against a doctrine known as "psychologism," which tended to reduce the laws of logic and mathematics to mere psychological principles governing the operation of the human mind.[17] On this view, that is to say, logic and mathematics don't describe objective reality, but merely the way the structure of our minds leads us to think about reality. There are obvious affinities between conceptualism and this sort of view, which derives from thinkers like Immanuel Kant (about whom we shall say something in later chapters). When you add to it (as Kant would not have) the suggestion that the way our minds are structured is determined by contingent and evolving social, historical, and cultural circumstances, the result is a very radical form of cultural relativism, on which all our concepts, as well as logic, mathematics, science, etc., are culturally conditioned and subject to revision, with no necessary connection to objective reality.

Radical, and totally incoherent, as are psychologism and conceptualism generally. For if we say that our concepts, standards of logic, etc., are determined not by any necessary match with objective reality but rather by the effects on our minds of contingent forces of history, culture, and the like, or even by biological evolution, then we have to give some account of exactly how this works – that is, we have to say precisely what biological and/or cultural forces were responsible, how they formed our minds, and so forth – and we will also have to give arguments in defense of this account. But such an account will necessarily have to appeal to various universals ("Darwinian selective pressures," "class interests," "genetic mutations," "social trends," etc.) and to scientific and mathematical principles governing the relevant processes; and defending it will require appeals to standards of logic. Yet these were the very things the view in question tells us have no objective validity, and (since they purportedly depend on our minds for their existence) did not exist before our minds did. Hence this sort of view completely undermines itself.

Suppose instead that, following Kant, the conceptualist or psychologist takes the less radical position that though our concepts and/or standards of logic and mathematics reflect only the operations of our own minds and not objective reality, this is a *necessary* fact about ourselves, something that could not be changed by either biological or cultural evolution. We are stuck, in other words, with the concepts and standards we have, and would-be social engineers are just out of luck. Would this save the view from collapsing into incoherence? Not at all. For again, the advocate of such a view is going to have to explain to us how he *knows* all this, and how our minds got that way in the first place, and if he appeals to concepts, logical standards, etc., that he's just got done telling us have no connection to objective reality and that depend on our minds for their existence, then he's effectively undermined his own case. On the other hand, insofar as he claims that it is a necessary fact about our minds that we have just the concepts, standards of logic, etc., that we do, then he's thereby claiming to have knowledge of the objective nature of things – specifically, of the objective nature of the workings of our minds – of the sort that was supposed to be ruled out by his theory. For to formulate and defend his claim he needs to appeal to certain universals (like "mind"), standards of logic, etc.; and again, his theory claims that these have no objective validity. So he's caught in a dilemma: if he insists, as his theory must lead him to, that our concepts, standards of logic, etc., have no objective validity, then he cannot so much as defend his own position; if he claims that they do have validity, so as to justify his claim to know about the objective nature of our minds, then he's just contradicted his own view in the very act of defending it. Again, the view is simply incoherent.[18]

Views like the ones in question are titillating and have, for obvious reasons, an emotional appeal to adolescents of all ages. But from a *rational* point of view, they are completely worthless; as David Stove once said, at the end of the day their proponents have little more to offer in their defense than "shit-eating grins."[19] In fairness, it should be noted that there are a great many naturalists, materialists, and atheists who would warmly agree with this harsh judgment. If some religious believers think that the secularists who dominate the academy are all relativists, they are very much mistaken. At least in academic philosophy departments dominated by "analytic philosophy," as most departments in the U.S. and U.K. are these days – other departments in the humanities, and philosophy departments outside these countries and/or dominated by "continental philosophy" are sometimes another story altogether – at least the more extreme forms of relativism, subjectivism, and the like are held in utter contempt.[20] We shouldn't blame secularists for crimes of which they are not guilty. What *is* true is that naturalists, materialists, and atheists often hold views which are *just as insane* as those held by extreme relativists, and they certainly all hold views that have *the same consequences* as extreme relativism does, even if this is not what they intend.

But I digress; we will get back to all that before long. The point for now is that formulating a plausible case for either conceptualism or nominalism is, at best, *very* hard to pull off. Nor is there much of an intellectual motivation for doing so other than trying to avoid realism. It is no good appealing (as is often done) to the famous principle of Ockham's razor as a motivation; for Ockham's razor tells us to opt for the simpler theory and avoid postulating the existence of something unless we need to, and the clear lesson of the history of the debate over universals, propositions, numbers and the like is that we *do* need to "postulate" their existence. Nominalism and conceptualism are "simpler" theories than realism only in the sense in which astronomy would be "simpler" if we denied the existence of stars and planets. One is tempted to say to opponents of realism: Give it up. You can't escape. Stop resisting. Go with it. But why many thinkers would roll naked through broken glass and lemon juice *not* to go with it will be evident by the end of this book, as we see the very conservative, and very religious, consequences of realism and allied notions.

Something like Plato's theory, then, seems clearly right. But the "something *like*" is important. For one can be a realist without going the whole hog for Plato's denigration of the senses and commitment to a mysterious realm of objects beyond time and space. This brings us at last to Aristotle.

Aristotle's metaphysics

With Aristotle, as with Plato, antiquity has delivered to us divergent accounts of his character. But the divergence pretty much boils down to this: Either he was more or less a kind and generous man of refinement, or he was more or less a vain and overly ambitious SOB. So far as I know, no one ever accused him of being a god. According to the ancient biographer Diogenes Laertius, Aristotle

was something of a dandy: "He used to indulge in very conspicu-
ous dress, and rings, and used to dress his hair carefully"; he also
"had a lisping voice."[21] But it's not what you think. He was married
at least once and maybe twice, had children with the different
women involved, and compared homosexuality to eating dirt.
(Plato had also condemned homosexuality as contrary to nature;
the Greek attitude toward homosexuality was far more complicated than popular clichés would have it, and not one that would be
recognized today as "liberal."[22])

Though modern thought is largely defined by its rejection of the
classical philosophical worldview, Plato has always had an easier
time speaking to moderns than Aristotle has. Aristotle is down-to-
earth, a champion of common sense and moderation. His writings,
or at least the ones we still have, are dry and dull reading, being, it
seems, mainly lecture notes. He lacks Plato's literary flair, and
eschews his more extreme positions. Like Plato, he is an elitist, but
unlike Plato, he is not given to utopian social theorizing. Even those
modern secularists and liberals who hate the metaphysics illustrated by Plato's allegory of the cave thrill to the idea that the common
man is in the grip of illusion and ought to be ruled by philosopher-
kings, even if *their* idea of a philosopher-king would have filled
Plato with abject horror. Aristotle, by contrast, is to them something
of a wet blanket, unwilling to mix his inegalitarianism with any
contempt for conventional opinion or even to express it in titillating
prose. Overall, then, Aristotle just isn't as "sexy" as Plato. His only
advantage is being right.

Like Plato, Aristotle is a realist in the sense we've been discussing. But he thinks Plato needs to be brought down to earth a
bit. For Aristotle, universals or forms are real, and they are not
reducible to anything either material or mental. Still, he thinks it is
an error to regard them as objects existing in a "third realm" of their
own. Rather, considered as they are in themselves they exist only
"in" the things they are the forms of; and considered as abstractions
from these things, they exist only in the intellect. Furthermore, even
the intellect relies on the senses in coming to know them. What all
this means exactly, how it differs from the views we've considered
so far, and why it matters, can only be understood in the context of
Aristotle's overall metaphysics – his description of the basic

principles and categories governing all reality, knowledge of which must inform any sound scientific, ethical, political, or theological inquiry. The reader should be warned, then, of two things. First, what follows in the next few pages will unavoidably be a little dry, abstract, and technical. Second, you had better pay strict attention anyway, so crack open a Jolt Cola and prop up your eyelids with toothpicks if you have to, because what I said earlier about the significance of realism in general goes double for Aristotle's version, which is the most powerful and systematic realist metaphysics ever developed (even if it was Aristotle's medieval followers, rather than the man himself, who completed this development).

How significant is Aristotle? Well, I wouldn't want to exaggerate, so let me put it this way: *Abandoning Aristotelianism, as the founders of modern philosophy did, was the single greatest mistake ever made in the entire history of Western thought.* More than any other intellectual factor – there are other, non-intellectual factors too, of course, and some are more important – this abandonment has contributed to the civilizational crisis through which the West has been living for several centuries, and which has accelerated massively in the last century or so. It is implicated in the disintegration of confidence in the rational justifiability of morality and religious belief; in the widespread assumption that a scientific picture of human nature entails that free will is an illusion; in the belief that there is a "mind-body problem" and that the only scientifically and philosophically respectable solution to it is some version of materialism; in the proliferation of varieties of relativism and irrationalism, and also of scientism and hyper-rationalism; in the modern world's corrosive skepticism about the legitimacy of any authority, and the radical individualism and collectivism that have followed in its wake; and in the intellectual and practical depersonalization of man that all of this has entailed, and which has in turn led to mass-murder on a scale unparalleled in human history. Its logical implications can also be seen in today's headlines: in the abortion industry's slaughter of millions upon millions of unborn human beings; in the judicial murder of Terri Schiavo (as Nat Hentoff aptly labeled it) and the push for euthanasia generally; in the mostly pointless and certainly point-missing debate between Darwinians and "Intelligent Design" advocates; in the movement for "same-sex marriage" and the sexual revolution generally; and a thousand other things besides.

"Surely You're Joking, Mr. Feser!" you might be thinking to yourself about now, with apologies to Richard Feynman. But I am not joking. I do realize it might *seem* far-fetched to link the abortion debate, say, to the thought of either a 4th century B.C. Greek philosopher or some nasty things said about him by Bacon and Hobbes (though, if I may say so, the sorts of people who would trace the Iraq war to Leo Strauss's lecture notes have no business accusing others of stretching things). Of course, I am not claiming that Aristotle sported a pro-life bumper sticker on his mule, or handed out "Bush for President" buttons at the Lyceum. Nor am I claiming that he would personally have agreed with, much less understood, everything ever defended in the name of his philosophical system. What I am saying is that it was the logical development of Aristotelian ideas (primarily by his medieval Scholastic admirers) that provided the most powerful and systematic intellectual foundation for traditional Western religion and morality – and for that matter, for science, morality, politics, and theology in general – that has ever existed. And it was the pulling of that first Aristotelian thread that has led to the unraveling of the once-seamless garment of Western thought – an unraveling that undoes not only the religious and moral worldview to which secularists would bid good riddance, but also *any* rational and moral standards by reference to which they could justify their own position. As I keep saying, we will see how all this works out in the chapters to follow. But having yet again issued a gigantic promissory note, let me get on with Aristotle's metaphysics, so that I can begin in the next chapter to pay off my debt to the reader.

A. Actuality and potentiality: The place to start talking about Aristotle is with Parmenides. You'll recall that he said that change and motion are impossible, and that if the senses tell us otherwise, so much the worse for them. You'll also recall thinking that he sounded like a nut. Aristotle might not have put it quite that way, though he certainly had no inclination whatsoever to take Parmenides' conclusion seriously. But he did take his *arguments* for that conclusion seriously, and regarded them as interesting enough to merit a detailed reply. Since few readers are likely to worry about whether Parmenides' specific arguments really work, I won't bother going into all the flaws that Aristotle pinpointed in them (though these are philosophically interesting and important). More relevant to our concerns is Aristotle's positive account of how, regardless of Parmenides' arguments, change really is possible at all.

Parmenides' claim was that something can't come from nothing, but that nothing was the only thing something new *could* come from, since the only thing there is other than what already exists (i.e. being) is non-being or nothing. Hence nothing new can come into existence, and change is impossible. Aristotle's reply is that while it is true that something can't come from nothing, it is false to suppose that nothing or non-being is the only possible candidate for a source of change. Take any object of our experience: a blue rubber ball, for instance. What can we say about it? Well, there are the ways it actually is: solid, round, blue, and bouncy. (These are different aspects of its "being," you might say.) And there are the ways it is not: square and red, for example; it is also not a dog, or a Buick Skylark, or innumerable other things. (The ball's squareness, redness, dogginess, etc., since they don't exist, are thus different kinds of "non-being.") But in addition to all this, we can distinguish the various ways the ball *potentially* is: red (if you paint it), soft and gooey (if you melt it), a miniature globe (if you draw little continents on it), and so forth. So being and non-being aren't the only relevant factors here; there are also a thing's various *potentialities*.

The distinction between *actuality* and *potentiality*, then, is the key to understanding how, contra Parmenides, change is possible. (The more traditional terminology, beloved of us fogeys, is "act" and "potency," but I will spare you that.) Parmenides says: If we say that a solid rubber ball can become soft and gooey, then it can't be the actual gooeyness itself that makes this possible, because it doesn't yet exist, and it can't be the non-existent gooeyness either, since what doesn't exist can't explain anything; so, again, the ball can never become gooey, and in general no sort of change is possible, regardless of what our senses tell us. Aristotle replies: Even if the gooeyness itself doesn't yet exist in the ball, the *potential* for gooeyness *does* exist in it, and this, together with some external influence that *actualizes* this potential (e.g. heat), suffices to show how the change can occur.

Pretty obvious, you might be thinking, and you'd be right. So why dwell on it? Here's one reason: Once you make this simple distinction between actuality and potentiality, you are on your way to seeing that *there is and must be a God*. Aristotle drew this inference himself, for reasons he develops at length in his famous arguments for an Unmoved Mover (or, as we might say today, an Unchanging Changer). We will be looking at Aquinas's version of this argument in the next chapter.

Further comments are in any case in order, for simple though it is, Aristotle's distinction is liable to be misunderstood. First of all, you might think, at least if you are a contemporary analytic philosopher, that a thing is "potentially" almost *anything*, so that Aristotle's distinction is uninteresting. For example, it might be said by such philosophers that we can "conceive" of a "possible world" where rubber balls can bounce from here to the moon, or where they move by themselves and follow people around menacingly, or some such thing. But the potentialities Aristotle has in mind are the ones rooted in a thing's nature as it actually exists, not just any old thing it might "possibly" do in some expanded abstract sense rooted in our powers of conception. Hence, in Aristotle's sense of "potential," while a rubber ball could potentially be melted, it could *not* potentially follow someone around all by itself.

Second, and as indicated already, Aristotle holds that even though a thing's potentials are the key to understanding how it can change, this is not the end of the story. An outside source of change is also necessary. For potential gooeyness, say, precisely because it is *merely* potential, cannot actualize itself; only something else (like heat) could do it. Consider also that if a potential could actualize itself, there would be no way to explain why it does so at one time rather than another. The ball melts and becomes gooey when you heat it. Why did this potential gooeyness become actual just at that point? The obvious answer is that the heat was needed to actualize it. If the potential gooeyness could have made itself actual all by itself, then it would have happened already, since the potential was there already.

So, no potential can actualize itself, and in this sense anything that changes requires something outside it to change it. This is true even of animals, which seem at first glance to change themselves; for what this always amounts to is really just one part of the animal being changed by another part. The dog "moves itself" across the room, but only insofar as the potential motion of the legs of the dog is actualized by the flexing of the leg muscles, and their potential to be flexed is actualized by the firing of the motor neurons, and the potential of the motor neurons to fire is actualized by other neurons, and so on and so forth. Thus we have the classic Aristotelian principle: *Whatever is changed is changed by another*, or, in its more traditional formulation, *Whatever is moved is moved by another*. (When Aristotelians speak of "motion," they mean "change" in general, not just motion in the sense of moving from place to place, which is what people usually mean by the word these days. "Why do they use the word in such a strange way?" you might ask. Actually, they don't use it in a strange way. The Aristotelian usage is the older usage; the newer usage is a novelty, and one that leads to all sorts of misunderstandings on the part of modern writers when they consider Aristotelian ideas and arguments. But more on this later.)

Third, while actuality and potentiality are fully intelligible only in relation to each other, there is an asymmetry between them, with actuality having metaphysical priority. A potential is always a potential *for* a certain kind of actuality; for instance, potential gooeyness is just the potential to be actually gooey. Furthermore, potentiality cannot exist on its own, but only in combination with actuality – hence there is no such thing as potential gooeyness all by itself, but only in something like an actual rubber ball. It is incoherent to speak of something both existing and being *purely* potential, with no actuality whatsoever. But it is not incoherent to speak of something as purely actual, with no potentiality (indeed, for Aristotle there is such a being, namely God – but again, more on this later). So, while for us to understand actuality and potentiality, we need to contrast them with each other; in the real world outside our minds actuality can exist on its own while potentiality cannot. As the very first of the famous "Twenty Four Thomistic Theses" has it ("Thomism" being the philosophical system deriving from

Thomas Aquinas, the greatest disciple of Aristotle): "Potency and Act divide being in such a way that whatever is, is either pure act, or of necessity it is composed of potency and act as primary and intrinsic principles."[23] (Helpful tip: You can always tell a Thomist at the beach or on the freeway, because you'll see this formula emblazoned either on the T-Shirt he's wearing or on the bumper of his car. I am hoping that this book will contribute to its revival as a catch-phrase.)

Fourth, a thing's various actualities and potentialities exist in a layered fashion and constitute a hierarchy, as I will now demonstrate with a paragraph full of somewhat dry technical distinctions. (Bear with me.) For example: Since you are a human being, you are a rational animal; because you are a rational animal, you have the power or faculty of speech; and because you have this power, you sometimes exercise it and speak. Your actually having the power of speech flows from your actually being a rational animal; it is a "secondary actuality" relative to your being a rational animal, which is a "primary actuality." And your actually exercising that power on some occasion is in turn a "secondary actuality" relative to your having the power – which, at least relative to the actual exercise of it, is "primary." (Note that you *have* the power even when you don't exercise it, e.g. when you are sleeping or competing in a breath-holding contest.) There are similar distinctions to be drawn with respect to potentiality. Suppose you don't speak German. You nevertheless have the potential to speak it, in the sense that you might learn it. Call this a "first potentiality" for speaking German. Now, even once you do learn it, you won't of course be speaking it all the time, even though you could speak it at any particular moment if you wanted to. You thus now have the potential to speak German in *another* sense. Call this a "second potentiality" for speaking German. Now acquiring this second sort of potentiality for speaking German – the ability to speak it at will – is also, of course, a kind of actuality, insofar as you now actually have the ability to speak it. So a second potentiality is also a kind of primary actuality; and when you really do go ahead and speak German, exercising your new ability, the act of speaking counts as a secondary actuality relative to this primary actuality. I could make further distinctions – and I know you want me to – but that's enough to make the point.

(I can almost hear the reader stifling a yawn; indeed, I can even just about hear his eyes glazing over. "What's the point of all this hair-splitting?" you're wondering. So here's one more promissory note: Unless you make these distinctions, you cannot fully understand the abortion and euthanasia debates, among other things. But don't take my word for it; keep reading.)

B. Form and matter: If Parmenides was wrong to deny the existence of change, Heraclitus was also wrong to claim that change is all that exists. For Aristotle, the right view, here as elsewhere, is somewhere in between the extremes. It might seem that Plato had already seen this; but in fact Plato more or less embraces both extremes at once, rather than repudiating them. For he concedes to Parmenides that the world of the senses does not correspond to reality in the strictest sense, and to Heraclitus that it is devoid of permanence. He might soften the errors somewhat, but he doesn't eliminate them. (Liberalism is like this: Purporting to offer a middle ground between radical individualism and collectivism, what it really gives us is a diabolical synthesis of the two, a bureaucratically managed libertinism. Conservatism, which sees the family rather than the individual or society as a whole as the fundamental social unit, is the true "third way." But I digress, and fear that comparing Platonism to liberalism does dirt on Platonism.)

Against Parmenides, Heraclitus, and Plato, Aristotle insists that common sense is right in affirming that the ordinary objects of everyday experience – tables, chairs, rocks, trees, dogs, cats, and people – are paradigmatically real. With Heraclitus, he holds that these real things undergo change; with Parmenides, he holds that what is real cannot be change alone; and with Plato, he holds that form is the key to understanding how something permanent under-lies all change. His basic idea is this: The ordinary objects of our experience are irreducible composites of potentiality and actuality, of the capacity for change and something that persists through the change. In particular, they are irreducible composites of *matter* and *form*. The blue rubber ball is composed of a certain kind of matter – namely rubber – and a certain form – namely, the form of a blue, round, bouncy object. The matter by itself isn't the ball; after all, rubber could also take the form of an eraser, or a doorstop, or any number of other things. The form by itself isn't the ball either; you can't bounce blueness, roundness, or even bounciness down the hallway, for they are mere abstractions. It is only the form and matter together that constitute the ball. Hence we have Aristotle's famous doctrine of *hylomorphism* (or "matter-formism," to convey the significance of the Greek *hyle* or "matter" and *morphe* or "form").

Now some of the forms a thing has are non-essential. A ball is still a ball whether it is blue or red. But other forms *are* essential. If the ball is melted down, it loses its round shape and bounciness; and for that very reason, it is no longer a ball at all, but just a puddle of goo. Those features that are essential to a thing comprise what Aristotelians call its *substantial form* – the form that makes a thing the kind of substance or thing that it is, its *essence*. Being round is part of the substantial form or essence of a ball; being blue is not. Being a rational animal is (according to Aristotelians) the essence or substantial form of a human being; having black or white skin is not part of this essence, since someone can be a rational animal, and thus a human being, whatever his skin color. As with actualities, forms come in a kind of hierarchy. There is the substantial form or essence of a thing (e.g. being a rational animal in the case of human beings); there are various properties of a thing that are not part of its essence per se but which necessarily flow from its essence (e.g. having the capacity for humor, which follows from being a rational animal); and there are a thing's "accidental" features, those which it may have or lack, gain or lose, without affecting its essence (e.g. being bald in the case of a human being).[24]

That it is only matter and form together that constitute a ball is part of what I mean by calling this composite "irreducible." What exists in the actual world is just the ball itself. The matter of the ball doesn't exist apart from the ball, at least not while the ball itself still exists. (Of course, you could melt it down, but in that case even though the matter would still exist, the ball wouldn't; and even then, though the matter would have lost the form of a ball, it would have taken on a new form.) The form of the ball doesn't exist by itself either; it only exists insofar as the rubber has taken on that specific form. So, form and matter *considered by themselves* are, in general anyway, mere abstractions; they exist in the mind, but not in reality. Still, they are *different* aspects of reality – in this case, of the ball. The form is not the matter and the matter is not the form. Even if, contra Plato, the form of the ball doesn't exist by itself; neither is it true to say after the fashion of materialism that the ball is "just a piece of matter." Nothing is *just* a piece of matter, for matter cannot exist without form, and form (being the principle that accounts for permanence) isn't material (matter being the principle that accounts for change).[25]

Related to this is the fact that form and matter, as Aristotle conceives of them, can only be understood in relation to each other. Form is paradigmatically what determines matter, and matter is defined in terms of its potential to take on different forms. That the distinction is a distinction between interdependent aspects of a thing is what makes a simultaneous reply to Parmenides, Heraclitus, and Plato possible. The blue rubber ball remains a rubber ball even after it is painted red because it retains the form of a rubber ball; and even when, as a result of melting, the ball goes out of existence and becomes a puddle of goo, the rubber itself persists through this change. Hence permanence is possible, despite what Heraclitus says. That the ball is composed of matter is also what makes it possible for it to change, contra Parmenides. And that the form is just the form *of* a particular hunk of matter shows that Plato is wrong to think of forms as generally existing completely independently of the material world.

The interrelationship between form and matter parallels the interrelationship between actuality and potentiality. But the two distinctions, though closely related, are not the same, for the latter distinction is more general than the former. In particular, while to have a certain form is always to be actual (rather than merely potential) in a certain way, to be actual is not always to have a certain form. For on the Aristotelian view, as we have noted, there is such a thing as a purely actual being (namely God), and such a being does not have a form, certainly not in the sense other things do. (You know the drill: more on this later.) Furthermore, while to be a material thing is always to have potentialities of various sorts, for a thing to have potentiality does not necessarily entail its being a material object. For there could be an *immaterial* thing that manifests potentiality insofar as it comes into existence at some point in time (thereby going from potential existence to actual existence).

What sort of thing might this be? Well – despite Aristotle's rejection of Platonism – a form, actually. This brings us to another parallel with the actuality/potentiality distinction, and also (sorry!) a further complication to the story. For form and matter, like actuality and potentiality, are asymmetrically related. Though we understand actuality and potentiality by reference to each other, actuality is nevertheless metaphysically prior to potentiality. Similarly, though we understand form and matter by reference to each other, form is metaphysically prior to matter. To be sure, with a purely material object like a ball, its form can never exist apart from its matter. And as we have said, matter can never exist apart from form. But there can also be such a thing as an immaterial object – Aristotle hints that (a part of) the human soul might be an example – and like everything else, such a thing would have a form. Hence it is possible, at least in principle and in some cases, for forms to exist without matter. Such forms would be immaterial particular things, though, not uninstantiated universals; hence this qualification to Aristotle's theory does not mark a return to Plato's view that forms are abstract universal natures in which different material things "participate," much less to the idea that forms in general exist apart from the material world.[26] (Aristotle himself just hints at all this; it was left to his medieval successors to develop it in detail, as we will see.)

Since Aristotle rejects these views of Plato's, his version of realism is often referred to as "moderate realism," as opposed to the "extreme realism" of Plato. (The views are also often just called "Aristotelian realism" and "Platonic realism.") Since it seems he is willing to allow that at least some forms can exist without matter, why does he reject Plato's view? One reason is that treating a form as something both universal – that is, instantiated in many things – but also existing independently as an object in its own right, as Plato does, seems to lead to various paradoxes. Take the Form of Man, for example. Individual men are men only because they participate in this Form, Plato says. But if the Form of Man is itself a kind of substance or thing, doesn't that entail that there must be some other Form that *it* participates in and by reference to which it counts as the Form of Man specifically? Don't we have to posit a Super-Form of Man over and above the Form of Man, in which both

2. Greeks Bearing Gifts

individual men and the Form of Man itself participate? Indeed, wouldn't we have to posit a Super-Super-Form of Man over and above that Super-Form, in which the Form of Man, the Super-Form, and individual men participate? We seem led into infinite regress, and absurdity.

This objection – known as the "Third Man" argument – was raised by Plato himself, and it has been inconclusively hashed over for millennia. A more telling consideration seems to be the following. Consider a universal like "animality" (i.e. the feature of being an animal). Every individual animal is either rational (as human beings are) or non-rational (as all other animals are). But what about animality itself, considered *as* a universal? Well, precisely because it is universal, it has to apply to both rational and non-rational animals. But it can't itself include both rationality and non-rationality, for these are contradictory. So we have to say that inherently it entails neither rationality nor non-rationality. But no genuine substance or thing can be *neither* rational nor non-rational; any existing thing has to be one or the other. Hence animality cannot be said to exist as a substance or thing in its own right; that is to say, it cannot be said to be a Platonic Form.

How does it exist, then? In the real, mind-independent world it exists only in actual animals, and always inseparably tied to either rationality or non-rationality. There is animality in Socrates, but it is there inseparably tied to his rationality, and specifically to his humanness. And there is animality in Fido, but it is there inseparably tied to non-rationality, and specifically to dog-ness. Animality considered in abstraction from these things exists only in the mind. The senses observe this or that individual man, this or that individual dog; the intellect abstracts away the differentiating features of each and considers the animality in isolation, as a universal. This is not nominalism, for it holds that universals exist. Nor is it conceptualism, for while it holds that universals *considered in abstraction from other features* exist only in the mind, it also holds that they exist in the extra-mental things themselves (albeit always tied to other features) and that the abstracted universals existing in the intellect derive from our sense experiences of these objectively existing things, rather than being the free creations of the mind. So realism is preserved, but in a more sober and down-to-earth way than

Platonism affords. We can have our cake and eat it too: There are objective essences, natures, or forms of things, just as Plato says; but our knowledge of them derives from the senses, and is grounded in ordinary objects of our experience, just as common sense holds.

C. *The four causes*: Whew! OK, I know you need a break. Trade the Jolt Cola in for a martini. (I just did, for what it's worth.) One more set of ideas, and then we're done with Aristotle for a while; and in this case the ideas are, I think you'll find, at least a little more concrete. They may also be the most important of all the philosophical concepts we've looked at so far. For if you don't understand Aristotle's four causes, then I dare say you don't understand anything at all. But then, we all *do* understand Aristotle's four causes, at least intuitively. You don't need a Ph.D. to do so; indeed, as in so many other areas, these days a Ph.D. is more likely to be an obstacle to understanding. What is needed is rather an explicit systematic account of what we all know intuitively, and the avoidance of certain deep and widespread modern philosophical errors which we'll consider in later chapters. Aristotle gives us both.

Go back to the rubber ball. Suppose you had never seen one before, and wondered what it is. A cursory examination would reveal to you that it is made out of rubber, and that it is spherical, uniformly solid, and bouncy. But that wouldn't tell you everything you'd need to know about it for a complete explanation. You might also ask "Where did this thing come from?" and seeing the words "Acme Ball Company, Made in USA" printed on it would tell you, if it wasn't obvious already, that it is not a natural object, but made in a factory somewhere. Even then you'd still have another question, and indeed the most important one: "What is it *for*?" The answer to that, of course, would be that it is a child's toy intended to provide amusement.

And there you have Aristotle's four causes. The first is what is traditionally called the *material cause* or underlying stuff that a thing is made out of, in this case rubber. Then we have the *formal cause*, which is the form, structure, or pattern that the matter exhibits, which in this case comprises such features as sphericity, solidity, and bounciness. As you can see, the material and formal causes of a thing are just its matter and form, considered as components of a complete explanation of it. Next we have the *efficient cause*, which is what brings a thing into being, or, more generally and technically, which actualizes a potentiality in a thing; in this case, that would be the actions of the workers and/or machines in the factory in which the ball was made, as they molded the rubber into a ball. Finally we have the *final cause*, which is the end, goal, or purpose of a thing, in this case providing amusement to a child. In combination, these causes provide a complete explanation of a thing. That doesn't mean that in asking about the ball, for example, you would not have further questions. You might ask "Where does rubber come from?" or "How do they mold it so perfectly?" or "Who made the factory and why?" But the answers will always be just further examples of material, formal, efficient, and final causes.

The four causes are completely general, applying throughout the natural world and not only to human artifacts. Take a bodily organ like the heart, for example. To understand what it is, you have to know its material cause, viz. that it is made out of muscle tissue of a certain sort. But there are lots of muscles in the body that aren't hearts, so you need to know more than that. You also need to know its formal cause, and thus such things as that the muscle tissue is organized into atria, ventricles, and the like. Then there is its efficient cause, which in this case would be the biological processes that determined that certain embryonic cells would form into a heart rather than, say, a kidney or brain. Finally, and again most importantly of all, there is its final cause, namely that it serves the function of pumping blood.

As I have said, everyone knows about the four causes implicitly even if they don't know them by that name. Still, there's more to be said, including some inevitable complications of a philosophical nature. (You knew it was coming.) These have to do with two considerations alluded to above: the need for an explicit and systematic account of the four causes, one which expands upon our commonsense knowledge and lays bare their nature, interrelationships, and implications; and the need to answer those errors which have clouded modern thinkers' understanding of Aristotle's doctrine. For now I will make only some cursory remarks about these matters, because we will be revisiting the four causes over and over again in the course of the next few chapters, gradually drawing out their deep and multifarious consequences, rebutting various misunderstandings and objections as they arise, and finally vindicating Aristotle's doctrine completely – and thus the implications that follow from it too – in Chapter 6.

Note first that as Aristotle understands the material and formal causes of a thing, they imply far more than the obvious fact that the ordinary objects of our experience are made up of some kind of stuff or other organized in a certain way. Aristotle's entire metaphysical scheme as we've considered it thus far – moderate realism, hylomorphism, the whole ball of wax – is implicated as well. A thing's formal cause is, at the deepest level, its substantial form or essence; its material cause entails that it has certain potentialities and lacks others; its formal cause, being its substantial form or essence, is shared by other things and known by the intellect via abstraction from experience; and so forth. To be sure, these various philosophical subtleties are built on common sense and do not contradict it, but they do go considerably beyond it.

Aristotle's notion of efficient cause – that which brings something into being – is often said, almost with a pose of magnanimity, to be an element of his position that has carried over largely unchanged into modern philosophy. (The old boy got something right after all, you see.) But this is an exaggeration at best, and certainly very misleading. In fact it is such a misleading exaggeration that I am tempted to say it is really a falsehood; certainly it is no compliment to Aristotle, given how deeply and notoriously problematic the notion of cause and effect has become in the always-unsafe hands of modern philosophers. For one thing, just as material and formal causation are deeply intertwined on Aristotle's account, so too are efficient causes and final causes. You simply cannot properly understand the one apart from the other; indeed, there *cannot be* efficient causes without final ones. And this is precisely why causation has become such a problem for modern thinkers. Famously, they deny that there really are any final causes at all, appearances notwithstanding. (One is tempted to compare such brazenness to that of Parmenides, except that this would be an insult to Parmenides.) This has led them into all sorts of paradoxes and incoherencies, which have only gotten more bizarre and intractable as the centuries have worn on. And yet, with the sort of supreme confidence that goes hand in hand with madness, or at least incorrigible foolishness, they refuse even to consider the possibility that Aristotle might have been right about final causes after all. But I am getting ahead of myself; we will return to all of this in time. Suffice it for now to say that Aristotle's notion of efficient causation is by no means easily identifiable with anything you'll find in the writings of the typical modern philosopher.

Another indication of this is that Aristotle would be mystified by the modern tendency to treat cause and effect as essentially a relation between temporally ordered events. The standard story goes something like this: Suppose a brick is thrown toward a window. That's one event. Now suppose the window shatters. That's another event. Obviously, the first event came before the second one. We also want to say (or so we are assured) that the first event *caused* the second one. But why do we say this? Many events are not caused by the events they follow. So why do we think things are different in this case? After all, even in this case it is at least "conceivable" that the first event could occur without the second. The throwing of the brick *could*, in theory, be followed by the brick's vanishing into thin air, or turning into a rabbit or a Snickers bar. Logically speaking, the events are "loose and separate," with no "necessary connection" between them. So maybe it's just the fact that they are "constantly conjoined" *in our experience* that leads us to think there is such a connection. Maybe the necessity is in *us* and not in the objective world; that is to say, maybe there really is no objective connection at all between bricks being thrown and windows shattering, and it's just the way our minds happened to be wired that makes us think there is. Maybe "cause and effect" is just a matter of there being regular or "lawlike" correlations between events, and science must rest content with discovering these correlations. Or maybe . . .

Aristotle's reaction to all of this would probably be like that of the caveman in one of those Geico car insurance commercials: "Yeah I have a response . . . uh, *what?!*" The way of posing the "problem" of cause and effect just described, and some of the phrases used in doing so, owe much to the Scottish philosopher David Hume (1711–1776) – a big hero to "New Atheists" and secularists in general, needless to say – and philosophers have been oohing and aahing over his "discovery" of this "problem" ever since. No doubt they consider it an improvement on anything Aristotle had to say. Well, to paraphrase Lloyd Bentsen: I've read Aristotle; Aristotle is a hero of mine; and Mr. Hume, sir, you are no Aristotle. In fact Hume's supposedly weighty conundrum is, as we shall see, just one of many "traditional" "problems" of philosophy that have arisen only since, and only *because* of, the abandonment of Aristotelianism. They mark a precipitous decline in philosophical understanding, not an advance; in particular, and contrary to the self-image of their peddlers, they manifest an appalling lapse of care and rigor in analysis and argumentation.

Suppose you asked your uncle (or whomever) what caused the broken window. Unless he's a philosopher, he'd probably say, "The brick did" – the brick, not "the event of the brick's being thrown." In other words, for common sense it is ultimately *things* that are causes, not events. Aristotle would agree. He would also say that the *immediate* efficient cause of an effect, and the one most directly responsible for it, is *simultaneous* with the effect, not temporally prior to it. In the case of the broken window, the key point in the causal series would be something like the pushing of the brick into the glass and the glass's giving way. These events are simultaneous; indeed, Aristotle would say that the brick's pushing into the glass and the glass's giving way are really just the same event, considered under different descriptions. Or, to take an example often used in discussions of Aristotle, we might think of a potter making a pot, where the shaping activity of the potter's hand and the soft clay's being shaped are simultaneous, and again, one and the same event being described in different ways. But in examples like these, there is no question of the causes and effects being "loose and separate" or lacking a "necessary connection"; to say that a brick's pressing through the glass might "conceivably" not be accompanied by the glass's giving way, or that a hand's shaping the clay might "conceivably" occur without the clay's being shaped, wouldn't pass the laugh test of even the most jaded modern philosopher (though I admit you can never be too sure).

Yet the analysis of any event ultimately resolves, for Aristotle, into a series of causes intimately related in just this way. Hence there is no room for Hume's "problem" even to arise. Hume and his acolytes miss this because their analysis remains at too crude a level – again, speaking glibly as they do of "the event of the brick's being thrown" followed by "the event of the window's shattering," ignoring all the fine-grained detail inherent in this sequence. (Hume had a reason for indulging in such crudity, namely his empiricist theory of knowledge, but to appeal to it in his defense would be to try to justify the crude in terms of the even more crude. More on this later.[27]) The attentive reader might have noticed that Aristotle's account seems to entail a *series* of *simultaneous* causes and effects, and might also wonder where such a series terminates and how it can be explained. Good questions; we'll discover the answers in the next chapter, when we examine Aquinas's arguments for the existence of God.

Also relevant to those arguments, as we'll see, is a further Aristotelian principle concerning efficient causation, namely that whatever is in the effect must in some sense be contained in the cause as well. The basic idea is that a cause cannot give to its effect what it does not have to give, and it can be illustrated by a simple example. Suppose you come across a puddle of water near an outdoor spigot. You will naturally conclude that the puddle was caused by the spigot, either because someone turned it on or because it is leaking. The effect is a puddle of water and the cause is something fully capable of producing that effect, since it contains water in it already. But now suppose instead that you come across a puddle of thick, sticky, dark red liquid near the same spigot. In this case you will *not* conclude that the spigot was the cause, at least not by itself. The reason is that there is nothing in the spigot alone that could produce this specific effect, or at least not every feature of the effect. The spigot could produce a puddle of liquid alright, and maybe even a puddle of vaguely reddish liquid if there was rust in the line, but not a puddle of thick, sticky, dark red liquid specifically. You would be likely to conclude instead that someone had spilled a can of soda pop near the spigot, or perhaps that someone had been bleeding heavily nearby it. Even if these possibilities had been ruled out and you had evidence that the puddle came from the spigot after all, you'd conclude that somehow such a thick red liquid (blood, soda, or whatever) had somehow been put into the water line, or that if it had not, then there must have been something on the ground that when mixed with water from the spigot chemically produced this thick red liquid. What you would never seriously consider is the suggestion that normal water from the spigot *all by itself* produced the red puddle. For there is just nothing in water by itself that could produce the redness, thickness, or stickiness of the puddle; ergo there must have been something in addition to the water that produced the effect.

As this example illustrates, the effect might be "contained in" the cause in various ways. It could be that the cause was itself red, as blood or cherry soda pop is red even before it causes a red puddle. But it could also be that the cause was not itself red but had the power to generate redness in the effect; for example, neither the water nor some chemical substance spread on the ground (a ground-up "Fizzy" drink tablet, say) might be red, yet will produce a thick red liquid when combined. Or, to take another example, the cause of a fire might itself be on fire, as when a torch is used to start a brushfire, or it may instead have the power to produce fire, as a cigarette lighter has even when it is not being used. The traditional way of making this distinction is to say that a cause has the feature that it generates in the effect "formally" in the first sort of case (e.g. when both the cause and the effect are red or on fire) and "eminently" in the second sort of case (e.g. when the cause is not itself red or on fire but has an inherent power to produce redness or fire). If a cause didn't contain all the features of its effect either formally or eminently, there would be no way to account for how the effect came about in just the way it did. Again, a cause cannot give to its effect what it does not have to give.

This is another piece of common sense that Humeans and other modern philosophers pretend to doubt, for the same silly reasons they pretend to believe that it is possible that a brick thrown toward a window might turn into a rabbit instead of breaking the window. It is also sometimes suggested that the principle in question is disproved by evolution, since if simpler life forms give rise to more complex ones then (it is claimed) they must surely be producing in their effects something they did not have to give.[28] In fact evolution does nothing to disprove the principle, and the suggestion that it does rests on the same kind of sloppy thinking that underlies Humean doubts about causation in general. Every species is essentially just a variation on the same basic genetic material that has existed for billions of years from the moment life began. On the Darwinian story, a new variation arises when there is a mutation in the existing genetic structure which produces a trait that happens to be advantageous given circumstances in a creature's environment. The mutation in turn might be caused by a copying error made during the DNA replication process or by some external factor like radiation or chemical damage. Now, just as water and a certain chemical agent are together sufficient to produce a red puddle even if the water by itself wouldn't be, so too do the existing genetic material, the mutation, and environmental circumstances together generate a new biological variation even though none of these factors by itself would be sufficient to do so. Thus, evolution no more poses a challenge to the principle that a cause must contain every feature of its effect either "formally" or "eminently" than the puddle example does. Indeed, as the physicist Paul Davies has pointed out, to deny that the information contained in a new kind of life form derives from some combination of preexisting factors – specifically, in part from the organism's environment if not from its genetic inheritance alone – would contradict the second law of thermodynamics, which tells us that order (and thus information content) tends inevitably to decrease within a closed system.[29]

We'll have more to say about the grounds and dramatic implications of Aristotle's conception of efficient causes in the next chapter. We'll also return then (and in each of the forthcoming chapters, for that matter) to the all-important topic of final causes. I said that Aristotle regards final causation – goal-directedness, purposiveness, something's pointing toward an end beyond itself – as extending well beyond the realm of human artifacts, indeed as pervading the natural world. I also gave the functions of bodily organs as an example, and it is indeed the most obvious and compelling sort of example to give. But Aristotle takes final causation or goal-directedness to exist throughout inorganic nature as well. The moon is "directed toward" movement around the earth, as a kind of "goal." Fire is directed toward the production of heat, specifically, rather than cold. Water is directed toward evaporation, then condensation, then precipitation, then collection, then evaporation again, in a cyclical fashion. And so forth. Most people, including many contemporary philosophers, deeply misunderstand what Aristotle means by this. They sometimes suppose, for example, that he is making the quite absurd claim that the moon is *consciously trying* to go around the sun, or that fire *wants* to produce heat. (Laughter ensues, and then everyone goes back to praising Hume for his supposedly far-more-sober suggestion that a brick could "conceivably" disappear into thin air or turn into a turnip.) But Aristotle never said or thought any such thing. His whole point, in fact, is that there is a kind of goal-directedness that exists *even apart from* conscious thought processes and intentions. For Aristotle, our conscious thought processes are really but a special case of the more general natural phenomenon of goal-directedness or final causality, which exists in the natural world in a way that is mostly totally divorced from any conscious mind or intelligence. The functions of various bodily organs (hearts, kidneys, livers, etc.) are the most obvious examples – the organs have these functions, and perform them, even though they are totally unconscious – but less complex forms of final causality are to be found throughout the inorganic realm.[30]

I have referred to final causes as "all-important" for several reasons, all of which will become increasingly evident as we see the myriad implications of this idea in subsequent chapters. One reason worth emphasizing here, though, is their inherently preeminent place among the four causes. Aquinas refers to the final cause as "the cause of causes," and for good reason. The material cause of a thing underlies its potential for change; but potentialities, as we've seen, are always potentialities *for*, or directed *toward*, some actuality. Hence final causality underlies all potentiality and thus all materiality. The final cause of a thing is also the central aspect of its formal cause; indeed, it determines its formal cause. For it is only because a thing has a certain end or final cause that it has the form it has – hence hearts have ventricles, atria, and the like precisely because they have the function of pumping blood. ("Form follows function," you might say, though Aristotle would have been horrified at modern architecture's simple-minded application of this principle.) And as I have said (though for reasons that can be made explicit only after we cover some more ground through to Chapter 6), efficient causality cannot be made sense of apart from final causality. Indeed, *nothing* makes sense – not the world as a whole, not morality or human action in general, not the thoughts you're thinking or the words you're using, not *anything at all* – without final causes. They are certainly utterly central to, and ineliminable from, our conception of ourselves as rational and freely choosing agents, whose thoughts and actions are always directed toward an end beyond themselves.

Yet modern philosophers, scientists, and intellectuals in general claim not to believe in final causality. I say "claim" because, like all normal human beings, they actually appeal to final causes all the time in their everyday personal lives, and even to a great extent in their professional lives. They contemplate and act on their goals, give their reasons for doing things, explain to their children what this or that body part is for. Biologists and other scientists constantly make reference to the functions of organs, to the role various species play relative to one another in the ecosystem, to future events toward which the stars, galaxies, and other astronomical bodies are inevitably moving, and so on and on, and couldn't possibly carry on their work unless they did so. At the same time, these thinkers are in thrall to an official ideology according to which Aristotle's doctrine of the four causes was somehow refuted by modern science. In particular, it is held that modern science shows that there are no formal or final causes, and that material and efficient causes are very different from what Aristotle and his successors took them to be. Any appearance of final causality is illusory, and descriptions that make reference to it are merely useful fictions that can be translated into descriptions that make reference instead to purposeless, meaningless, goal-free causes and effects.

Let me be very clear about something. However widely accepted, these claims are, each and every one of them, simply untrue. They are false. Wrong. Mistaken. Erroneous. Non-factual. Not the case. And that is putting it much too mildly: If one were to use the proper technical jargon common in traditional Australian philosophy (at least according to Professor A.W. Sparkes's very fine dictionary of philosophical terms) one would characterize them as "bullshit."[31] Here are the facts. First, early modern philosophers and scientists never came remotely close to disproving Aristotle's doctrine of the four causes. Some of them did (as we will see) offer some feeble and easily rebutted objections, but for the most part it was simply decided to carry on scientific and philosophical practice *as if* one needed to appeal only to two (at most) of the four causes, and to ignore the others. Far from being a "discovery," the rejection of the four causes was a sheer *stipulation*, an act of pure intellectual willfulness. Second, this rash move immediately created a number of serious philosophical problems that have never been settled to this day, but instead have only gotten progressively worse; indeed, these problems have led contemporary philosophers to conclusions historically unprecedented in their bizarreness and absurdity. Third, the original stipulative character of this move has been largely forgotten with the passing centuries, and philosophers' and scientists' faulty collective memory has transformed it into the "discovery" they falsely regard it as having been. Fourth, for this reason, the *bizarreries* and absurdities to which contemporary intellectuals have been led by their rejection of the four causes have been embraced as further surprising "discoveries" or "results" of philosophical inquiry, rather than recognized for what they are: a *reductio ad absurdum* of the premises laid down by their intellectual ancestors, and thus of the entire modern philosophical picture of the world to which they are committed. That they *do* indeed constitute a *reductio ad absurdum* – a set of manifest falsehoods that refute the premises that led to them – is, as we will see by the end of this book, beyond reasonable doubt.

* * *

If you are still with me after all that – and you can put the Jolt Cola and toothpicks away now, I think (keep the martini if you like) – then you now know something crucial about Aristotle: Say of him what you will, he doesn't oversimplify things. But neither does he make them needlessly complicated. The structure of the world just happens to be as complex as he describes it, no more (perhaps) but no less either; or at any rate that, again, is something I claim we will see by the end of the book. More to the point, his account of the metaphysical structure of reality, far from being empty verbiage or of mere academic interest, has dramatic implications for religion, morality, and science that will repay the effort we have put into understanding it.

In this respect the heritage that Aristotle and the other Greek philosophers left us is, as they say, the gift that keeps giving. Yet modern thinkers have regarded it with suspicion of the sort more appropriately directed toward that most infamous of Greek gifts, the Trojan Horse. Given their own commitments, they are right to do so. In the hands of medieval Christians, Jews, and Muslims, the work of Plato and Aristotle was used to demolish the intellectual foundations of the pagan culture that produced them. If resurrected today, it would do the same to the simultaneously newer and shabbier paganism that has supplanted the religious heritage of the West. In the next chapter we will begin to see why.

3. Getting Medieval

In their book *Three Philosophers: Aristotle, Aquinas, Frege*, Elizabeth Anscombe and Peter Geach relate a story about St. Thomas Aquinas according to which he once came upon "a holy nun who used to be levitated in ecstasy." His reaction was to comment on how very large her feet were. "This made her come out of her ecstasy in indignation at his rudeness, whereupon he gently advised her to seek greater humility."[1]

Supreme unflappability was one of the hallmarks of Aquinas's character, along with a towering intellect, personal holiness, and single-minded devotion to God. Held captive by his brothers in the family castle in their failed effort to prevent him from joining the Dominicans, he took the opportunity to memorize the entire Bible and the four books of the *Sentences* of Peter Lombard. When the brothers upped the ante by sending a prostitute into his room, he famously chased her away with a flaming brand snatched from the fireplace and then used it to draw a cross on the wall, before which he prayed for, and received, the gift of lifelong chastity. He could become so absorbed in a chain of abstract reasoning or in prayer that he would sometimes forget where he was, fail to perceive the people around him, or even fail to notice the flame from a candle he was holding as it burned his hand. His writings come to some eight million words, including the massive *Summa contra Gentiles* and the *Summa Theologiae*, each of which clocks in at five thick volumes in the currently available popular editions.[2] The latter remained unfinished: Toward the end of his life Aquinas had a mystical experience, after which he said he could write no more given that "all that I have written seems to me like straw compared with what has now been revealed to me."[3]

One wonders how he would have reacted to the mental and moral midgets now being marketed as "New Atheists," who peddle stale "refutations" of theism that were themselves refuted long before Aquinas came on the scene. Perhaps he would "get medieval" with them – not in the Quentin Tarantino sense (fun as *that* would be to see) but in the Thomas Aquinas sense of humbly arguing them into the ground in about five minutes before snacking on some herring and heading over to afternoon Mass. Or perhaps, paraphrasing his remark to the levitating nun, he would simply note how very big their mouths are, and – given the worthlessness of what has come out of those mouths – counsel them to greater humility. Certainly he would be amused should they dismiss the nun story as a pious legend, given the whoppers some of them tell about Aquinas in their bestselling anti-Bible tracts.

What Aquinas didn't say

Wanda: But you think you're an intellectual, don't you, ape?

Otto: Apes don't read philosophy.

Wanda: Yes, they do, Otto. They just don't understand it.

A Fish Called Wanda (1988)

One cannot help but think of *A Fish Called Wanda* when one reads Richard Dawkins's *The God Delusion*; or at least I can't. You might think this is because the movie prominently features a snobbish Englishman or two, but that isn't the reason. It's rather (of all people) Otto, Kevin Kline's boorish American diamond thief, who most brings to mind the good professor.

Dawkins may well be a fine biologist – I really have no idea, though I suppose the fact that he teaches at Oxford might say something in his favor. But then, I teach at a community college, so what the hell do I know? Well, this for starters: that where *philosophy* is concerned, Richard Dawkins evidently knows about as much as Richard Dawson, though I admit that this may be an insult to Mr. Dawson. The one certain difference between them is that Dawson has never had the temerity to think his proficiency in his own field – hosting television game shows – qualified him to speak on philosophical matters. Yet the ideas on which Professor Dawkins's reputation with the general public rests are not biological ones, but philosophical ones – even if, in some cases, they are philosophical ideas *disguised* as biological ones.

Which brings us back to *A Fish Called Wanda*. Otto fancies himself a thinker; in particular, a philosopher. The trouble is, he is absolutely innocent of any real understanding of philosophy, though also clueless about his own cluelessness, which is where the comedy comes in. It is left to Jamie Lee Curtis's character Wanda to disabuse him of his delusions of competence. "Aristotle was *not* Belgian," she informs him; "the central teaching of Buddhism is *not* 'Every man for himself'"; and so on.

Had Wanda been looking over Dawkins's shoulder as he wrote *The God Delusion*, she might have let him in on a few things too: "Aquinas never rested any of his arguments for God's existence on the claim that 'There must have been a time when no physical things existed'; indeed, rather famously, he deliberately refrains from doing so"; "It isn't true that Aquinas gives 'absolutely no reason' to think that the First Cause of the universe is omnipotent, omniscient, good, etc.; in fact he devotes many hundreds of pages, across several works, to proving just this"; "The Fifth Way has nothing to do with Paley's 'watchmaker' argument; actually, even the most traditional followers of Aquinas often reject Paley with as much scorn as evolutionists do"; "St. Anselm was not trying to prove God's existence to God Himself"; and so on. And on, and on.[4] Indeed, Ms. Curtis could have filmed a whole *sequel* to her movie, filled with nothing but philosophy jokes of which Dawkins and his ridiculous book are the butt. Let us hope that she would have been kinder to Dawkins than she was to poor, dumb Otto. Anyway, devout evolutionist that he is, Dawkins, like his hero T.H. Huxley, would presumably not take too great offense at being compared to an ape.

Among the delusions of Richard Dawkins, then, is that he has anything of any interest whatsoever to say about philosophical matters, such as: whether talk about biological functions can be reduced to talk about patterns of efficient causation; what the nature of the human mind is; or in this case, whether God exists. (We will be looking at the first two questions ourselves in later chapters, and at the last one in this chapter.) One is almost tempted to think Dawkins's research for the philosophical chapters of his book consisted entirely of a quick thumbing through of *Philosophy for Dummies*. Almost, except for this: Though I haven't read *Philosophy for Dummies*, I would not want to insult its author, Thomas Morris, who is a very capable philosopher indeed, and the author of several rigorous and widely esteemed academic works on technical philosophical subjects. In recent years he has turned to writing for a popular audience. But since even the work in question seems not to have been "dumbed down" enough for the Charles Simonyi Professor of the Public Understanding of Science at Oxford University, Dr. Morris might want to consider a simplified sequel aimed at the "New Atheist" audience. He could call it *Philosophy for Dawkins*.

I will give Dawkins this much, however: Unlike his fellow "New Atheists," he does seem to realize that if you are going to mouth off about what a gang of idiots religious thinkers are, you had better try to make some effort actually to *refute* them, and especially the most eminent among them. And there are many very eminent ones indeed, several of whom were referred to in Chapter 1. But they don't get more eminent than Thomas Aquinas, who is widely considered, even by secular philosophers, to be the greatest philosopher of the Middle Ages, and among the greatest philosophers, period – certainly in the top ten, probably in the top five – of all time. He is also, of course, more or less the official philosopher of the Roman Catholic Church and esteemed as the greatest Christian philosopher even by many Protestants. Hence, it can safely be said that if you haven't both understood Aquinas and answered him – not to mention Anselm, Duns Scotus, Leibniz, Samuel Clarke, and so on, but let that pass – then you have hardly "made your case" against religion. Yet Dawkins is the only "New Atheist" to offer anything even remotely like an attempt to answer him, feeble as it is.

Christopher Hitchens, who directs a snotty barb or two at Aquinas, is mostly content to bluff his way through a few stock objections to the "design argument" of William Paley (every atheist's favorite whipping boy), tarting up the presentation with some evolutionary-theoretic trivia cribbed from this month's *Scientific American* or wherever. His main contribution to our intellectual life, here as elsewhere, is to prove by example that a journalist who *reads* more than most of his colleagues do by no means thereby *understands* more. "Still," I hear you saying, "he *is* a mere journalist, so what did you expect?" Well I certainly did not expect him to do *better* than the professional philosophers among the New Atheists. For Sam Harris, though he even finds room in the bibliography of *The End of Faith* to cite *me* (of all people), says *nothing* about Aquinas. Indeed, he says precious little of philosophical substance at all regarding the classical arguments for God's existence, trotting out the sorts of criticisms that anyone who's read a recent introductory philosophy of religion textbook knows are easily answered, and aimed at caricatures. This might be excusable in a non-philosopher like Hitchens or Dawkins (though not when they're shooting off their mouths about philosophical matters), but it is alarming coming from someone who trumpets his credentials as "a graduate in philosophy from Stanford University," and who deigns, forsooth, to set the whole country straight vis-à-vis religion with his *Letter to a Christian Nation* – a book which, despite its absurdly pretentious title, reads like something Madalyn Murray O'Hair's publisher would have rejected as too superficial. Since Harris is a dead ringer for comedian Ben Stiller, one wonders whether the whole thing is an elaborate publicity stunt – an Andy Kaufman wresting match, only with anti-religious fallacies instead of anti-feminist chokeholds. But then one notices in Harris's bio that he moved on from his undergraduate study of philosophy to seek "a doctorate in neuroscience." His B.A. having qualified him, he thinks, to dismiss the great religious thinkers of the West without having read them, perhaps his next feat will be to perform brain surgery without a single lesson. But before you ask for volunteers, Sam, here's a quick *Letter to a Stanford Graduate*: A little learning is a dangerous thing; drink deep or taste not the Pierian spring (etc.). Since you're such a hotshot, I trust I needn't cite the literary reference.

The really disgusting spectacle, though, comes from Daniel Dennett, who unlike Harris is no philosophical neophyte or dilettante, but a long-established "big name" academic philosopher with a great many peer-reviewed articles and books on his resumé. In a 448-page tome devoted to "breaking the spell" of religion, he devotes a total of *three pages* to addressing the traditional philosophical arguments for God's existence. Most of this is given over to a simplistic evaluation of St. Anselm's ontological proof – never a favorite with philosophical defenders of religion anyway, though far more complex, interesting, and worthy of consideration than Dennett lets on – and to the ritualistic kicking of poor, pathetic Paley. (What *would* atheists do without him?) And what about the cosmological argument – *the* central argument in the history of philosophical theology, and the one to which Aristotle, Maimonides, al-Ghazali, Aquinas, Duns Scotus, Leibniz, Clarke, et al., devote the bulk of their attention? Dennett gives it a paragraph. Worse, he devotes most of the paragraph to the stupid "Everything has a cause, so what caused God?" caricature that none of these thinkers ever defended; and while he graciously allows that there are more sophisticated versions of the argument, he dismisses them with the suggestion that only those with a patience for "ingenious nitpicking about the meaning of 'cause'" and "the niceties of scholastic logic" could ever find them of interest.[5]

Imagine Dennett's reaction if some creationist similarly dismissed Darwinian arguments as so much "ingenious nitpicking about the meaning of 'adaptation'" and "the niceties of population genetics." He would be outraged, and rightly so. And yet Mr. "Bright" himself is not above the same intellectual dishonesty when the target is religion. The author of a sympathetic recent study of Dennett's philosophy acknowledges that the "consensus evaluation" of Dennett's work among his academic peers is that while it is "undeniably creative and important," it "lacks philosophical depth and is not systematic."[6] Dennett's colleague and fellow Darwinian Michael Ruse was even more blunt in a now-notorious email exchange between them, in which he wrote: "I thought your new book is really bad and not worthy of you. . . . I think that you and Richard [Dawkins] are absolute disasters in the fight against intelligent design . . . what we need is not knee-jerk atheism but serious grappling with the issues – neither of you are willing to study Christianity seriously and to engage with the ideas."[7] Somehow, though, Dennett, like his fellow New Atheist lightweights, has been able to parlay an appallingly meager understanding of religion into a reputation for Serious Secularist Thought. Such a development calls for an investigation into the sociology, and perhaps also the psychopathology, of the secularist readership, who will apparently swallow anything their gurus shovel at them. Since I've been coining possible book titles, here's another one for anyone who wants to do the job: *Not so Bright: Daniel Dennett as a Marketing Phenomenon*.

But enough of this unpleasantness. Let us turn to Aquinas. To understand his arguments for God's existence, you need first to understand what is wrong with the way philistines like Dawkins read them, or rather misread them. Like many who are not familiar with philosophical modes of argumentation, Dawkins assumes that Aquinas is engaged in a kind of empirical theorizing, "postulating" God's existence as a "hypothesis" to "explain" certain pieces of "data." That is, he thinks Aquinas's reasoning is analogous to the sort of reasoning a detective engages in when he infers from a cigarette butt and the size of a shoe print that the suspect was probably a six-foot-tall smoker, or that an astronomer engages in when he infers from the observed wobble of a certain distant star that there is probably a large planet orbiting it. This everyday sort of reasoning is inherently probabilistic and therefore always at least somewhat tentative. It is always at least possible, for example, that the suspect was actually five-feet tall and just wearing oversized shoes, or that there are two small planets rather than one large one orbiting the star in question. Which hypothesis is more likely to be true depends on such considerations as whether it violates the principle of Ockham's razor by postulating more entities than are strictly necessary to account for the evidence, whether it is consistent with other hypotheses that we have good independent reason to think are probably true, and so forth. When understood in this light, arguments for God's existence inevitably come to seem like what are called "God of the gaps" arguments: "Here is something science hasn't yet explained; probably God is the explanation." Dawkins, Harris, et al., come along and have little trouble coming up with some imaginative materialistic explanation of the evidence in question, and even if the proposed explanation is unsupported or farfetched, it serves rhetorically to undermine any confidence their hapless readers might otherwise have in the whole enterprise of arguing for God's existence.

But Aquinas does *not* argue in this lame "God of the gaps" manner, and neither do any of the great philosophical theologians referred to above (Aristotle, Maimonides, Duns Scotus, Leibniz, et al.). I will admit that some theists do argue this way: Paley did, and "Intelligent Design" theorists influenced by him do as well. But their faulty methodology should not be read back into thinkers who would have had no truck with it. Why atheists are so fixated on Paley, I cannot say, unless it is precisely because he is such an easy target: If he didn't exist, atheists would have had to invent him, or find some other straw man to beat. Aquinas, as is well known, always painstakingly considered all opposing arguments, and always made a point of attacking an opponent's position at its strongest point. (This contrast is one reason I compare the moral character of the New Atheists so unfavorably to that of Aquinas, and it is a reason they will be hard-pressed to dismiss à la Hume as a mere "monkish virtue.") An old and fondly remembered professor of mine, who was a very militant atheist, always had a soft spot for Aquinas and some of the other medieval Scholastics, whose brilliance he readily acknowledged. Compared to them, he would say, the sorts of apologists beloved of contemporary evangelicals "are like a pimple on the ass of an athlete." That is a bit harsh; some "God of the gaps" arguments do point to real difficulties with the naturalistic position, and can be reformulated in more adequate terms. Still, it is true that some arguments common in popular religious apologetics have done real damage to the public understanding of the traditional arguments for God's existence, and precisely (as we shall see) because they have foolishly taken on board certain modern philosophical assumptions that tend unwittingly to give the game away to naturalism.

What Aquinas *is* doing can be understood by comparison with the sort of reasoning familiar from geometry and mathematics in general. Take the Pythagorean theorem, for example. Once you understand the axiomatic method, the definition of triangularity, and so forth, and then reason through a particular proof of the theorem, you can see that the theorem must be true, and necessarily so. It is not a "hypothesis" "postulated" to "explain" certain "evidence," and it is not merely "probable." Anyone who suggested that there might be some other "explanation" of the "evidence" more in line with Ockham's razor, or that the Pythagorean theorem was simply a "theorem of the gaps" that might be undermined by further "research," would simply demonstrate thereby that he didn't know what he was talking about. Geometry doesn't work that way. It doesn't involve the formulation and testing of hypotheses, after the fashion of empirical science. This hardly makes it less rational than empirical science; it just shows that the sort of argumentation used in empirical science is not the only kind of rational argumentation that there is. Of course, it might turn out that some particular proof for a geometrical theorem has a flaw in it somewhere, in which case it would fail as a proof; geometers aren't infallible any more than empirical science is. But the reason it would fail is not that there is some evidence it failed to take account of, or that its conclusion was less probable all things considered. It would just be because there was a logical fallacy somewhere in the proof. Geometrical reasoning, and mathematical reasoning in general, is all-or-nothing. The premises are indubitable, and in any argument that appeals to them, the conclusion either follows necessarily from those premises, in which case we have no choice but to accept it, or it does not follow, in which case the argument is worthless. If the theorem is going to be proved, some other, airtight argument is going to have to be discovered. Either way, there is no question of "weighing evidence," of "hypotheses," of the "balance of probabilities," etc.

Now Aquinas's arguments, like Plato's and Aristotle's, are metaphysical in character, not scientific. Contrary to the common muddleheaded use of the word "scientific" as if it were a synonym for "rational," that doesn't mean they are not rational arguments; it just means they are of a species of rational argument different from the scientific (that is, if by "science" we mean modern empirical science – Aristotle and his medieval successors used the term in a broader sense, which included metaphysics). They are in this respect like geometrical arguments. They are also like geometrical arguments in being all-or-nothing, though unlike geometrical arguments in that they take empirical premises, rather than pure abstractions, as their starting points. Scientific arguments start from empirical premises and draw merely probabilistic conclusions. Mathematical arguments start from purely conceptual premises and draw necessary conclusions. Metaphysical arguments of the sort Aquinas is interested in combine elements of both these other forms of reasoning: they take obvious, though empirical, starting points, and try to show that from these starting points, together with certain conceptual premises, certain metaphysical conclusions follow necessarily. And the empirical starting points are always so general that there is no serious doubt of their truth: for example, they will be premises like "More than one object is red," or "We observe change going on in the world around us." Hence Plato and Aristotle argue in their different ways that, given the nature of things as we observe them, there must necessarily be forms or universals that are neither purely mental nor reducible to matter. Hence Aquinas argues that, given that we observe things that exist, undergo change, and exhibit final causes, there necessarily must be a God who maintains them in existence at every instant. Now as with geometrical arguments, it is always possible that someone attempting a metaphysical demonstration has made a mistake somewhere; metaphysical reasoning is not infallible. But as with geometry, the *kind* of mistake involved will not be a failure to consider all the empirical evidence, a violation of Ockham's razor, or any other such thing. And even if someone claims to doubt the empirical premises appealed to – as, for example, Parmenides would claim to doubt that change ever occurs – it will typically be doubt of the sort that derives from some competing metaphysical theory, rather than from some scientific discovery of heretofore-unknown evidence. In general, the starting points of metaphysical arguments aren't matters of scientific controversy, but rather premises concerning that which science, like common sense, necessarily takes for granted.

Part of the problem with Dawkins's criticisms of Aquinas, then (and of the other New Atheists' criticisms of certain other religious arguments), is that they fail to understand the difference between a scientific hypothesis and an attempted metaphysical demonstration, and illegitimately judge the latter as if it were the former. Of course, they might respond by claiming that scientific reasoning, and maybe mathematical reasoning too, are the only legitimate kinds, and seek thereby to rule out metaphysical arguments from the get go. But there are two problems with this view (which is known as "scientism" or "positivism"). First, if they want to take this position, they'll need to defend it and not simply assert it; otherwise they'll be begging the question against their opponents and indulging in just the sort of dogmatism they claim to oppose. Second, the moment they attempt to defend it, they will have effectively refuted it, for scientism or positivism is *itself* a metaphysical position that could only be justified using metaphysical arguments. Of its very nature, scientific investigation takes for granted such assumptions as that: there is a physical world existing independently of our minds; this world is characterized by various objective patterns and regularities; our senses are at least partially reliable sources of information about this world; there are objective laws of logic and mathematics that apply to the objective world outside our minds; our cognitive powers – of concept-formation, reasoning from premises to a conclusion, and so forth – afford us a grasp of these laws and can reliably take us from evidence derived from the senses to conclusions about the physical world; the language we use can adequately express truths about these laws and about the external world; and so on and on. Every one of these claims embodies a metaphysical assumption, and science, since its very method presupposes them, could not possibly defend them without arguing in a circle. Their defense is instead a task for metaphysics, and for philosophy more generally; and scientism is shown thereby to be incoherent.[8]

As the philosopher and historian of science E.A. Burtt stated in his classic *The Metaphysical Foundations of Modern Physical Science*,

> even the attempt to escape metaphysics is no sooner put in the form of a proposition than it is seen to involve highly significant metaphysical postulates. For this reason there is an exceedingly subtle and insidious danger in positivism. If you cannot avoid metaphysics, what kind of metaphysics are you likely to cherish when you sturdily suppose yourself to be free from the abomination? Of course it goes without saying that in this case your metaphysics will be held uncritically because it is unconscious; moreover, it will be passed on to others far more readily than your other notions inasmuch as it will be propagated by insinuation rather than by direct argument. . . . Now the history of mind reveals pretty clearly that the thinker who decries metaphysics . . .

> if he be a man engaged in any important inquiry, he must
> have a method, and he will be under a strong and constant
> temptation to make a metaphysics out of his method, that is,
> to suppose the universe ultimately of such a sort that his
> method must be appropriate and successful. . . . But inas-
> much as the positivist mind has failed to school itself in
> careful metaphysical thinking, its ventures at such points
> will be apt to appear pitiful, inadequate, or even fantastic.[9]

Burtt could have been writing about the New Atheists, for his
words describe them "to a T." Dawkins in particular, as we shall
see, constantly tries to frame the debates over the existence of God
and the nature of the human mind as if they hinged on evolution,
attempting thereby to transform the Darwinian method of analysis
he is most comfortable with into a general metaphysic that holds
the master key to every scientific and philosophical problem.
Precisely because he is a non-philosopher doing high-falutin' metaphysics disguised as straight science, his metaphysics is very bad
indeed – or as Burtt might say, "pitiful" and "inadequate" where
religion is concerned, and downright "fantastic" when Dawkins's
"selfish gene" and "meme" theories carry him altogether into fairy-
land. But because this bad metaphysics is held by him more or less
unconsciously, he has been able very effectively to propagate it by
insinuation rather than argument to countless readers, and to
remain blissfully unaware that there is any serious alternative to it.

This brings us to the second thing to keep in mind when examining Aquinas's arguments for the existence of God – and for the
immortality of the soul and the natural law conception of morality
too, as we shall see –which is that the specific metaphysical principles in terms of which they are formulated are classical rather than
modern ones; in particular, they are Aristotelian ones. That is why
we spent a long chapter examining the classical tradition from
Thales to Aristotle. Without that background, you simply cannot
understand the arguments in question, and not only where Aquinas
is concerned; for most of the great philosophical theists owe much
to Platonism and/or to Aristotelianism. Needless to say, Dawkins
and Co. are, here as elsewhere, utterly clueless.

Third, as indicated already, Aquinas does not argue from the
claim that "everything has a cause," nor, contrary to what Dawkins
thinks, does he argue that the universe had a beginning and that

God must have been the cause of that beginning. His aim is to show that given that there are in fact some causes of various sorts, the nature of cause and effect entails that God is necessary as an uncaused cause of the universe *even if we assume that the universe has always existed and thus had no beginning.* The argument is not that the world wouldn't have got started if God hadn't knocked down the first domino at some point in the distant past; it is that it wouldn't exist *here and now*, or undergo change or exhibit final causes *here and now* unless God were *here and now*, and at every moment, sustaining it in being, change, and goal-directedness.

Fourth, I need to make a general remark about Aquinas's famous "Five Ways," the arguments that Dawkins focuses on. These are taken from a short section at the beginning of the massive *Summa Theologiae* – a passage no longer than a couple of pages in a modern book – and Dawkins, like many other commentators, treats them as if they were intended to form all by themselves a complete case for the existence of God. In fact the *Summa Theologiae*, despite its length and the difficulty some of its concepts pose for the modern reader, was written as a primer for novices in theology, not an advanced text. Moreover, the Five Ways themselves were intended merely as a brief summary of arguments that were generally familiar to the readers of the time, and Aquinas leaves the detailed elaboration of some of them to other works, such as the *Summa Contra Gentiles*. He also develops some of the relevant points, such as the reasons why we must attribute omnipotence, omniscience, and the like to the Unmoved Mover or First Cause, in very great detail in the sections of the *Summa* immediately following the Five Ways. Anyone at all familiar with the *Summa* and with even very basic Aquinas scholarship would know all of this. Thus it is a very serious lapse in scholarly competence and/or intellectual integrity for someone like Dawkins, an Oxford don who sees fit to pour scorn on the scholarly acumen and intellectual honesty of others, to treat the Five Ways as if they constituted Aquinas's complete case for God's existence, to ignore Aquinas's responses to various objections, and to tell his readers that Aquinas gives "absolutely no reason" for certain claims that, as I have said, he actually devotes many hundreds of pages to defending. Presumably Dawkins would not appreciate it if an opponent ripped two pages out of context from one of his popular works, and then purported to refute his entire body of work in biology on the basis of a few sarcastic criticisms of it. Yet that is, in effect, what he does to Thomas Aquinas – a man who was, we may safely say, a thinker of far greater consequence than Richard Dawkins can ever hope to be.

One last preliminary point. Many secularists seem hell-bent (if you'll pardon the expression) on pretending that religious people in general believe in a God so anthropomorphic that only a child or the most ignorant peasant could take the question of His existence seriously even for a moment. I know I've heard the stupid "Easter Bunny" comparison often enough to make me want to scream, and from purportedly educated people who would not countenance some ignoramus who dismissed particle physics on the grounds that he couldn't bring himself to believe in something as silly as billions of little billiard balls bouncing around inside his coffee cup. It is hard to see any honorable reason for this tendency, since it doesn't take much reading in the great works of philosophical theology to know that the anthropomorphic characterization of "what religious people believe" is a travesty, certainly when applied to the best representatives of religious thought.

To understand what serious religious thinkers *do* believe, we might usefully distinguish five gradations in one's conception of God:

1. God is literally an old man with a white beard, a kind if stern wizard-like being with very human thoughts and motivations who lives in a place called Heaven, which is like the places we know except for being very far away and impossible to get to except through magical means.

2. God doesn't really have a bodily form, and his thoughts and motivations are in many respects very different from ours. He is an immaterial object or substance which has existed forever, and (perhaps) pervades all space. Still, he is, somehow, a person like we are, only vastly more intelligent, powerful, and virtuous, and in particular without our physical and moral limitations. He made the world the way a carpenter builds a house, as an independent object that would carry on even if he were to "go away" from it, but he

nevertheless may decide to intervene in its operations from time to time.

3. God is not an object or substance alongside other objects or substances in the world; rather, He is pure being or existence itself, utterly distinct from the world of time, space, and things, underlying and maintaining them in being at every moment, and apart from whose ongoing conserving action they would be instantly annihilated. The world is not an independent object in the sense of something that might carry on if God were to "go away"; it is more like the music produced by a musician, which exists only when he plays and vanishes the moment he stops. None of the concepts we apply to things in the world, including to ourselves, apply to God in anything but an analogous sense. Hence, for example, we may say that God is "personal" insofar as He is not *less* than a person, the way an animal is less than a person. But God is not literally "*a person*" in the sense of being one individual thing among others who reasons, chooses, has moral obligations, etc. Such concepts make no sense when literally applied to God.

4. God as understood by someone who has had a mystical experience of the sort Aquinas had.

5. God as Aquinas knows Him now, i.e. as known in the beatific vision attained by the blessed after death.

Further gradations between some of these are no doubt possible, but this will suffice for our purposes. Obviously, each grade represents an advance in sophistication over the previous one. Grade 1 represents a child's conception of God, and perhaps that of some uneducated adults. Grade 2 represents the conception of some educated religious believers, of popular apologetics, and of arguments like Paley's "Design argument." Grade 3 is the conception of classical philosophical theology: of Augustine, Anselm, Aquinas, and other such thinkers. Grades 4 and 5 are attainable only if granted supernaturally by God. Now the lower grades are not necessarily without their value. Some individuals, and certainly young children, find it difficult to understand God in anything but grade 1 terms, and such imagery can be more or less useful in giving them at least a rudimentary idea of Him. For example, while God is not literally a wise old man, thinking of Him as a wise old man is at least far closer to the truth than thinking of Him as an animal, since unlike an animal he is not less than personal (even if He is infinitely *more* than a human person). (Compare the way in which it is useful to have children think of molecules as little balls joined together by sticks, even though this is not literally what they are.) Grade 2 is better still than even the best grade 1 imagery, since it eliminates the limitations inherent in physical imagery, which cannot apply to God. But it is still inferior and too anthropomorphic compared to grade 3, which is about the best we can do with unaided reason.

What I am calling grade 3 enshrines Aquinas's famous doctrine of analogy, on which the language we use to refer to God is not used in the same or "univocal" sense in which it is applied to things in this world (as we might describe a fire engine and a Stop sign as being "red" in exactly the same sense), but neither is it used in a completely different or "equivocal" sense (the way that a tree has "bark" and a dog has a "bark" in entirely different senses). Rather, it is used in an *analogical* sense, as when you say that you "see" the tree in front of you and also that you can "see" that the Pythagorean theorem must be true. Obviously you don't see the truth of the theorem in exactly the same sense in which you see a tree, but there is an analogy between vision and intellectual insight that makes the use of the term appropriate in both cases. Similarly, God is not personal, or good, or powerful, or intelligent in the *same* sense in which a human being is, but He can nevertheless correctly be described in these terms if they are understood analogously; while there is nothing in God that is even analogous to evil, or weakness, or stupidity, so that these terms cannot be applied to Him at all.

How do we know which terms do and do not apply? Short of divine revelation, we can know this only by examining the arguments for God's existence and their implications. It is to that task that we now turn. Do keep in mind, though, that it is not a serious reply to the arguments to say "I don't believe in the Easter Bunny either," any more than this would be a serious reply to a scientist trying to convince you of the existence of transitional species, or quarks, or universal gravitation.

The existence of God

There are many serious arguments for the existence of God – the philosopher Alvin Plantinga has suggested that there are at least "two dozen or so" – but they are not all equally fundamental or powerful.[10] One that is worth mentioning in passing given the themes of the previous chapter derives from St. Augustine, and can be summarized in the following way. As we have seen, it is very hard to avoid realism about universals, propositions, and numbers and other mathematical objects. For the reasons we examined, the existence of these entities in some form or other cannot reasonably be denied, and it is implausible to regard them either as material things or as dependent on the human mind for their existence. We also saw that there are serious problems with understanding them according to Plato's version of realism – as abstract objects existing in their own right in a "third realm" – as opposed to Aristotle's. At the same time, it is also hard to see how they could exist apart from *any* mind whatsoever: a proposition, for example, just seems clearly to be the sort of thing that exists only as entertained or contemplated by a mind. Furthermore, it seems implausible to say, as Aristotle apparently would, that triangularity (for example), though neither material nor entirely mental, would go completely out of existence if every particular triangular thing and every mind that might think about triangularity went out of existence. For wouldn't it still be true in that case that the angles of a triangle add up to 180 degrees? Wouldn't other geometrical truths remain as true as they ever did? But if universals, propositions, and mathematical objections are eternal and necessarily existing entities that cannot plausibly exist apart from a mind, and such a mind could not (for the reasons we have seen) be a finite or limited mind like ours, it follows that they must exist in an eternal and infinite mind. But such a mind is exactly what God is supposed to be. Hence it follows that God exists.[11]

Aquinas does not defend this argument himself, but he and many other medieval Scholastic philosophers did endorse the idea that universals and the like exist as "thoughts" in the divine intellect, a conclusion that fits in nicely with the understanding of God entailed by their own favored arguments, and which contributes to unifying and completing the metaphysical picture of the world given to us by Plato and Aristotle. The position that results when one combines Aristotle's version of realism with Augustine's conception of universals as existing in God's mind has a name of its own: Scholastic realism.[12]

Though Aquinas is a Scholastic realist, his Aristotelianism leads him to prefer arguments for God's existence that begin from premises more obviously known through sensory experience. He gives several such arguments, and the famous Five Ways are just some of them. For brevity's sake, I will discuss only three of Aquinas's arguments here, but the sample is representative.[13]

A. The Unmoved Mover

Aquinas thought that the most evident of the arguments for God's existence was that which showed that the very existence of change requires that there be a first unchanging changer of everything that changes, which analysis reveals is identical to God as usually understood. Versions of this argument were given by Aristotle, and Aquinas presents versions of his own in the *Summa contra Gentiles* (at length) and as the first of the Five Ways in the *Summa Theologiae* (in a truncated form). The traditional name for this argument is "the argument from motion," since "motion" is the traditional Aristotelian term for what nowadays we'd just call "change." [14]

Remember that for Aristotle, change or motion always involves a transition from potentiality to actuality. And since a potential is by itself just that – merely potential, not actual or real – no potential can make itself actual, but must be actualized by something outside it. Hence a rubber ball's potential to be melted must be actualized by heat; hence the potential of an animal's leg to move must be actualized by the firing of the motor neurons; and so forth. Remember also that Aristotle takes the immediate efficient cause of a thing to be simultaneous with it. The immediate cause of a pot's being curved, for example, is the curved position of the potter's hand as he molds it.

Now, by the same token, the curved position of the potter's hand is itself immediately caused by whatever events in his nervous system keep the muscles in his hand flexed in such-and-such a way. But of course, we can also point to other, less immediate causes of the curved position of his hand. For example, it was remotely caused by the fact that his girlfriend asked him last week to make a pot for her; for he wouldn't be sitting there right now curving his hand in just that way if she hadn't made this request. This brings us to a crucial distinction Aquinas and other medieval philosophers made between two kinds of series of causes and effects, namely "accidentally ordered" and "essentially ordered" series (or causal series *per accidens* and *per se*, for you fans of Scholastic Latin). To take a stock example, consider a father who begets a son, who in turn begets another. If the father dies after begetting his son, the son can still beget a son of his own, for once in existence the son has the power to do this all by himself. He doesn't need his father to remain in existence for him to be able to do it. If we imagine an ongoing series of fathers begetting sons who in turn beget others – and of course, such series really do exist all around us – then we can observe that in every case, each son has the power to beget a son of his own (and thus become a father) even if his own father, or any previous father in the series, goes out of existence. Considered as a "causer" of sons, each member of this series is in this sense independent of the previous members. Hence the series is "accidentally ordered" in the sense that it is not essential to the continuation of the series that any earlier member of it remain in existence. And in the same way, the potter's curving his hand in making the pot occurs even though his girlfriend's request happened a week ago. The causal link between the request and the hand's curving is also "accidental" insofar as the latter exists in the absence of the former.

But it would not exist in the absence of the firing of the motor neurons. Here we have an "essentially ordered" causal series, and we have one precisely because the cause in this case is (unlike the girlfriend's request) simultaneous with the effect. The hand is held in the position it is in only because the motor neurons are firing in such-and-such a way; take away the neural activity, and the hand goes limp. Or, once again to make use of a stock example, if we think of a hand which is pushing a stone by means of a stick, the motion of the stone occurs only insofar as the stick is moving it, and the stick is moving it only insofar as it is being used by the hand to do so. At every moment in which the last part of the series (viz. the motion of the stone) exists, the earlier parts (the motion of the hand and of the stick) exist as well. The stone, and the stick itself for that matter, only move because, and insofar as, the hand moves them; indeed, strictly speaking it is the hand alone which is doing the moving of the stone, and the stick is a mere instrument by means of which it accomplishes this. The series is "essentially ordered" because the later members of the series, having no independent power of motion on their own, derive the fact of their motion and their ability to move other things from the first member, in this case the hand. Without the earlier members, and particularly the first one, the series could not continue.

Now an accidentally ordered series, like the fathers begetting sons who beget more sons (and indeed like the countless other causal series familiar from everyday experience that extend backwards in time), could, in Aquinas's view, in theory go back forever into the past. He doesn't think any such series does in fact go back forever, but he also doesn't think it can be *proved* through philosophical arguments that they don't. That is to say, he doesn't think it can be proved, and doesn't try to prove, that the universe had a beginning.[15] The reason is that, since in an accidentally ordered series the members of the series have their causal powers independently of the operation or even existence of earlier members, there is nothing about the activity of the members existing here and now that requires that we trace it back to some first member existing in the past. But things are very different with essentially ordered causal series. These sorts of series paradigmatically trace, not backwards in time, but rather "downward" in the present moment, since they are series in which each member depends *simultaneously* on other members which *simultaneously* depend in turn on yet others, on so on. In this sort of series, the later members have no independent causal power of their own, being mere instruments of a first member. Hence if there were no first member, such a series would not exist at all. If the last member of such series does in fact exist, then (as the motion of the stone does in our example), the series cannot, even in theory, go back infinitely: there must be a first member.

Now I suppose I should apologize to Dennett at this point for "nitpicking about the meaning of 'cause'" (and by an appeal to "Scholastic logic" at that). On the other hand, most of Dennett's peers in contemporary analytic philosophy – some of whom have, to their credit, indulged in a great deal of "nitpicking about the meaning of 'cause'" themselves, even if not in a Scholastic vein – would refer to this sort of activity, not as "nitpicking," but rather as "precision," "striving for clarity," "careful argumentation," "avoiding sloppy thinking," "not being a hack," or even just "doing philosophy." And Dennett, you'll recall, is known to these same peers as a thinker who "lacks philosophical depth and is not systematic." So, perhaps I'm not the one who owes the apology after all. In any event, without distinctions like the ones I've been making, you simply cannot understand Aquinas's arguments, which is no doubt why Dennett (and Dawkins, and Harris, and Hitchens) show no sign of understanding them.

Anyway, with this background in place we can proceed to the argument itself. Consider once again the hand, stone, and stick. The stone, as I have said, moves only insofar as the stick moves, and the stick moves only insofar as the hand moves. More technically, but more precisely, the stone's potentiality for motion is actualized by the stick, but only because, simultaneously, the stick's potentiality for motion is actualized by the hand. That's where we had left things, treating the hand, for purposes of illustration, as a first mover. But of course, in fact the hand is not really the first member of the series at all. It moves only because the arm moves it, and the arm and hand together move only because the relevant muscles flex, which is in turn due to the firing of certain neurons. That is to say, the hand's potentiality for motion is actualized by the arm, and the arm's potentiality for motion is actualized by the muscles, and the muscles' potentiality for motion is actualized by the nerves; and again, all of this is simultaneous. But even this isn't the end of the series. It continues on, through a number of simultaneous steps, to ever-deeper levels of reality. The motion of the stone depends on the motion of the hand, which depends on the motion of the stick, which depends on the firing of the neurons, which depends on the firing of other neurons, all of which depends on the state of the nervous system, which depends on its current molecular structure, which depends on the atomic basis of that molecular structure, which depends on electromagnetism, gravitation, the weak and strong forces, and so on an so forth, all simultaneously, all here and now. The actualization of one potential depends on the simultaneous actualization of another, which depends on the simultaneous actualization of another, which depends on the simultaneous actualization of another, which depends on . . .

How far can it go? Not that far, actually; certainly not to infinity. For what we have here is an essentially ordered causal series, existing here and now, not an accidentally ordered one extending backwards into the past. And an essentially ordered series, of its nature, must have a first member. All the later members of such a series exist at all only insofar as the earlier ones do, and those earlier ones only insofar as yet earlier ones do; but were there finally no first member of the series, there'd be no series at all in the first place, because it is only the first member which is in the strictest sense really *doing* or *actualizing* anything. The later members are mere instruments, with no independent, actualizing power of their own. Suppose you see the caboose of a train pulling out of the station, and demand to know what is pulling it. A freight car, you are told. And what is pulling that? Another freight car. And that? Yet another freight car. All true enough; but none of these answers really explains anything, because the freight cars, like the caboose, have no independent power of motion of their own, and so no appeal to freight cars explains anything, even if the series of cars pulling the caboose went on to infinity. What is needed is an appeal to something that does have the power of movement in itself, such as an engine car. Similarly, should you see (though a hole in a fence say) a paint brush coating the fence with paint, and ask what is causing it to do so, the answer "the brush handle" will not explain anything, since a brush handle has no independent power of movement. And this wouldn't change in the least even if we imagined that the brush handle was infinitely long. Again, the only genuine explanation would be something that did have independent power of movement and could therefore move the otherwise inert brush. The same thing is true of the sequence beginning with the moving stone. No member of the series has any independent causal power of its own, but derives what it has from something earlier in the series. As with the railway cars and the paint brush, this series too must terminate in a first mover which moves all the others, indeed moves *through* all the others.

Now, a first mover in such a series must be itself unmoved or unchanging; for if it was moving or changing – that is, going from potential to actual – then there would have to be something outside *it* actualizing *its* potential, in which case it wouldn't be the first mover. Not only must it be un*moved*, though, it must be un*movable*. For notice that, especially toward the "lower" levels of the series we were considering – the nervous system's being actualized by its molecular structure, which is in turn actualized by its atomic structure, etc. – what we have is the potential existence of one level actualized by the existence of another, which is in turn actualized by another, and so forth. To account for the actualization of the potential motion of the stone we had eventually to appeal to the actualization of the potential existence of various deeper levels of reality.[16] But then the only way to stop this regress and arrive at a first member of the series is with a being whose existence does not need to be actualized by anything else. The series can only stop, that is to say, with a being that is *pure actuality* (or "Pure Act," to use the Scholastic phrase), with no admixture of potentiality whatsoever. And having no potentiality to realize or actualize, such a being could not possibly move or change. That a stone is moved by a hand via a stick, then – and more generally, that things change at all – suffices to show that there is and must be a first Unmovable Mover or Unchangeable Changer.

That is all pretty abstract, I realize; so much so that it might seem jarring when Aquinas goes on to say: ". . . and this we call God." What he means by this is that, whatever else people might have in mind when they use the expression "God," they mean to refer to whatever being is the ultimate explanation of the processes of change we observe in the world around us. It turns out that there really is such a being; and it also turns out that what it means for there to be such a being is for there to be a being describable in philosophical terms as "Pure Actuality," even if this has (of course) never occurred to most people who believe in God.

"Well, uh, OK, then," you might be thinking; "but what does that have to do with God as the average person understands Him?" A lot, actually. For once we have this much in hand, we can go on to deduce all sorts of things about what a being of Pure Actuality would have to be like, and it turns out that such a being would have to be like the God of traditional Western religious belief. As I mentioned above, Aquinas devotes a great deal of attention, and hundreds of pages, to this question, as did the other great classical philosophical theologians. Hence we have the section *Questions on God* from the *Summa Theologiae*, which in the new edition edited by Davies and Leftow runs to 287 pages; the 300 or so pages of Book One of the *Summa contra Gentiles*, about two-thirds of which is devoted to deriving the divine attributes; the gigantic treatise *De Potentia Dei* (*On the Power of God*); and so on. Countless other thinkers of stature have also addressed the question at length and with philosophical rigor over the centuries; to take just two random examples from a glance over at the bookshelf, there is (from the 18th century) Samuel Clarke's famous *Demonstration of the Being and Attributes of God*, and (from the 20th century) Reginald Garrigou-Lagrange's *God: His Existence and His Nature*, Book Two of which devotes over 500 pages to the matter. And yet, Dawkins, as I have said, tells us that there is "absolutely no reason" to think that the Unmoved Mover, First Cause, etc. is omnipotent, omniscient, good, and so forth. Perhaps what he meant to say was "absolutely no reason, apart from the many thousands of pages of detailed philosophical argumentation for this conclusion that have been produced over the centuries by thinkers of genius, and which I am not going to bother trying to answer." So, a slip of the pen, perhaps. Or, maybe Dawkins simply doesn't know what the hell he's talking about.

Obviously, this is a big topic (the nature of an Unmoved Mover, I mean, not Dawkins's ignorance – though that does seem to be pretty vast too). Suffice it for our purposes to say the following. First, there cannot possibly be more than one being who is Pure Actuality; hence the argument from motion leads inevitably to monotheism. One reason for this (there are others, one of which we'll examine when we look at the next argument for God's existence) is that in order for there to be two (or more) purely actual beings, there would have to be some way of distinguishing them, some feature that one of them had that the other lacked; and there just couldn't be any such feature. For to lack a feature is just to have an unrealized potentiality, and a purely actual being, by definition, has no unrealized potentialities. So if we said, for example, that one purely actual being was more powerful than another, and that that is what distinguished him from the other one, then we'd be saying in effect that the other purely actual being had failed to realize his potential for power as fully as the first had – which makes no sense given that we're talking about a purely actual being, with no potentialities of any sort. So, again, there is no feature that one purely actual being could have that another could lack, and thus no way even in theory to distinguish one purely actual being from another. So there couldn't be more than one.

A being of Pure Actuality, lacking any potentiality whatsoever, would also have to be immaterial, since to be a material thing entails being changeable in various ways, which a purely actual being cannot be. Such a being would not come into existence or go out of existence – both of these being instances of change – but simply exist always. In fact, he would have to be eternal or outside of time and space altogether, since to be within time and space also entails changeability. The Unmoved Mover is in any event that to which every motion or change in the material universe – not just moving stones, but melting glaciers, orbiting moons, budding flowers, growing boys and girls, and so on through all of nature – traces back. Being the common first member of all the various essentially ordered causal series that result in these instances of change, the Unmoved Mover is outside and distinct from them all, as that which sustains the entire world in motion from instant to instant.

Now recall the Aristotelian principle that a cause cannot give what it does not have, so that the cause of a feature must have that feature either "formally" or "eminently"; that is, if it does not have the feature itself (as a cigarette lighter, which causes fire, is not itself on fire), it must have a feature that is higher up in the hierarchy of attributes (as the cigarette lighter has the power to generate fire). But the Unmoved Mover, as the source of all change, is the source of things coming to have the attributes they have. Hence He has these attributes eminently if not formally. That includes every power, so that He is all-powerful. It also includes the intellect and will that human beings possess (features far up in the hierarchy of attributes of created things, as we will see in the next chapter), so that He must be said to have intellect and will, and thus personality, in an analogical sense. Indeed, he must have them in the highest degree, lacking any of the limitations that go along with being a material creature or otherwise having potentiality. Hence He not only has knowledge, but knowledge without limit, being all-knowing.

Does this mean that the Unmoved Mover has what we would regard as negative or defective features too – blindness, disease, heroin addiction, etc., "eminently" if not "formally"? Not at all. For every such feature is what the Scholastics called a "privation," the absence of a positive feature rather than a positive feature in its own right. Hence sight, for example, is a positive attribute, being just what an animal's visual apparatus (comprising the eyes, optic nerves, relevant brain areas, etc.) makes possible when it is realizing its natural potentialities, that is, functioning according to its essence and final cause. But blindness is not a different positive attribute from sight; it is rather a negative attribute, the absence of sight, a failure to realize a natural potentiality. The same thing is true of disease, of moral character flaws (as we will see in a later section), and of every other feature we would naturally consider a defect. The Unmoved Mover, being a purely actual being devoid of potentiality, cannot meaningfully be said to have any of these features even "eminently" (whatever that would mean in this case). In fact, since to have a positive feature or perfection is just to actualize a potentiality, and the Unmoved Mover, the source of all such features, is purely actual, with no unactualized potentiality, He can only be said to have every perfection (and no defect) eminently, and thus to be perfect and all-good (again, in an analogical sense – not being a creature with potentialities to actualize, the Unmoved Mover isn't "good" in the sense in which a human being might be said to be good, e.g. striving to fulfill his moral obligations).

To show that an Unmoved Mover exists, then, is just to show that there is a single being who is the cause of all change, Himself unchangeable, immaterial, eternal, personal (having intelligence and will), all-powerful, all-knowing, and all-good. It is, in short, to show that there is a God.

No doubt a "New Atheist" reading this will already be sputtering some response or other; but judging from the writings of such people, there is also no doubt that the response will be superficial, ill-informed, and dogmatic, long on attitude and short on understanding. I have noted *ad nauseam* that the "No one's ever shown

that the first cause would be omnipotent, omniscient, good, etc."
objection – which, to be fair to Dawkins, is very common in the
atheist literature (which is no doubt where he picked it up from) –
is an urban legend, sustained by the fact that atheists tend to read
only each other's books and not the writings of the religious
thinkers they're supposedly refuting. I have also said that the premise "Everything has a cause" plays no role in Aquinas's arguments,
and that is obviously true here: He never says "Everything has a
cause" or even "Everything is in motion" (which would invite the
reply that God must therefore have a cause or be moving), but
rather simply notes that there are *some* things that are caused to
move, which is all he needs for the argument to get going. And then
there is the fact that, contrary to what most atheists seem to think,
Aquinas, like many other philosophical theologians, is not interested in trying to prove that the universe had a beginning and that
God must have started it off some time in the distant past (which
might seem to invite the reply that He may not be around now).[17]
Rather, he argues that even if the universe had no beginning in
time, there would still have to be an Unmoved Mover keeping it
going here and now, and at any other moment that it exists, past or
future. Since the standard objections to arguments like Aquinas's
are based on misunderstandings like these, it should be obvious
that the standard objections are worthless.

We can also now see how inept and uncomprehending
Dawkins is when he alleges that Aquinas makes the "entirely
unwarranted assumption that God himself is immune to the
regress" of movers, and that "it is more parsimonious to conjure up,
say, a 'big bang singularity.'"[18] This is like saying that it would be
"entirely unwarranted" to "assume" that a triangle is what you get
when you draw a three–sided polygon, and that it would be "more
parsimonious to conjure up, say, a point or a line." For where an
essentially ordered causal series is in question, it is *necessarily* the
case (and not a matter of probability, hypothesis, or "assumption")
that it has a first member, just as it is necessarily the case that three-
sided polygons are triangles, have angles adding up to 180 degrees,
and so on. And where that first member is a purely actual being, it
follows, not with probability, but *necessarily* (so the argument continues) that it has the various divine attributes and thus must be

God, rather than a "big bang singularity" or what have you. There are no mere "assumptions" involved here, nothing "unwarranted," and nothing to which questions of "parsimony" are at all relevant. Aquinas's claim is that if we start with the fact of motion and an understanding of what essentially ordered causal series entail, we will be led as a matter of metaphysical inevitability to an Unmoved Mover having the defining attributes of God; it is not a matter of there being a "gap" in our scientific knowledge that we might "postulate" has God as one possible explanation among others. As I have said, Dawkins's problem is that he doesn't know the difference between probabilistic empirical theorizing and strict metaphysical demonstration, and thus misreads an attempt at the latter as if it were the former. That is not to say that Aquinas might not be mistaken at some point in the argument – though obviously I don't think he is – but if you're going to show that he is, you first need to understand what *kind* of argument he is giving, and thus what *kind* of mistake he'd be making if he's made one at all.

For similar reasons, certain other common responses to the Unmoved Mover argument are wide of the mark. It is sometimes suggested, for instance, that Aquinas is beholden to an outdated Aristotelian physics and astronomy; and it is true that the examples he gives to illustrate his points are sometimes made in terms of scientific claims we now know to be false. But there is nothing in the argument itself that requires the truth of Aristotle's scientific theories, only of his metaphysical ones. The illustrations are *mere* illustrations, and can easily be replaced with better ones. In particular, the analysis of motion or change as a transition from potentiality to actuality is a metaphysical analysis that is deeper than any empirical scientific theory. Theories of the latter sort merely give us different accounts of the specific physical mechanisms by which the transition from potentiality to actuality occurs in the material world, and can never call into question the distinction itself, which can only be evaluated by philosophical means.

More specifically, Newton's principle of inertia – that a body in motion tends to stay in motion unless acted upon from outside – is sometimes claimed to undermine Aquinas's view that whatever is moving must here and now be moved by something else. For if it is just a law of physics that bodies will, all things being equal, remain in motion, then (so the objection goes) there is no need to appeal to anything outside them to account for their continued movement. But this is irrelevant to Aquinas's argument, for three reasons. First, Newton's principle applies only to "local motion" or movement from one place to another, while Aquinas's Aristotelian conception of motion is broader and concerns change in general: not just movement from place to place, but also changes in quality (like water's becoming solid when it freezes), changes in quantity (like its becoming hotter or colder by degrees), and changes in substance (as when hydrogen and oxygen are combined to make water). So, even if we were to grant that the local motion of an object needn't be accounted for by reference to something outside it, there would still be other kinds of motion to which Aquinas's argument would apply. Second, whether or not an object's transition from place to place would itself require an explanation in terms of something outside it, its acquisition or loss of momentum *would* require such an explanation, and thus lead us once again to an Unmoved Mover. Third, the operation of Newton's first law is itself something that needs to be explained: It is no good saying "Oh, things keep moving because, you know, that's just what they do given the principle of inertia"; for we want to know *why* things are governed by this principle. To that one might respond that it is just in the *nature* of things to act in accordance with the principle of inertia. And that is true; it is also, for reasons we will examine in our last chapter, a very Aristotelian thing to say (*meta*physically speaking, that is, even if not in regard to Aristotle's own pre-Newtonian physics). But for that reason it is a very *Thomistic* thing to say, and thus hardly something that would trouble Aquinas. For it just leads to the further question of what is the cause of a thing's existing with the nature it has, and that takes us once again back up a regress that can only terminate in a purely actual Unmoved Mover. It also takes us to our second argument.

B. The First Cause

In order for the universe to undergo change, it obviously must exist. In particular, it must persist in existence from moment to moment. So why does it do so? Suppose it is suggested that the universe has always existed, or that it oscillates from Big Bang to Big Crunch to

Big Bang over and over again, or that it is really a "multiverse" consisting of many branching baby universes, per the speculations of physicists desperate to keep the divine foot out of the door the Big Bang seems to have opened. Fine and dandy, but all of this is completely irrelevant to the question I just asked, which is the question Aquinas is interested in.[19] Remember that, for purposes of proving God's existence, Aquinas doesn't care about the Big Bang or whether the universe had a beginning. The question isn't about what got things started or how long they've been going, but rather *what keeps them going*.[20]

Is there just something in their natures that allows them to do so? Definitely not. For consider the nature or essence of any of the things that make up the physical universe – people, for example. Suppose we agree with Aristotle that the essence of a human being is to be a rational animal. Does knowing that essence tell you whether there are any people? Does it tell you, say, whether Socrates, or George Bush, or Bruce Wayne exists? Not at all. You do know that George Bush exists, of course, but not because you know his essence; rather, you know it because you've met him, or heard about him, or seen him on television. And Socrates doesn't exist anymore, while Bruce Wayne never existed at all outside of the *Batman* comics and movies. So there's nothing about the nature or essence of being human that entails one way or the other whether any human being exists. And the same thing is obviously true of the other inhabitants of the physical world, be they rocks, trees, planets, or whatever. Moreover, all of these things come into existence and go out of existence all the time, which shows by itself that there's nothing about their nature that entails that they must exist. Consider also that, supposing unicorns have an essence – being horse-like and having horns on their heads, say – that obviously doesn't tell you whether they exist either. In fact they don't exist, but you wouldn't know that just from knowing their essence; a child, on first hearing about them, might think they do exist, as just another kind of horse. And the same thing would be true of elves, fairies, Smurfs and the like, if they have essences. Whether it's people or trees, unicorns or elves, their essence is one thing and their existence (or lack thereof) another, and the first doesn't entail the second. But then, the essences or natures of the things in the universe can't be what accounts for their continuing to exist from moment to moment.

This distinction between essence and existence – between *what* a thing is and *that* it is – is famously central to Aquinas's philosophy, and it relates to Aristotle's distinction between actuality and potentiality. Remember that the ordinary objects of our experience – people, dogs, cats, trees, rocks, etc. – are in Aristotle's view composites of form and matter, where the form is the essence or nature of the thing and the matter is what has taken on that form, nature, or essence. So, for example, there is the form or essence of a human being – being a rational animal – and there is the matter that makes up the human body, which has this form or essence. Now, relative to matter, the form or essence is "actuality" – it actualizes the potential in the matter, in this case making it a living human body rather than a cat or an apple. But as we've just seen, there's nothing about a form or essence per se that guarantees that it exists or informs anything. Like George Bush, Socrates and Bruce Wayne, being human beings, are composites of form and matter, but unlike Bush they aren't real, since Socrates is dead and Bruce Wayne is fictional. So, though "actual" relative to matter, a form or essence is only "potential" relative to existence or being. Existence or being is what "actualizes" a form or essence.[21]

Now if the essence of a thing and the existence of the thing are distinct in this way – there is nothing in the former that entails the latter – then something needs to put them together if the thing is to be real. That "something" obviously can't be the thing itself, for to give itself existence, a thing would have to exist already, and the whole point is that since existence still needs to be added to its essence it *doesn't* exist already. So, nothing can cause itself; whatever comes into existence, or more generally whatever must have existence added to its essence in order for it to be real, must be caused by another. This is the "principle of causality" (also sometimes known as a version of the "principle of sufficient reason").[22] Notice that it does *not* say that "Everything has a cause" – something which, as I have said, Aquinas never asserted or would have asserted. The principle says only that *what does not have existence on its own* must have a cause.

Now Hume famously attacks this principle, claiming that we can easily "conceive" a thing coming into being without a cause, so that the principle is at the very least doubtful. What he has in mind is something like this. Imagine the surface of a table with nothing on it. Now imagine a bowling ball suddenly appearing – pop! – in the middle of it, "out of nowhere" as it were. There, you've just conceived of something coming into being without a cause, right?

Well, no, actually. It really is amazing that this argument has gotten the acclaim and attention it has over the centuries, given how very feeble it is. One problem with it is that it assumes quite falsely that to imagine something – to form a certain mental image – is the same as to conceive it, in the sense of forming a coherent intellectual idea of it. But imagining something and conceiving it in the intellect simply aren't the same thing. You can form no clear mental image of a chiliagon – a thousand-sided figure – certainly not one that's at all distinct from your mental image of a 997-sided figure or a 1002-sided figure. Still, your intellect can easily grasp the concept of a chiliagon. You can form no mental image of a triangle that is not equilateral, isosceles, or scalene. But the concept of triangularity that exists in your intellect, which abstracts away from these features of concrete triangles, applies equally to all of them. And so forth. Like many empiricists, Hume conflates the intellect and the imagination, and his argument – indeed, his philosophy in general – sounds plausible only if one follows him in committing this error.

For another thing, as Elizabeth Anscombe has pointed out, to imagine something appearing suddenly isn't even to *imagine* it (let alone conceive it) coming into existence without a cause.[23] Suppose the situation described really happened to you: a bowling ball suddenly appears on your table. What would be your spontaneous reaction? Would you say, "Wow, Hume was right! Look, a bowling ball came into existence without a cause!" More likely you'd say, "Where the hell did *that* come from?" – a question that implies that there is a source, a *cause*, from which the bowling ball sprang. Then you'd *look* for that cause: a hole in the ceiling maybe, or a magician's trick; if nothing this mundane can be found, you might even consider something exotic like a mad scientist testing a teleportation device, or a bizarre and otherwise astronomically improbable quantum fluctuation in the table. Even if you could somehow rule these explanations out, it is unlikely you'd resign yourself to the world's irrationality and have your valet fetch Hume's *Treatise* for you from the bookshelf (as Louis XVI had *his* valet fetch a volume of Hume's *History of England* when he learned he was to be executed). You'd probably just think, "I guess I'll never know what caused it" – *what* caused it, not whether it was caused. In any case, there's simply nothing about the situation Hume describes that amounts to imagining something coming into existence with *no* cause, as opposed to coming into existence with an *unknown or unusual* cause.

But it's worse for Hume even than that. Anscombe also asks us to consider how we'd go about determining whether the sort of scenario we've been describing really is a case of something *coming into existence* in the first place, as opposed, say, to merely reappearing from somewhere else where it had already existed. And the answer is that the only way we could do so is by making reference to some *cause* of the thing's suddenly being here as being a *creating* cause, specifically, rather than a *transporting* one. Thus, the only way we can ultimately make sense of something coming into being is by reference to a cause. What Hume says we can easily conceive not only hasn't been conceived by him, it seems likely *impossible* to conceive.[24]

So the principle of causality seems secure. Not that it was ever much in serious doubt even among atheists themselves, who implicitly take it for granted whenever they trumpet this or that finding of science. For science itself – which is, after all, in the business of searching for the causes of things – takes for granted the principle of causality and couldn't proceed without it. I daresay that there has really only ever been one motive for seriously doubting the principle (or pretending seriously to doubt it anyway) and that is to block arguments for a first cause of the universe. And even then, it has never been doubted consistently, given atheists' purported attachment to science.

How does the principle get us to a first cause? When we consider that the essence of everything within the universe is distinct from its existence, so that each of these things must be caused by something outside itself, we can see that the same thing must be true of the universe as a whole. And in that case, the universe must have a cause outside itself. Now at this point a standard move is to claim that this argument commits the "fallacy of composition." If every brick in a certain wall weighs a pound, it doesn't follow that the whole wall weighs only a pound; so (the objection continues) the fact that everything in the universe requires a cause outside itself doesn't entail that the universe as a whole does. The trouble with this objection is that not every instance of this sort of reasoning from part to whole commits a fallacy. For example, if every brick in a wall built out of children's Lego blocks is red, then the wall as a whole must be red. And the case of the universe as a whole is surely like this. If a roomful of physical objects needs a cause outside itself, so do two rooms full; if a city full of physical objects needs a cause outside itself, so does a country full of them; if a planet full of physical objects needs a cause outside itself, so does a solar system . . . There is no reason whatsoever to doubt that the same thing is true when we reach the level of the physical universe as a whole.

Now Hume is bound to pop up again at this point with another widely parroted but worthless objection. If every specific thing within the universe as a whole has a cause – this person was caused by his parents, that house was caused by its builders, that species was caused by natural selection, and so forth – what is left to be explained? This might seem plausible if we are thinking of tracing causes backwards in time (it isn't, actually, but I'll let it pass for the sake of argument).[25] But remember that what is in question here is not what events in the past led to what exists here and now, but rather what it is that keeps the things that exist, here and now, in existence here and now. Your mother gave birth to you, but she's not what's sustaining you in being here and now; what's doing that is going to be something like the current state of the cells of your body, which is in turn sustained by what's going on at the molecular level, and the atomic level, along with gravitation, the weak and strong forces, and so forth – all of these things being things whose essence is distinct from their existence and thus need a cause outside themselves. In other words, what we've got here is once again an "essentially ordered" causal series, which, for reasons we saw earlier, must of metaphysical necessity terminate in a first cause. Even when we consider the physical universe as a whole, then, we have something that down to its last detail consists of elements whose essence is distinct from their existence, and thus cannot account for their continued existence from moment to moment.

Hence, everything in the universe, and indeed the universe as a whole, must be sustained in being here and now by a cause outside it, a First Cause which upholds the entire series. But could this being itself be just another entity composed of essence and existence? If so, then it would not truly be a first cause at all, for it would require something outside *it* to explain its own existence, and the regress would continue. No, the only thing that could possibly stop the regress and explain the entire series would be a being who is, unlike the things that make up the universe, not a compound of essence and existence. That is to say, it would have to be a being whose essence *just is* existence; or, more precisely, a being to whom the essence/existence distinction doesn't apply at all, who *is* pure existence, pure being, full stop: not *a* being, strictly speaking, but Being Itself.

What would this First Cause be like? Note first that, as pure being or existence, He would also be Pure Actuality, and thus everything said about the Unmoved Mover would be true of Him; indeed, it is obvious that the First Cause and the Unmoved Mover are identical. Hence, equally obviously, the First Cause is God. He would also, as Being Itself, exist "necessarily" rather than "contingently." That is, whereas the ordinary objects of our experience of their nature are the sorts of things that need not have existed – they do in fact exist, but things could have gone differently – the First Cause could not possibly have failed to exist. (Hume, being his usual overrated self, famously asked why the universe itself might not be the necessary being, and did not stay for an answer. But the answer, as should be obvious by now, is that since the universe is undergoing change and is composed of essence and existence, it cannot be either Pure Actuality or Being Itself, and thus cannot be a necessary being in the relevant sense.)

What is even clearer from this argument than from the Unmoved Mover argument, though (though it is also deducible from that one) is that God would have to be an *absolutely simple* being. By "simple" I don't mean "easy to understand" – considering the level of abstraction the present argument requires us to think at, He is obviously not simple in *that* sense. What I mean is simple as opposed to composite, or being composed of parts. Physical things are composed of parts: not just our arms, legs, bodily organs, etc., but, more fundamentally from a metaphysical point of view, our form or essence on the one hand, and our matter on the other. Angels, not being material, are pure forms or essences on Aquinas's view, but even with them their essence needs to be combined with existence in order for them to be real, so that they too are composite. But the First Cause, since He is not a composite of essence and existence but just *is* pure existence itself, is simple. There are no parts or components in Him, not even metaphysical ones. Several things follow from this. First, God, not having an essence distinct from His existence, does not fall under a genus or general category. With us, there is the general category or essence "being human," and then there are the various individual human beings who fall under it, and who are distinguished from one another by the different parcels of matter which compose their bodies. Each of us is one existing instance among others of the general category or essence. But God is not one instance of a category or essence, not one particular existing thing of a general type. He is, again, pure Existence or Being Itself, rather than a compound of existence and essence. This is another reason there cannot even conceivably be more than one God: Since there is no divine essence distinct from the divine existence, there is no general category under which various distinct divine beings could fall, and thus no sense to be made of the idea of there being this God, that God, the other God, and so forth.[26]

It also follows that, when we speak of God as being powerful, intelligent, good, and so forth, we are not describing features that exist in a distinct way in God Himself. *Our* minds can only have a clear grasp of intellect, power, goodness, etc., as distinct attributes, since they exist distinct from one another in the things of our experience. But *in God* they exist as one: God's power *is* His intellect, which *is* His goodness, and so forth; they are but different ways of referring to what is in itself the same thing, Being Itself. The intelligence, power, goodness, etc., that exist in the world of created things are but fragmented and imperfect reflections of what exists in a unified and perfect way in the First Cause. This is, to be sure, a difficult idea to get one's mind around. But that shouldn't be surprising, unless we assume that *everything* that exists *must* be completely transparent to our intellects – an assumption that is totally unwarranted and implausible even from a "naturalistic" point of view (indeed, especially from a naturalistic point of view, as we shall see). Reason reveals to us that there is a God, and also tells us to some extent what He is like; but in doing so it also reveals to us that God is not something we should expect to be able fully to grasp, given the limitations on our intellects.

C. *The Supreme Intelligence*

The divine intellect is the particular focus of the last argument for God's existence we want to look at, which is Aquinas's Fifth Way. Dawkins, like many other atheistic critics, thinks this is more or less the same argument as William Paley's famous "Design argument." Paley's argument was roughly this: The universe is extremely complex and orderly, like a human artifact, only more so; and while it is theoretically possible that it could have arisen via completely impersonal forces, it is more probable that it was designed by some sort of intelligent being. Paley focuses on living things, their various organs, and their adaptation to their environments as the most powerful evidence of the complexity in question. His successors in the "Intelligent Design" movement do the same thing, arguing – not implausibly in some cases – that this or that biological structure is so "irreducibly complex" that it is overwhelmingly unlikely to have arisen through impersonal processes. Appealing to Darwinism, Dawkins and the other New Atheists respond – also not implausibly – that this is "God of the gaps" reasoning that is constantly vulnerable to being overthrown by further scientific research, which may well reveal (as it has done in the past) mechanisms by means of which what seems irreducibly complex can be accounted for in terms of more simple, impersonal, unthinking forces of nature.

Bizarrely, Dawkins seems to have gotten it into his head that his evangelical Darwinism will be sure to win over even the fundamentalist *hoi polloi* if sold to them as an exercise in "consciousness-raising," and he repeats this stupid '60s-era expression like a mantra throughout *The God Delusion*. For that matter, he also calls for "atheist pride" to take its rightful place alongside "gay pride"; meditates earnestly on John Lennon's "Imagine"; gives a nod to the feminist demand for "Herstory"; and drops in an approving reference to Robert Pirsig's *Zen and the Art of Motorcycle Maintenance*. I half expected to see him in a Nehru jacket and love beads on the book's dust cover photo. Grooviness, apparently, is next to Godlessness.

But if Dawkins is stuck in a time warp, it isn't in the 1960s that we will find him. For Dawkins, it is always *1860*, and it is T.H. Huxley rather than Aldous Huxley who is his guru. The enemy is always Soapy Sam Wilberforce, and arguments for God's existence, whatever their actual formulation and the intentions of their authors, are somehow always "really" about Paley, creationism, Darwin, and evolution. Dawkins is like the bore at a cocktail party who somehow always manages to bring the discussion back around to his own pet obsession of the moment. The one thing in the world he knows anything at all about is evolution; ergo, the debate about God's existence is "really" about his specialty. Or, as the '60s burnouts whom Dawkins apparently admires started to say in the '70s: "It's all about me."

Well, if Dawkins really wants his consciousness raised, he should love this little revelation: Aquinas's Fifth Way has nothing to do with either Paley's design argument or the creation/evolution debate. This is awful luck for a monomaniacal Darwinist afflicted with Dawkins's strange intellectual variation on Narcissistic Personality Disorder, but there it is. It is also something that is not terribly difficult to find out if only one bothers actually to read Aquinas's works and serious books about him. Philosopher Christopher Martin complained in his 1997 book on Aquinas that Dawkins seemed fixated on attacking Paley's argument for God's existence, as if there were no others.[27] That was over ten years ago; and like the Bourbons, Dawkins seems to have forgotten nothing, and learned nothing. If you'll forgive my quoting the Geico cavemen once again: "Next time, maybe do a little research."

One crucial difference between Aquinas and Paley is that whereas Aquinas is an Aristotelian committed to the objective reality of each of Aristotle's "four causes," Paley is a "modern" philosopher who, in common with other modern philosophers (as we'll see in Chapter 5), rejects Aristotle's metaphysics and denies that formal and final causes really exist in nature, or at least denies that we can have any knowledge of them. Another difference is that whereas Aquinas is attempting to provide a strict and airtight *metaphysical demonstration* of the existence of God, Paley – like the "Intelligent Design" theorists who follow him – is arguing instead on the basis of empirical probabilities, and claiming only to show that *some* sort of cosmic designer (maybe the God of traditional theism, but possibly something less grand) is *more probably* (but not certainly) the cause of the universe than any impersonal force. One consequence of these differences is that while Darwinian explanations of various biological phenomena are a serious challenge to the arguments of Paley and "Intelligent Design" theorists, they are almost totally irrelevant to Aquinas's Fifth Way; and I say "almost" totally irrelevant not because they might slightly hurt the Fifth Way, but because, on the contrary, if anything they slightly *help* Aquinas.

How can this be? Paley, as a "modern" thinker who rejects Aristotle's idea of final causes – purposiveness or goal-directedness existing objectively in the natural world – accepts the notion that in some sense the world is a vast machine. On this "mechanical" picture of the universe as a kind of clockwork, everything that exists in the physical world is made up of (or "is reducible to") purely material parts which by themselves have no goal, purpose, or meaning, and these parts interact with other bits of material stuff according to a stripped-down version of Aristotle's "efficient cause." How this is supposed to work became ever more mysterious as a result of Hume's critique of the principle of causality and other developments in modern philosophy (again, see Chapter 5), but the basic idea, to simplify a bit, is this: What exists objectively in the physical world are just mindless, purposeless, meaningless particles of matter bouncing around, knocking into each other in certain regular ways. Sometimes the particles combine to form larger and more complicated arrangements, thus giving rise to rocks, trees, dogs, human bodies, mountains, planets, etc. And there might be certain identifiable regularities in the way this happens. But even these more complex things have no *inherent* purpose, goal, meaning, or function, and they are not instances of fixed essences or substantial forms either; for there are (so it is claimed) no final causes or formal causes in the world, but just "matter in motion." Now if it can be shown – and this is what Paley and his successors try to show – that certain of these complex arrangements of bits of matter are statistically highly unlikely to occur apart from intelligent design, then that would make it probable that there is a designer of some sort who is causing these arrangements. On the other hand, if it can be shown instead – by means of Darwinian evolutionary theory, say – that any or all of these arrangements could in fact come about through unintelligent impersonal processes, then that drastically lowers the probability that any intelligent designer is involved. And since intelligence itself must somehow be just one more phenomenon among others explicable in terms of the "mechanical" processes constituted by meaningless chains of cause and effect between material elements, the probability that any designer would be an immaterial being beyond the physical world (à la the God of traditional theism) is arguably very low indeed.[28]

Now Aquinas, I think, would be completely disgusted by this whole way of framing the debate over God's existence – and that includes the Paley/"Intelligent Design" side of it, which more or less gives away the store to the skeptics by adopting the modern "mechanistic" conception of nature, and is thus reduced to a pathetic "God of the gaps" strategy. But its deficiencies from the point of view of apologetics are not the main problem with this conception of nature. Its main problem is that it is just *false*, and demonstrably so. From a Thomistic point of view, Paley and Co. have sold their birthright for a mess of pottage; and while the Darwinians have been unquestionably thuggish and often dishonest in their critiques of the "Intelligent Design" movement, to the extent that ID proponents have followed Paley in trading in Aristotle for a basically mechanistic picture of the physical universe, they have been "asking for it."

This is especially lamentable given that, as I have said, an evolutionary account of the origin of species doesn't undermine the Fifth Way in the least, and might even slightly help it. Now let me be clear about what I do and do not mean by this. I am *not* saying that either Aquinas or a follower of Aquinas could or should accept so-called "theistic evolutionism," if that is understood as entailing that *every* aspect of the biological realm, including every aspect of human nature, can be explained in terms of purely physical processes like natural selection. In fact I would say that while many biological phenomena might be so explained, there are others – such as our capacity to form general concepts and to reason on the basis of them – which, as we will see later, *demonstrably cannot* be explained in terms of evolution or in any other materialistic way.[29] What I *am* saying is that even if, *per impossibile*, everything in the biological realm could be explained by means of natural selection, this would not affect *the Fifth Way* specifically at all, even if it would affect other positions Aquinas takes. And since, as far as a follower of Aquinas is concerned, the evolutionary process would itself, even in that case, manifest final causality or goal-directedness, it would simply constitute one more example of the general phenomenon that forms the starting point of Aquinas's argument, and in that sense therefore at least slightly help his case.

What is that case? At one level, it is extremely simple. The universe is filled with natural regularities; this is uncontroversial. These include the regularities manifested in the biological realm – the way the heart pumps blood, thus keeping an organism alive, or the way a species is so adapted to its environment that its members can reliably find sources of food, reproduce themselves, and so forth – but Aquinas is not especially interested in these over any others. Indeed, unlike Paley and "Intelligent Design" proponents, he is not, for the purposes of the Fifth Way, particularly interested in *complexity* per se at all. The regularity with which the moon orbits the earth, or the regularity of the way a struck match generates fire – both very simple examples compared to eyes, hearts, species, and the like – are no less important. Indeed, they are *more* important for his argument. For life is a fairly rare phenomenon, confined so far as we know only to the earth. But the far simpler causal regularities I have been speaking of are completely general, and pervade the physical universe. Indeed, they largely constitute the physical universe, which can be thought of as a vast system of material elements interacting according to regular patterns of cause and effect.

But there is no way to make sense of these regularities apart from the notion of final causation, of things *being directed toward an end or goal*. For it is not just the case that a struck match regularly generates fire, heat, and the like; it regularly generates fire and heat *specifically, rather than* ice, or the smell of lilacs, or the sound of a trumpet. It is not just the case that the moon regularly orbits the earth in a regular pattern; it orbits the earth *specifically, rather than* quickly swinging out to Mars and back now and again, or stopping dead for five minutes here and there, or dipping down toward the earth occasionally and then quickly popping back up. And so on for all the innumerable regularities that fill the universe at any moment. In each case, the causes don't simply *happen* to result in certain effects, but are evidently and inherently *directed toward* certain specific effects as toward a "goal." As we saw when we first looked at Aristotle's notion of final causality, this doesn't mean they are *consciously trying* to reach these goals; of course they are not. The Aristotelian idea is precisely that goal-directedness can and does exist in the natural world even apart from conscious awareness.

Still, it is very odd that this should be the case. One of the raps against final causation is that it seems clearly to entail that a thing can produce an effect even before that thing exists. Hence to say that an oak tree is the final cause of an acorn seems to entail that the oak tree – which doesn't yet exist – in *some* sense causes the acorn to go through every state it passes through as it grows into the oak, since the oak is the "goal" or natural end of the acorn. But how can this be? Well, consider those cases where goal-directedness *is* associated with consciousness, viz. in us. A builder builds a house; he is a cause that generates a specific kind of effect. But the reason he is able to do this is that the effect, the house, exists as an idea in his intellect before it exists in reality. That is precisely how the not-yet-existent house can serve as a final cause – by means of its form or essence existing in someone's intellect, if not (yet) in reality. And that seems clearly to be the *only* way something not yet existent in reality can exist in any other sense at all, and thus have any effects at all: that is, if it exists in an intellect.

Now go back to the vast system of causes that constitutes the physical universe. Every one of them is directed toward a certain end or final cause. Yet almost none of them is associated with any consciousness, thought, or intellect at all; and even animals and human beings, who are conscious, are themselves comprised in whole or in part of unconscious and unintelligent material components which themselves manifest final causality. Yet it is impossible for anything to be directed toward an end unless that end exists in an intellect which directs the thing in question toward it. And it follows, therefore, that the system of ends or final causes that make up the physical universe can only exist at all because there is a Supreme Intelligence or intellect outside that universe which directs things toward their ends.

Notice that there is absolutely nothing in this argument that has to do with the allegedly "irreducible complexity" of eyeballs or mitochondria, or any other such mainstays of the creation-versus-evolution debate. Even if the universe consisted of nothing but an electron orbiting a nucleus, that would suffice for the Fifth Way. Notice also that, here as elsewhere, Aquinas doesn't care, for the purposes of proving God's existence, how the universe got started or even whether it ever did. All that matters is that there are various causes *here and now* which are *here and now* directed to certain ends, and the argument is that these couldn't possibly exist at all if there were not a Supreme Intellect *here and now* ordering them to those ends. And this *includes* those causes operative in biological evolution. Nor is this a matter of "probability," but of conceptual necessity: it is not just *unlikely*, but *conceptually impossible* that there could be genuine final causation without a sustaining intellect.

Does this conflict with Aristotle's view that final causes exist even where there is no consciousness? No, and to see why not we might consider the analogy of language. If we consider the words, sentences, and other linguistic items that we speak or write, record on tape or print in a book, it is obvious that they get their meaning only from the community of language users that produces them, and ultimately from the ideas expressed by those language users in using these linguistic items. Apart from such users, the things we have written or recorded would be nothing more than meaningless splotches of ink and sound waves. Still, once produced, these linguistic items, and language in general, take on a kind of life of their own. The words and sentences written in books and recorded on tape retain their meaning even when no one is thinking about them; indeed, even the words and sentences recorded on a book or on a tape sitting in a dusty corner of a library somewhere, not having been looked at for decades and completely forgotten, still retain their meaning for all that. Moreover, language has a structure that most language users themselves are unaware of, but which can be studied by linguists. And so forth. But if the community of language users should disappear entirely – if every language user died off as a result of a plague, say – then the recorded words that were left behind *would* in that case revert to nothing more than meaningless splotches and sounds. While the community of language users exists, its general background presence is all that's required for the meaning to persist in the physical sounds and markings, even if some of those sounds and markings are not the focus of anyone's attention at any particular moment. But if the community disappears altogether, the meaning goes with it. By analogy – and it is only an analogy, and not an exact one – I would suggest that the relationship of the Supreme Intelligence to the system of final causes in the world is somewhat like the relationship between language users and language. The Supreme Intelligence directs things toward their ends, but the system he thereby creates in doing so has a kind of "independence" insofar as it can be studied (as Aristotle studied it) without reference to the Supreme Intelligence Himself, just as linguists can study the structure of language without paying attention to the intentions of this or that language user. The ends are in one sense just "there" in unconscious causes like the meaning is just "there" in the words once they have been written. Still, if the Supreme Intelligence were to cease his directing activity, final causes would immediately disappear, just as the meaning in the words would disappear if the community of language users disappeared altogether.

Could such a Supreme Intelligence possibly be anything less than God? It could not. For whatever ultimately orders things to their ends must also be the ultimate cause of those things: To have an end is just part of having a certain nature or essence; for that nature or essence to be the nature or essence of something real, it must be conjoined with existence; and thus whatever determines that things exist with a certain end is the same as what conjoins their essence and existence, that is, what causes them. But as we have seen, the ultimate or First Cause of things must be Being Itself. Hence the Supreme Intelligence cannot fail to be identical with the

First Cause and thus with the Unmoved Mover, with all the divine attributes. The arguments all converge on one and the same point: God, as conceived of in the monotheistic religions.

There can be no doubt, then, that the Supreme Intelligence which orders things to their ends cannot fail to be Pure Being and therefore also cannot fail to be absolutely simple. All this simply follows inexorably from the logic of the argument. This is worth emphasizing, because Dawkins makes a very big deal about how "complex" the "Designer" would have to be, and thus how he would Himself be in need of further "explanation." Indeed, this is, he tells us, his "central argument," and Harris trumpets it as well (though only because he read it in Dawkins, who seems oddly to have been ceded the title of "house philosopher" by the other New Atheists, including the philosophers among them).[30] Dawkins even proudly gives it a separate entry in the index ("argument, author's central, 157–8"). This is very helpful, because the busy reader scanning the index will be glad to find when he turns to pages 157–8 that if the "central argument" of *The God Delusion* is this bad, he needn't waste his time reading the rest of it. Indeed, since the central anti-theistic argument presented by Dennett, Harris, and Hitchens is pretty much the same as Dawkins's, he needn't waste his time reading their books either.

Now Dawkins's "central argument" is directly presented against Paley – the New Atheists' obsession, whom if he were still alive might look into getting a restraining order against them – but it is also intended to apply to Aquinas, whom Dawkins incompetently supposes is giving the same argument as Paley. In fairness to Paley, about whom I have said some pretty harsh things myself, I should note that his argument isn't quite as bad as Dawkins and his parrots take it to be. Read a book like Richard Swinburne's *The Existence of God* if you want to see why the usual objections to it are greatly overrated. But, having now cut Paley some slack, I want to emphasize again that he simply doesn't matter, and wouldn't get nearly the attention he does get from the New Atheists if he hadn't made himself such an attractive punching bag by effectively conceding all their main premises. What does matter is how Dawkins's "central argument" fares against the classical sort of teleological argument represented by Aquinas's Fifth Way, and considered in that light it is totally worthless. If you want to say that Darwinism is a "simpler hypothesis" and thus "more probable" than Paley's designer vis-à-vis the question of the "complexity" of biological organs and the like, that may or may not be a good objection to Paley; certainly you can make the case. But it is completely irrelevant against the Fifth Way, because (a) that kind of "simplicity" is not what Aquinas is talking about when he calls God "simple," (b) Aquinas is not trying to explain the "complexity" of organs or of anything else in the first place, and (c) his argument is not an attempt to weigh probabilities, but an attempt at a metaphysical demonstration in which the conclusion follows necessarily from the premises. Given the existence of final causation, of essentially ordered causal series, the essence/existence distinction, and so forth, it simply follows deductively that there is a Supreme Intelligence who is Pure Being and thus absolutely simple. Or at any rate, if you are going to fault this argument, you first have to understand and evaluate it on its own terms. It won't do to substitute some Paleyan straw man to attack, simply because that's all you know and all you are competent to say anything about.

I realize, of course, that many will reply that there is still a fatal flaw in Aquinas's argument insofar as final causes don't exist. The moderns, they will allege, were right to deny their existence, as well as the existence of what Aristotle called formal causes. Well, it's true that many people say this. But they are wrong to say it. The reality of formal and final causes is rationally unavoidable, as we will see by the end of this book. You can no more coherently deny their existence than you can deny the existence of your own mind and your own actions – even if some have tried, incoherently, to deny these too. Indeed, Dawkins himself falls into Aquinas's trap when in the course of "refuting" him he casually alludes to the "goal-seeking behavior" of insects.[31] But before turning to all that, we need to say a little more about what follows if there *are* formal and final causes.

4. Scholastic Aptitude

Aquinas's arguments for God's existence show how certain Aristotelian metaphysical ideas that might seem at first glance too abstruse to have any practical relevance – such as the distinction between actuality and potentiality, the principle that effects are contained in their causes either "formally" or "eminently," and that final causality pervades the natural order – in fact have the most dramatic consequences for the debate between religion and atheism. We want now to examine how some of these principles (and others we've looked at, such as Aristotle's "hylomorphism") were applied by Aquinas and the Scholastic tradition in general to a defense of the immortality of the soul and the natural law conception of morality. I can even, at long last, promise some racy sex talk. (Well, sort of.) The reader deserves a little excitement in the midst of all this technical philosophy, though I trust it is by now obvious why we have had to "get metaphysical" to the extent we have. No pain, no gain, and all that. (Anyway, if you think *this* is tedious, try plowing through Dennett's application of the methods of "evolutionary psychology" – viz. the relentless piling of one sheer speculation upon another for hundreds of pages – in the attempt to "explain" religion "naturalistically"; or Harris's flaky venture into Eastern meditation, which will leave you aching to get to the end of *The End of Faith*. If these guys don't believe in purgatory, they should read their own books.)

The soul

Aristotle, it will be remembered, held that the objects of our everyday experience are composites of form and matter, of a nature or essence on the one hand and a parcel of material stuff that takes on that form, nature, or essence on the other. This is as true of living things as of anything else. And for Aristotle, a *soul* is just the form or essence of a living thing. It is important not to misunderstand this. Someone with some crude misconception about what Aristotle or Aquinas must think a soul is supposed to be – like Dennett, no doubt, or Dawkins – might say "What grounds does Aristotle have for saying that a *soul* is what gives a living thing's body its essence or form? What superstition!" But the form or essence of a living thing is just what Aristotle (and Aquinas) *mean* by the word "soul." They aren't saying, "We hypothesize that the soul, as popularly understood, is what gives a thing its nature"; they're saying "By 'soul' we simply mean to refer to the nature of a living thing, whatever that turns out to be." So the reader should not think of some ghostly object of the sort that floats away from a body after death, as in the movies, because that's simply not what they have in mind. The soul is just a kind of form.

It should for that reason also not be seen as odd that Aristotle and Aquinas think of living things in general, including plants and non-human animals, as having souls. All they mean by this is that a plant or an animal has the form or essence characteristic of a living thing. They do *not* mean that when your favorite fern or dog dies, its soul goes to heaven. It doesn't go anywhere but out of existence, since like the forms of rocks and tables, the forms of plants and non-human animals are mere abstractions considered by themselves, and have no reality apart from the particular material things they are the forms of. The soul of a plant is what Aristotelians call a "nutritive soul"; and that is just a form or essence that gives a thing that has it the powers of taking in nutrients, growing, and reproducing itself. The soul of a non-human animal is called a "sensory soul," and it is just a form or essence that gives a thing that has it both the powers of a nutritive soul, and also an animal's distinctive powers of being able to sense the world around it (by seeing, hearing, etc.) and to move itself (by walking, flying, etc.). When we come to human beings we have what is called a "rational soul," which includes both the powers of the nutritive and sensory souls and also the distinctively human powers of intellect and will: that is, the power to grasp abstract concepts – namely, the forms or essences of things – and to reason on the basis of them, and freely to choose between different possible courses of action on the basis of what the intellect knows. As all of this indicates, the relationship between kinds of souls illustrates the Aristotelian idea that there is a hierarchy of forms: the sensory soul incorporates and adds to the powers of the nutritive soul, and the rational soul in turn incorporates and adds to the powers of both the nutritive and sensory souls, so that there is a natural hierarchical relationship between them.

The superiority of the rational soul goes beyond its place at the top of this hierarchy, however. As we have seen, a thing's having a certain form goes hand in hand with its having a certain final cause or natural end, or a hierarchically ordered set of final causes or natural ends. A plant is ordered toward taking in nutrients, growing, and reproducing itself; those are the ends nature has given it. An animal has these ends too, along with the ends entailed by its distinctive powers of sensation and locomotion. Notice, though, that some of these ends are subordinated to the others. The point of nutrition, for example, is just to enable a plant or animal to carry out its other ends, such as growing and reproducing. Now a human being has all of these ends too, but on top of them he has the ends or final causes entailed by being rational and having free will. Rationality – the ability to grasp forms or essences and to reason on the basis of them – has as its natural end or final cause the attainment of truth, of understanding the world around us. And free will has as its natural end or final cause the choice of those actions that best accord with the truth as it is discovered by reason, and in particular in accord with the truth about a human being's own nature or essence. That is, as we shall see, exactly what morality is from the point of view of Aristotle and Aquinas: the habitual choice of actions that further the hierarchically ordered natural ends entailed by human nature. But the intellect's capacity to know the truth is more fully realized the deeper one's understanding of the nature of the world and the causes underlying it. And the deepest truth about the world, as we have seen, is that it is caused and sustained in being by God. The highest fulfillment of the distinctively human power of intellect, then, is, for Aristotle and Aquinas, to know God. And since the will's natural end or purpose is to choose in accordance with the furtherance of those ends entailed by human nature, the highest fulfillment of free choice is to live in a way that facilitates the knowing of God. All the other powers of the soul, including the nutritive and sensory powers, also have their own ends or final causes, but they are all subordinate in human nature to this distinctive and overarching end.

The human soul, then, though it is, at the first level of analysis, just the form or essence of the living human body, turns out on deeper analysis to have a divine end or purpose which raises it above plant and animal souls in dignity. But the truth about the human soul goes beyond even this. Note that the powers of nutritive and sensory souls are completely tied to the material stuff that makes up the living things they are the souls of. Nutrition and growth require the taking in and alteration of bits of matter, and reproduction involves transforming bits of matter into something that is like the thing doing the transforming. An animal's sensing the world around itself requires the use of bodily organs (eyes, ears, tongues, etc.), as does its moving about (legs, fins, wings, etc.). If there is no matter to make up the various physical organs that carry out these functions, the functions simply cannot be carried out. Hence if the matter that makes up a plant or animal goes away, the soul goes with it, for there is nothing left to underlie the operation of its powers. That is why I said earlier that the soul of a plant or non-human animal does not "go to heaven," or anywhere else, when it dies. If there is a sense in which plants and non-human animals have souls, then, they do not have immortal souls.

Now the rational soul, since it includes the powers of the nutritive and sensory souls, cannot fail to be to a very great extent dependent on matter for its operations. Like plants and animals, we need bodily organs if we are to fulfill our abilities to take in nutrients, grow, reproduce, and move about and sense the world around us. But things are very different with the power of intellect. This power *cannot possibly* require a material or bodily organ for its operation. Why not? There are a number of reasons, some of which we'll be examining in the next two chapters. But for now let us focus on a reason of the sort emphasized by Aquinas and other Scholastic thinkers (and to a lesser and less conclusive extent by Aristotle).[1] Central to the intellect's operation is its grasp of forms, essences, or universals, and other abstractions like propositions – the sorts of things we spent so much time discussing in Chapter 2. As we saw in that chapter, however, these things cannot be in any way material: this or that triangle is a material thing, but the form or essence *triangularity* is not; snow is material, but the proposition *that snow is white* cannot be; and so forth. But the immaterial nature of these things entails that the intellect which grasps them must itself be immaterial as well. How so?

Consider first that when we grasp the nature, essence, or form of a thing, it is necessarily one and the same form, nature, or essence that exists both in the thing and in the intellect. The form of triangularity that exists in our minds when we think about triangles is *the same form* that exists in actual triangles themselves; the form of "dogness" that exists in our minds when we think about dogs is *the same form* that exists in actual dogs; and so forth. If this weren't the case, then we just wouldn't really be thinking about triangles, dogs, and the like, since to think about these things requires grasping what they are, and what they are is determined by their essence or form. But now suppose that the intellect is a material thing – some part of the brain, or whatever. Then for the form to exist in the intellect is for the form to exist in a certain material thing. But for a form to exist in a material thing is just for that material thing to be the kind of thing the form is a form of; for example, for the form of "dogness" to exist in a certain parcel of matter is just for that parcel of matter to be a dog. And in that case, if your intellect was just the same thing as some part of your brain, it follows that that part of your brain would become a dog whenever you thought about dogs. "But that's absurd!" you say. Of course it is; that's the point. Assuming that the intellect is material leads to such absurdity; hence the intellect is not material.

Consider also that when you think about triangularity, for example, as you do when proving a geometrical theorem, it is necessarily *perfect* triangularity that you are contemplating, not some approximation of it. Triangularity as your intellect grasps it is entirely determinate or exact. (Of course your mental image of some triangle might not be determinate, but indeterminate and fuzzy. But to form a mental image of something, you'll remember, is not the same thing as to grasp it with your intellect.) Now the thought you are having must be as determinate as triangularity itself, otherwise it just wouldn't *be* a thought about triangularity per se, but only a thought about some approximation of triangularity. But material things are never determinate in this way; any material triangle, for example, is always only ever an approximation of triangularity. It follows, then, that any thought you might have about triangularity is not something material; in particular, it is not some process occurring in the brain. And what goes for triangularity goes for *any* thought, since any thought is going to involve universals, propositions, numbers or the like, which we have seen are all abstract and determinate in a way material objects and processes never can be.

Related to this is the fact that universals are, well, *universal*, and every material thing is particular. Triangularity is not identical to this or that particular material triangle. But suppose a thought about the universal triangularity was something material. Then, presumably, the "triangularity" part of this material thought would consist of some physical representation of triangularity in the brain somewhere (in the form of a neuronal firing pattern or some such thing). But no such physical representation could possibly count as the universal triangularity, because like any other physical representation of a triangle, this one too would be just one particular material thing among others, and not universal at all. Hence, again, there is just no sense to be made of the idea that thought is a purely material operation of the brain.

Now I can almost hear a Dennett or Dawkins reading this and responding: "But how is postulating 'ectoplasm' or some such thing any better as an explanatory hypothesis? What about Ockham's razor? What about neuroscience?" But Aquinas and other Scholastic writers who defend arguments like the foregoing are not "postulating" anything, they are not offering an "explanatory hypothesis," and they certainly don't believe in "ectoplasm." (For the uninitiated, "ectoplasm" is a ghostly kind of stuff that writers like Dennett are constantly accusing critics of materialism of believing in. It plays the same sort of straw-man role in his writings on the mind that Paley does in Dawkins's writings on religion.) Here, as elsewhere, the arguments we are considering are attempts at what I have been calling metaphysical demonstration, not probabilistic empirical theorizing. In each case, the premises are obviously true, the conclusion follows necessarily, and thus the conclusion is obviously true as well. That, at any rate, is what the arguments claim. If you're going to refute them, then you need to show either that the premises are false or that the conclusion doesn't really follow. Otherwise you have no rational basis for not accepting them. Appealing to further neuroscientific research, Ockham's razor, etc., is just beside the point; if the arguments work, then the immateriality of the intellect is *itself* a datum that any respectable neuroscientific theory will have to be consistent with, and any theory that seemed to deny it would itself be violating Ockham's razor. The "findings of neuroscience" couldn't refute these arguments any more than they could refute "2 + 2 = 4." For Aquinas's claim isn't a "soul of the gaps" analogue to "God of the gaps" arguments. He is not saying: "Gee, the mind is mysterious, and there's still a lot we don't know about the brain. So I speculate that there might be some ghostly object floating around in there." Rather, he is saying that given the facts about universals, etc., and our thoughts about them, it is *conceptually impossible* (not merely improbable) for the intellect to be material, whatever else might be true of it. So whatever neuroscience might discover – and there is of course a lot that it has discovered, and will continue to discover – one thing we know it *won't* "discover" is that thought is a material operation of the brain, any more than it will "discover" that 2 + 2 = 5.

If Aquinas doesn't think of the intellect as a piece of "ectoplasm," then, how does he conceive of it? We've already seen how: as a power of the soul, which is itself a kind of form, nature, or essence, and where a form, nature, or essence is but a *component* of a substance or thing, not a complete substance or thing in its own right. The form of a rock isn't a complete substance; only the form of the rock and the matter of the rock together constitute a thing or substance, that is, a rock. Similarly, the soul of a man isn't a complete substance; only the soul and body (i.e. the form and matter) together constitute a thing or substance, that is, a man. It isn't the soul that thinks when a man uses his intellect; it is the man himself who thinks, just as it is the man himself, and not the soul, who grows taller, digests his food, and walks around. For this reason, it is not at all surprising that human thought should be very closely correlated with certain brain events even if it is not identical to any of them. Since the soul is the form of the body, including the brain, the connection between them is in many ways like the connection between the form of some particular table – its round shape, its having four legs, its being brown, etc. – and the matter that makes up the table; that is, it is bound to be very close indeed. When the intellect determines that a certain course of action is the best one to take and the will follows it, the body proceeds to move in a way that constitutes the action. The operation of intellect and will constitute in this case is the formal-cum-final cause of the action, of which the firing of the neurons, flexing of the muscles, etc. are the material cause. Then there is the fact that even though the intellect itself operates without any bodily organ, it does depend indirectly on the senses for the raw material from which it abstracts universals or essences (e.g. it abstracts the universal "triangularity" from particular triangles it has perceived). And the sense organs, along with the brain events associated with perceptual experiences, are material.

But precisely because the operations of the intellect are not directly dependent on the matter of the brain, the parallel with the form of a table is not exact. If the soul can, unlike the form of a table, *function* apart from the matter it informs (as it does in thought), then it can also, and again unlike the form of a table, *exist* apart from the matter it informs, as a kind of incomplete substance. Remember that from an Aristotelian point of view, there is an asymmetry between actuality and potentiality, and between form and matter (the latter distinction being a special case of the former, which is more general). Usually actuality and potentiality are combined, and potentiality can never exist without actuality; but actuality can and does exist without potentiality, namely in God, who is Pure Actuality. Similarly, form and matter are usually combined, and matter can never exist without form; but form can exist without matter, and does in this case, at least after death when the matter of the body is no longer informed by the soul, its form. Unlike the souls of plants and animals, then, the rational soul is immortal, on Aquinas's view. Whereas the body dies precisely when and because the soul or form of the body is no longer giving structure and function to the matter of the body – just as a table goes out of existence when the matter composing it no longer has the form of a table – the soul itself, partially operating and thus existing as it does apart from the body even when informing it, does not thereby die. For a thing to perish is just for it to lose its form. But the soul doesn't lose its form, because it *is* a form. That doesn't mean that a human being continues to exist after death, for a human being is a composite of form and matter, and it is only a part of him – the form or soul – that carries on. Still, it is the highest and most distinctive part of him.

When does the rational soul's presence in the body begin? At conception. For a soul is just the form – the essence, nature, structure, organizational pattern – of a living thing, an organism. And the human organism, as we know from modern biology, begins at conception. Now Aquinas did not know this; given the flawed biological information available to him in his day, he thought that the human organism came into existence some time after conception, though long before birth. Despite the fact that he still thought abortion was immoral at *any* point after conception, some "pro-choice" advocates have tried to make hay out of this, but their efforts are in vain. Once you add Aquinas's metaphysics to modern biology, there can be no doubt that the soul is present from conception, and thus that a human being exists from conception.[2]

Of course, the features essential to human beings as rational animals – being able to take in nutrients, to sense the world around them, to think, and so forth – are not fully *developed* until well after conception. But that doesn't mean that they aren't *there*. Remember Aristotle's distinction between actuality and potentiality. Rationality, locomotion, nutrition, and the like are present even at conception "in potency" or as inherent potentialities. And as you'll recall, this doesn't mean "potential" in the loose and far-fetched sense in which a rubber ball might "potentially" roll by itself or spontaneously combust, due to some bizarre quantum fluctuation. It doesn't even mean "potential" in the sense in which a rubber ball might potentially be melted down and made into something else, e.g. an eraser. It means "potential" in the sense of a capacity that an entity already has within it by virtue of its nature or essence, as a rubber ball *qua rubber ball* has the potential to roll down a hill even when it is locked in a cabinet somewhere. And in this sense a zygote has within it the potentiality for or "directedness toward" the actual exercise of reasoning, willing, and all the rest that a rubber ball doesn't have, that a sperm or egg considered by themselves don't have, and that even a skin cell, despite having the full complement of human DNA within it, doesn't have unless it is re-directed *away* from *its* natural end (i.e. functioning as part of the skin) by a scientist attempting to clone someone. To allude to another distinction made earlier, the zygote, given its nature or form, has rationality as a "primary actuality" even if not yet as a "secondary actuality," and these other things don't; they have at best only the capacity to be *turned into* something that has this primary actuality. Hence Harris's sarcastic claim that "every time you scratch your nose, you have committed a Holocaust of potential human beings" demonstrates, not any fault with the pro-life position, but only his own inability to make precise conceptual distinctions.[3] The skin cells on your nose might well be "potential human beings," in the loose sense in which a rubber ball is a "potential eraser." But a zygote is *not* a "potential human being" or a "potentially rational animal." Rather, it is an *actual* human being and thus an *actual* rational animal, just one that hasn't yet fully realized its inherent potentials. Harris and his ilk might want to ignore the importance of this distinction, but that it *is* a genuine distinction cannot rationally be denied.

Far from any of this being undermined by modern science, it is *confirmed* by it. For the nature and structure of DNA is exactly the sort of thing we should expect to exist given an Aristotelian metaphysical conception of the world, and not at all what we would expect if materialism were true. The reason is that the notions of DNA, of the gene, and so forth are utterly suffused with goal-directedness and potentiality. It is no accident that terms like "encoding," "information," "instructions," "blueprint" and the like are often used to describe the workings of DNA, for there is no other way coherently and informatively *to* describe those workings; and yet the notion of being encoded, or being information, or being a set of instructions, or being a blueprint all involve directedness of something toward an end beyond itself, and thus final causality. To have a certain trait "in the DNA" *just is* to have as a "primary actuality" the potential to realize it as a "secondary actuality." Aristotle would no doubt have had little patience for contemporary pop psychology, but he might have found useful one of its catchphrases as a way of describing those contemporary biologists who think they have significantly moved beyond him: they are "in denial." Compared to the way in which final causality has – in actual practice, if not in theory and rhetoric – maintained its grip on biological thinking, the Darwinian "revolution" is a trivial blip on the continued silent and unacknowledged hegemony of Aristotle. The unhealthy fixation of Dawkins, Dennett, and Co. on the relatively insignificant Paley has kept them from seeing this fatal difficulty with their position. They have been frantically shooting their flit guns at a gnat even while an elephant grinds them into paste under its feet. But again, I am getting ahead of myself; we will return to all of this later.

Given the facts about the soul's "entrance" into the body, there should be no mystery about when it "leaves." Again, the soul is just the form of the human organism, so it is necessarily there as long as the living organism is. Hence it "leaves" only when the organism dies; and that means *death*, not severe brain damage, and not a person's lapsing into a "persistent vegetative state." Though a person might not be capable of exercising his rationality, it is there nonetheless in potentiality, since the soul – the form, nature, or essence of the living organism – is still there, and rationality is part of this form, nature, or essence. As Plato and Aristotle agree, for something to fail to instantiate a form or essence perfectly does not mean that it fails to instantiate it at all. Thus even poor Terri Schiavo, since she was still alive and thus still had a rational soul, was no less a rational animal than her husband and the judges who together condemned her to death, even if, unlike them, she could not exercise her rationality. And for that reason, depriving her of the food she needed was as much an act of murder as depriving any other innocent and helpless human being of food would have been. For the same reason, and as has already been implied, given Aristotelian metaphysics together with the facts of modern biology, abortion necessarily counts as murder at *any* point from conception onward, and *whatever* the circumstances of the conception, including rape and incest. For a zygote, being a human organism and thus in possession of the form or essence of a human organism (i.e. a rational soul), has the same right to life that any innocent human being has. Of course, some would deny that innocent human beings per se really have a right to life, and we will address this issue presently. The point for now is that if you do agree that every innocent human being has a right to life, then you cannot consistently fail to take a "pro-life" position and thus favor outlawing *all* abortions (and all forms of euthanasia too) just as you'd favor outlawing any other form of murder.

One final note about the rational soul. Given that it functions and thus exists independently of matter, it cannot possibly have been generated by purely material processes. And so a *complete* explanation of it in evolutionary terms is in principle impossible. That doesn't mean that evolutionary theory is completely irrelevant. Since it is the form of a rational animal, the matter a rational soul informs must be complex enough to sustain those material operations that it relies on in an indirect way, such as sensation. In principle, evolutionary theory could explain how living things got to such a level of complexity that it was possible for an animal to exist which was capable of having a rational soul. But the actual existence of the rational soul itself would have to come from outside the evolutionary process. Yet we have already shown that there is a God, and that the rational soul, unlike any other kind of soul, is ordered toward the knowledge of God. Thus we have a ready explanation of the existence of rational souls: direct creation by God. This is not some ad hoc appeal to a *deus ex machina*; for we have, again, already established that there is a God and that the soul is both immaterial and directed toward knowing Him. And an evolutionary process itself, like everything else that exists, would have to be sustained in being by Him from moment to moment anyway. An appeal to God is thus theoretically natural, even inevitable.

Notice in any event that at every point in Aquinas's account of the soul, as at every point in his arguments for God's existence, the appeal is to what follows rationally from such Aristotelian metaphysical notions as the formal and final causes of a thing. There is no appeal to "faith," or to parapsychology, ghost stories, near-death experiences, or any other evidence of the sort materialists routinely dismiss as scientifically dubious. Whatever one's ultimate appraisal of these arguments, the New Atheist's pretense that a religious view of the world can only ever be the result of wishful thinking rather than objective rational argumentation is thereby exposed as a falsehood, the product, if not of willful deception, at least of inexcusable ignorance of the views of the most significant religious thinkers. That alone suffices to show that the arguments of Dawkins and his gang are worthless. For even if, *per impossibile*, their atheism turned out to be correct, they would not have arrived at it by rational means, shamelessly caricaturing as they do the best arguments for the other side, when they are not ignoring them altogether.

Natural law

The same thing can be said of the New Atheists' attitude toward the moral views defended by religious believers, including the traditional sexual morality so hated by secularists. That these views can only be regarded as superstitious, without rational foundation, motivated by bigotry, etc., is a familiar enough cliché, and the New Atheists have nothing to add to it – other than Richard Dawkins's proposal to replace the Ten Commandments with a list that includes "Enjoy your own sex life (as long as it damages no one else)."[4] Combine this with his proposal to replace religious instruction for children with something more progressive, and his weird outrage over the "hysteria" he thinks surrounds the treatment of pedophiles – his own boyhood victimization by a pedophile was, he kindly shares with us, "embarrassing but otherwise harmless"[5] – and you get some truly creepy vibes about the direction in which secularist "values education" might go. (You can forget whatever Father Smith or Sister Mary taught you in parochial school, kids; Uncle Dick is here to tell you what it really means to love each other.)

But since I just ate, I'd rather leave aside Dawkins's bid to become the New Moses for the swinger set (though note once again how secularism apes religious motifs even as its proponents furiously deny making a religion of their hatred of religion). The point I want to emphasize is that, far from having no rational basis, the moral views now associated in the secularist mind with superstition and ignorance in fact follow inexorably from a consistent application of the metaphysical ideas we've traced back through Aquinas and the other Scholastic thinkers to Plato and Aristotle, the very greatest of the Greek founders of the Western intellectual tradition. In particular, this classical metaphysical picture entails a conception of morality traditionally known as *natural law theory*.[6]

Like so many of the ideas and arguments we've looked at already, natural law theory is very badly misunderstood by those who criticize it. The usual objections go like this: "If it's wrong to go against nature, then isn't it wrong to wear glasses, ride bicycles, etc., since these aren't natural but artificial?" "If what's good is what's natural, isn't everything we do therefore good, since everything that happens in nature is by definition 'natural'?" "If homosexuality is genetic, doesn't that show that it's natural too?" And so on, tiresomely and cluelessly.

Perhaps it is obvious from what's been said already what is wrong with these objections, but if not, here it is. The "nature" of a thing, from an Aristotelian point of view, is, as we've seen, the form or essence it instantiates. Hence, once again to haul in my triangle example, it is of the essence, nature, or form of a triangle to have three perfectly straight sides.[7] Notice that this remains true even if some particular triangle does not have three perfectly straight sides, and indeed even though (as I've repeated *ad nauseam*) every material instance of a triangle has some defect or other. The point is that these are *defects*, failures to conform to the nature or essence of triangularity; the fact that such defective triangles exist in the natural world and in accordance with the laws of physics doesn't make them any less "unnatural" *in the relevant sense*.

When we get to biological organs, we have things whose natures or essences more obviously involve certain final causes or purposes. So, for example, the function or final cause of eyeballs is to enable us to see. But suppose someone's eyeballs are defective in some way, making his vision blurry. In that case, to wear eyeglasses isn't contrary to the natural function of eyeballs; rather, it quite obviously restores to the eyeballs their ability to carry out their natural function. Bicycles don't do this, of course, but they do extend, rather than conflict with, the ability of the legs to carry out their natural function of allowing us to move about.

Finally, to round out this initial reply to some standard bad objections to natural law theory, while it is true that some defenders and critics of traditional sexual morality seem to worry themselves endlessly about whether homosexuality has a genetic basis, the question is actually largely irrelevant, and they shouldn't waste their time. For it is quite obvious that the existence of a genetic basis for some trait does not *by itself* prove *anything* about whether it is "natural" in the relevant sense. To take just one of many possible examples, that there is a genetic basis for clubfoot doesn't show that having clubfeet is "natural." Quite obviously it is *un*natural, certainly in the Aristotelian sense of failure perfectly to conform to the essence or nature of a thing. And no one who has a clubfoot would take offense at someone's noting this obvious matter of fact, or find it convincing that the existence of a genetic basis for his affliction shows that it is something he should "embrace" and "celebrate." Nor would it be plausible to suggest that God "made him that way," any more than God "makes" people to be born blind, deaf, armless, legless, prone to alcoholism, or autistic. God obviously *allows* these things, for whatever reason; but it doesn't follow that He positively *wills* them, and it certainly doesn't follow that they are "natural." So, by the same token, the possibility of a genetic basis for homosexual desire doesn't by itself show that such desire is natural. Homosexual activists often breathlessly cite this or that alleged "finding" that such a basis exists; someday they might even cite something plausible. "Whatever, dude," as the kids say. Even if it is established beyond a reasonable doubt that there is such a basis, with respect to the question of the "naturalness" of homosexuality, this would prove exactly zip.

Of course, that by itself does not show that homosexuality is immoral either. After all, having a clubfoot is not immoral, and neither is being born blind or with a predisposition for alcoholism. These are simply afflictions for which the sufferer is not at fault, and can only call forth our sympathy. On the other hand, if someone born with normal feet wanted to *give* himself a clubfoot through surgery, we would find this at the very least irrational; and if someone concluded from his having a genetic predisposition for alcoholism that regularly drinking to excess would be a worthwhile "lifestyle" for him to pursue, then we would regard him as sorely mistaken, *even if* he could do this in a way that allowed him to hold down a job, keep his friends and family, and avoid car accidents. Even amid the depravity of modern civilization, most people realize that the life of an alcoholic is simply not a good thing, even if the alcoholic himself *thinks* it is and even if he "doesn't hurt anybody else." We know in our bones that there is something ignoble and unfitting about it. In the same way, should it turn out that a desire to molest children has a genetic basis, no one would conclude from this that sexual attraction toward children is a good thing, *even if* the person who has it was able to satisfy his disgusting urges without actually touching any children. We all know in our bones that someone obsessed with masturbating to pictures of naked toddlers is sick, and not living the way a human being ought to live, even if he never leaves the darkness of his own room and his own soul.

Now I realize, of course, that many readers will acknowledge that we do in fact have these reactions, but would nevertheless write them off as *mere* reactions. "Our tendency to find something personally disgusting," they will sniff, "doesn't show that there is anything objectively wrong with it." This is the sort of stupidity-masquerading-as-insight that absolutely pervades modern intellectual life, and it has the same source as so many other contemporary intellectual pathologies: the abandonment of the classical realism of the great Greek and Scholastic philosophers, and especially of Aristotle's doctrine of the four causes. For we need to ask *why* there is a universal, or near universal, reaction of disgust to certain behaviors, and *why* certain traits count as unnatural even if there is a genetic factor underlying them. And when the "evolutionary psychologists," "rational choice theorists," and other such Bright Young Things and trendies have had their say, there can still be no satisfying answer to these questions that does not make reference to Aristotelian final causes – even if only because there can be no satisfying explanation of almost *anything* that doesn't make reference to final causes.

Let's back up then, and see what morality in general looks like from a point of view informed by Aristotelian metaphysics, and then return later on to the question of sexual morality in particular. Like Plato, Aristotle takes a thing's form, essence, or nature to determine the good for it. Hence, a good triangle is one that corresponds as closely as possible to the form of triangularity, its sides drawn as perfectly straight as possible, etc. A good squirrel is one that has the typical marks of the species and successfully fulfills the characteristic activities of a squirrel's life, e.g. by not having broken limbs, not gathering stones for its food rather than acorns, etc. So far this is obviously a non-moral sense of "good" – the claim isn't that triangles and squirrels are deserving of moral praise or blame – and corresponds closely to the sense in which we might think of something as a "good specimen" or "good example" of some kind or class of things. But it is the foundation for the distinctively moral sense of goodness.

Even from the squirrel example it is obvious that for any animal there are going to be various behaviors that are conducive to its well being and others that are not, and that these latter will be bad for it whatever the reason it wants to do them. So, to return to an obvious example from Chapter 2, if a squirrel has some genetic mutation that makes it want to lay itself out spread-eagled on the freeway, the fact that it enjoys doing this obviously does not entail that it is good for it to do so. Or, to take another but less obvious example from Chapter 2, if you somehow conditioned a squirrel to live in a cage and eat nothing but toothpaste on Ritz crackers, to such an extent that it no longer wanted to leave the cage, scamper up trees, and search for acorns, etc., even when given the chance, it wouldn't follow that the life of a Colgate addict is a good life for this particular squirrel. The sickly thing is simply not as healthy and "happy" a squirrel as he would have been had he never got himself into this fix, even if he has (of course) no way of knowing this. And again, this would remain true even if the squirrel had a genetic predisposition to like the taste of Colgate and dislike the taste of acorns, one that was not present in other squirrels. That predisposition simply wouldn't "jibe" with the overall structure of the natural physical and behavioral characteristics that are his by virtue of his instantiating the nature of a squirrel, however imperfectly. The predisposition would be a defect, like a puzzle piece that won't fit the rest of the puzzle.

Now, when we turn to human beings we find that they too have a nature or essence, and the good for them, like the good for anything else, is defined in terms of this nature or essence. Unlike other animals, though, human beings have intellect and will, and this is where moral goodness enters the picture. Human beings can *know* what is good for them, and *choose* whether to pursue that good. And that is precisely the natural end or purpose of the faculties of intellect and will – for like our other faculties, they too have a final cause, namely to allow us to understand the truth about things, including what is good for us given our nature or essence, and to act in light of it. Just as a "good squirrel" is one that successfully carries out the characteristic activities of a squirrel's life by gathering acorns, scampering up trees, etc., so too a good human being is one who successfully carries out the characteristic activities of *human* life, as determined by the final causes or natural ends of the various faculties that are ours by virtue of our nature or essence. Hence, for example, given that we have intellect as part of our nature, and that the purpose or final cause of the intellect is to allow us to understand the truth about things, it follows that it is good for us – it fulfills our nature – to pursue truth and to avoid error. So, a good human being will be, among many other things, someone who pursues truth and avoids error. And this becomes moral goodness insofar as we can choose whether or not to fulfill our natures in this way. To choose in line with the final causes or purposes that are ours by nature is morally good; to choose against them is morally bad.

"But *why* should we choose to do what is good for us in this Aristotelian sense?" someone might ask. The answer is implicit in what has been said already. The will of its very nature is oriented to pursuing what the intellect regards as good. You don't even need to believe in Aristotelian final causes to see this; you know it from your own experience insofar as you only ever do something because you think it is in some way good. Of course you might also believe that what you are doing is morally evil – as a murderer or thief might – but that doesn't conflict with what I'm saying. Even the murderer or thief who knows that murder and stealing are wrong nevertheless thinks that what he's doing will result in something he regards as good, e.g. the death of a person he hates or some money to pay for his drugs. I mean "good" here only in this thin sense, of being in some way desirable or providing some benefit. And that is all Aquinas means by it when he famously tells us that the first principle of the natural law is that "good is to be done and pursued, and evil is to be avoided." This is not meant by itself to be terribly informative; it is meant only to call attention to the obvious fact that human action is of its nature directed toward what is perceived to be good in some way, whether it really is good or not.

But when we add to this the consideration that the good for us is *in fact* whatever tends to fulfill our nature or essence in the sense of realizing the natural ends or purposes of our various natural capacities, then there can be no doubt as to why someone ought to do what is good in this sense. For you do by nature want to do what you *take* to be good for you; reason reveals that what is *in fact* good for you is acting in a way that is conducive to the fulfillment of the ends or purposes inherent in human nature; and so if you are rational, and thus open to seeing what is in fact good for you, you will take the fulfillment of those ends or purposes to be good for you and act accordingly. This may require a fight against one's desires and such a fight might in some cases be so extremely difficult and unpleasant that one might not have the stomach for it. But that is a problem of will, not of reason. It doesn't show that the rational thing is not to struggle against one's desires, but only that doing the rational thing can sometimes be extremely difficult and unpleasant. An obvious illustration of this is what happens when someone decides to stop drinking to excess: He previously thought drinking to excess was a good thing to do, or at least not a habit worth struggling against; then he realizes that it is not a good thing to do, and in fact that it would be good to stop doing it; and so he decides to stop doing it. Now he may well find that implementing this decision is extremely difficult; he may even come to find it so difficult that he starts to think it impossible. But that doesn't mean that to stop drinking to excess really isn't what is good for him, and thus what reason recommends. It only shows that his will has become so extremely corrupted that he is unable, or nearly unable, to do what it is good and rational for him to do. And notice this remains true whether or not his excessive drinking was in some way facilitated by some genetic factor. The presence of such a factor would not show that excessive drinking is good for him after all, but only that because of some tragic defect outside his control, he finds it more difficult than other people do to do what is good and rational. This would certainly reduce his culpability, and justify us in treating him with greater compassion and understanding than we might treat someone without such a handicap, but it would *not* justify revising our judgment that what he is doing is objectively bad and irrational.

Now modern philosophers, over-impressed as always by David

Hume, have thought that there is a frightfully difficult problem of "deriving an 'ought' from an 'is'" or upholding morality in light of the "fact/value distinction." There are facts, and then there are values, you see, and knowing any number of things about the first – about what *is* the case – can (so it is said) never tell you anything about the second – what *ought* to be the case. To confuse the two is to commit the "naturalistic fallacy." And so forth. The usual genuflecting to Hume's supposed genius ensues, as does an industry of producing fruitless attempts to solve the "problem" of justifying ethical judgments in light of this purported chasm between objective reality and moral value.

Well, there *is* such a problem if, as modern philosophers have done, one denies the reality of formal and final causes. But for those who avoid this foolish and ungrounded denial – such as Aristotle and Aquinas – there is no problem at all, and what has been said already shows why. Like everything else, human beings have a formal cause – their form, essence, or nature – and this formal cause entails certain final causes for their various capacities. So, for example, our nature or essence is to be rational animals, and reason or intellect has as its final cause the attainment of truth. Hence the attainment of truth is good for us, just as the gathering of acorns is good for a squirrel. These are just objective facts; for the sense of "good" in question here is a completely objective one, connoting, not some subjective preference we happen to have for a thing, but rather the conformity of a thing to a nature or essence as a kind of paradigm (the way that, again, a "good" triangle is just one which has perfectly straight sides, or a "good" squirrel is one that isn't missing its tail). We are also by nature oriented to pursuing what we take to be good. That is another objective fact, and for the same reasons. But then, when the intellect perceives that what is in fact good is the pursuit of truth, it follows that if we are rational what we will value is the pursuit of truth. "Value" – or rather, as the ancients and medievals would put it, the good – follows from fact, because it is built into the structure of the facts from the get-go.[8]

All of this falls apart if we deny that anything has a final cause or that there are forms, essences, or natures in the Aristotelian sense; and of course, Hume, like the moderns in general, denies just this. If there are no Aristotelian forms, essences, or natures, then there is no such thing as what is good for human beings by nature. If there are no final causes, then reason does not have as its purpose the attainment of truth or knowledge of the good. What we are left with are at best whatever desires we actually happen to have, for whatever reason – heredity, environment, luck – but these will be subjective preferences rather than reflective of objective goodness or badness. And the most reason can do is tell us how we can fulfill these desires; since there are no natures or essences of things, nor any final causes or natural purposes either, it cannot tell us what desires we *ought* to have. Thus can Hume say such things as that reason is the "slave of the passions," and that there is nothing contrary to reason in preferring that the whole world be destroyed rather than that my little finger gets scratched. Thus can nearly universal reactions of disgust at certain sexual practices, which from an Aristotelian point of view are nature's way of getting us to avoid what is contrary to her purposes, be written off as mere prejudices. And over two centuries of imbibing this kind of thinking is what has made possible the Peter Singers of the world, who can see nothing wrong with necrophilia or bestiality if that is what someone really wants to do no matter how hard we try to talk him out of it. Dr. Strangelove of Princeton is the direct intellectual descendant of "le bon David" of Edinburgh; and we are led thereby to number 3,456 (or whatever – I've lost count) on the list of idiocies that have come about as a result of the abandonment of Aristotelian final causes.

To be sure, the hardcore Humeans in the audience probably won't be troubled by this; "we're just following the argument where it leads," and all that. Well, I'm not done kicking Hume yet, not by a long shot. But note just for the moment that your boy didn't push his own argument through consistently, and not just because, unlike Singer, he didn't use it to try to justify every perversion he could think of. If there really are *no* final causes, then what's all this stuff about reason being the slave of the passions? For if there are no final causes, then reason cannot be the "slave" of – that is, inherently oriented toward the furtherance of – anything at all. And if there really are *no* essences, natures, or universals, what was the nominalist Hume doing writing a *Treatise of Human Nature*? Merely describing what happened to be going on in his own head circa 1739? In that case, "thank you for sharing," David, but if I want to read the introspective reflections of a plump Scotsman, I think I'll wait for George Galloway's memoirs. Maybe he'll describe for us the thrill he felt helping his pal Saddam maintain his bloody grip on Iraq for at least a few weeks longer – which, while disgusting and evil to be sure, sounds at least a little more gripping than Hume's going on endlessly about "impressions and ideas."

Anyway, let's return now to the question of the natural law approach to sexual morality, something Aquinas deals with in (among other places) part 2 of book 3 of the *Summa contra Gentiles*. This is a big topic, and one I'd frankly rather not address at all. For one thing, it really needs a book of its own to do it justice; all I can do is scratch the surface here. For another, I fear that broaching it might only reinforce the tiresome cliché that natural law moralists are "obsessed with sex." In fact if you look at any standard volume on ethics written from a traditional natural law theory point of view, you'll find that it deals with sexual morality at no greater length than it treats of other moral topics – capital punishment, war and peace, property rights, social justice, and so forth. That reflects the natural law view that sexual activity, however important, is just one relatively small part of life among others, not the be all and end all of our existence. It is only those who object to this who can be called "obsessed with sex," and what we have in the case of people who make this accusation against natural law theory is a pretty obvious example of what the pop psychologists call "projection." But the "New Atheists," it seems, must be numbered among these projectors, and it is important to correct their distortions.

Suppose, then, that things really do have final causes, including our various biological capacities. Then it is hardly mysterious what the final cause or natural purpose of sex is: procreation. And procreation is inherently heterosexual. That someone might successfully clone a human being someday is no evidence to the contrary, for I am speaking about the way things exist in nature, not the way they might be altered to further some end of ours. It is also irrelevant that people might indulge in sex for all sorts of reasons other than procreation, for I am not talking about what *our* purposes are, but what *nature's* purposes are, again in the Aristotelian sense of final causality. Now it is true of course that sexual relations are also naturally pleasurable. But giving pleasure is not the final cause or natural end of sex; rather, sexual pleasure has as its own final cause the getting of people to engage in sexual relations, so that they will procreate. This parallels the situation with eating: Even though eating is pleasurable, the biological point of eating is not to give pleasure, but rather to provide an organism with the nutrients it needs to survive; the pleasure of eating is just nature's way of getting us to do what is needed to fulfill this end. When analyzing the biological significance of either eating or sex, to emphasize pleasure is to put the cart before the horse. Procreation (and nutrition in the case of eating) "wears the trousers," as it were; pleasure has its place, but it is secondary.

Notice also that nature makes it very difficult to indulge in sex without procreation. There is no prophylactic sheathe issued with a penis at birth, and no diaphragm issued with a vagina. It takes some effort to come up with these devices, and even then, in the form in which they existed for most of human history they were not terribly effective. Moreover, human experience indicates that people simply find sexual relations more pleasurable when such devices are not used, even if they will often use them anyway out of a desire to avoid pregnancy. Indeed, this is one reason pregnancy – even when cut short by abortion – is so very common even in societies in which contraception is easily available: People know they could take a few minutes to go buy a condom, but go ahead and indulge in "unprotected" sex anyway. As this indicates, sexual arousal occurs very frequently and can often be very hard to resist even for a short while. And that last resort to those seeking to avoid pregnancy – the "withdrawal" method – is notoriously unreliable. Even with the advent of "the pill," pregnancies (though also abortions) are as common as rain; and even effective use of the pill – which has existed only for a very brief period of human history – requires that a woman remember to take it at the appointed times and be willing to put up with its uncomfortable side effects.

So, the final cause of sex is procreation, and the final cause of sexual pleasure is to get us to indulge in sex, so that we'll thereby procreate. And we're built in such a way that sexual arousal is hard to resist and occurs very frequently, and such that it is very difficult to avoid pregnancies resulting from indulgence of that arousal. The obvious conclusion is that the final cause of sex is not just procreation, but procreation in large numbers. Mother Nature very obviously wants us to have babies, and lots of them. And before you write all this off as just so much rationalization of prejudice, keep in mind that everything said so far, apart from the reference to final causes, would be endorsed by Darwinians as a perfectly accurate description of the biological function of sex, whether or not they would agree with the moral conclusions natural law theorists would draw from it. Not that you need Darwinism, or Aristotelianism for that matter, to tell you this. It is, I dare say, blindingly obvious, and if there is anyone at all who would challenge it you can be sure that is owing to a desperate attempt to rationalize certain *liberal* prejudices by keeping the natural law theorist from getting out of the starting gate.

Now in light of all this, it does seem that Mother Nature has put a fairly heavy burden on women, who, if "nature takes its course," are bound to become pregnant somewhat frequently. She has also put a fairly heavy burden on children too, given that unlike non-human offspring they are utterly dependent on others for their needs, and for a very long period. This is true not only of their biological needs, but of the moral and cultural needs they have by virtue of being little rational animals. They need education in both what is useful and right, and correction of error. In human beings, procreation – generating new members of the species – is not just a matter of producing new organisms, but also of forming them into persons capable of fulfilling their nature as distinctively *rational* animals. So, nature's taking its course thus seems to leave mothers and offspring pretty helpless, or at any rate it would do so if there weren't someone ordained by nature to provide for them. But of course there is such a person, namely the father of the children. Fathers obviously have a strong incentive to look after their own children rather than someone else's, and they are also, generally speaking and notoriously, jealous of the affections of the women they have children with, sometimes to the point of being willing to kill the competition. Thus Mother Nature very equitably puts a heavy burden on fathers too, pushing them into a situation where they must devote their daily labors to providing for their children and the woman or women with whom they have had these children;

and when "nature takes its course" these children are bound to be somewhat numerous, so that the father's commitment is necessarily going to have to be long-term.

The teleology or final causality of sex thus pushes inevitably in the direction of at least some variation on the institution of marriage, and marriage exists for the purpose of generating and nourishing offspring not only biologically but culturally. Everything else is subordinated to this in the sense that it wouldn't exist without, and loses its point without, the overall procreative end. Sex is pleasurable, but only because this is nature's way of pushing us into doing what is necessary for procreation; husbands and wives often feel great affection for one another, but this tendency is put in them by nature only because it facilitates the stability of the union that the successful generation and upbringing of children requires. Keep in mind that I am, again, not talking about the conscious purposes of human beings; obviously, individual human beings often value sexual pleasure and companionship more than reproduction. I am talking about *nature's* purposes, about final causes. If human beings didn't reproduce sexually, sexual organs wouldn't exist at all, and neither would sexual pleasure. Hence neither would romantic love or marriage exist. Human beings might still have affection for one another, but this affection wouldn't have any of the distinctive features we associate with the feelings that exist between lovers, or between husbands and wives or parents and children. All of these pleasures and affections exist in nature only because sexual reproduction does, and thus their point is to facilitate procreation, again in the full sense of not only generating, but also rearing, children.

That is the big-picture view of the teleology or final causality of sex. Let's turn now momentarily to the small picture, focusing on the sexual act itself. If we consider the structure of the sexual organs and the sexual act as a process beginning with arousal and ending in orgasm, it is clear that its biological function, its final cause, is to get semen into the vagina. That is why the penis and vagina are shaped the way they are, why the vagina secretes lubrication during sexual arousal, and so forth. The organs fit together like lock and key. The point of the process is not just to get semen out of the male, but also into the female, and into one place in the female in particular. All of this too is blindingly obvious, and no one can reasonably deny it or would deny it when looking at things from a biological point of view, whether or not they think any moral conclusions follow from it. Of course, there is more going on here than just plumbing. Women can have orgasms too, sexual pleasure can be had by acts other than just vaginal penetration, and all sorts of complex and profound other-directed passions are aroused in a man and woman during the process of lovemaking that go well beyond the simple desire to get semen into a certain place. But from the point of view of biological final causes, all of this exists only so that men and women will engage in the sexual act, so that it will result in ejaculation into the vagina, so that in turn offspring will be generated at least a certain percentage of the time the act is performed, and so that father and mother will be strengthened in their desire to stay together, which circumstance is (whatever their personal intentions and thoughts) nature's way of sustaining that union upon which children depend for their material and spiritual well-being. Every link in the chain has procreation as its final cause, whatever the intentions of the actors.

Now if there really are Aristotelian natures, essences, final causes, etc., then the lesson of all this for sexual morality should be obvious. Since the final cause of human sexual capacities is procreation, what is good for human beings in the use of those capacities is to use them only in a way consistent with this final cause or purpose. This is a *necessary* truth; for the good for us is defined by our nature and the final causes of its various elements. It *cannot possibly* be good for us to use them in any other way, whether an individual person thinks it is or not, any more than it can possibly be good for an alcoholic to indulge his taste for excessive drink or the mutant squirrel of our earlier example to indulge his taste for Colgate toothpaste. This remains true whatever the reason is for someone's desire to act in a way contrary to nature's purposes – whether simple intellectual error, habituated vice, genetic defect, or whatever – and however strong that desire is. That a desire to act in such a way is very deeply entrenched in a person only shows that his will has become corrupted. A clubfoot is still a clubfoot, and thus a defect, even though the person having it is not culpable for this and might not be able to change it. And a desire to do what is bad is still a desire to do what is bad, however difficult it might be for someone to desire otherwise, and whether or not the person is culpable for having a tendency to form these desires (he may not be).

This doesn't mean that individuals must always intend to have children with every sexual act. This may not be on their minds at all; they may just be in an amorous mood. Nor does it mean that the only act consistent with nature's purposes is immediate penetration and ejaculation into the vagina. All sorts of lovemaking might precede this. It *does* mean, though, that every sexual act has as its natural *culmination*, its proximate final cause, ejaculation into the vagina, and that the man and woman involved in such an act cannot act in a way to prevent this result, nor act to prevent the overall process from having conception as an outcome, whether or not that outcome is what they have in mind in performing the act, and whether or not that outcome would be likely to occur anyway even in the absence of their interference. It also means, partly for reasons evident from the foregoing, that they may indulge in this act, in a way that is consistent with its procreative final cause or natural end (understood in the broad sense of not only generating children but also rearing them, with the need for stability that that entails), *only* if they are married to one another.

It should be obvious that abortion is automatically ruled out as well, since it constitutes a particularly violent interference with nature's purposes. But there are other reasons too why abortion is immoral, and indeed especially wicked. The growth of a new human being in his or her mother's womb is not simply one natural process among others; it is the beginning of that relationship among human beings that is perhaps the closest of all, that between mother and child. A mother's natural instinct is to protect her child at all costs, especially when it is at its most vulnerable; the womb ought therefore to be the safest place in the world. The will to override that instinct – not only in a mother, but in a father who consents to or aids in the act of abortion – necessarily manifests an extraordinary degree of perversity and moral corruption.

We have also seen that an unborn child counts as a human being from conception onward. And every human being has a natural right to life, which can be lost only in the way other rights (such as the right to liberty) can be lost, viz. by committing a serious crime. Obviously, no unborn child is guilty of doing any such thing.

Now Aquinas himself does not have a theory of individual rights; that is a concept that only later becomes prominent in Western thought. But later Scholastic philosophers influenced by him did have such a theory. The basic idea is this. Nature has set for us certain ends, and the natural law enjoins on us the pursuit of those ends. We also live in society with others – man being a social animal as well as a rational one, as Aristotle noted – and these others also have ends set for them by nature. But we can all pursue these ends only if our fellow human beings do not interfere with that pursuit. Hence the existence of the natural law entails that we have certain rights against interference with that pursuit; and since there is no greater interference than being killed, it follows that every human being has, at least until he forfeits it by committing a serious crime, a right not to be killed. This also entails many other rights (such as a right to personal liberty that is strong enough to rule out chattel slavery as intrinsically immoral – the claim made by some that natural law theory would support slavery as it was known in the United States is a slander.[9]) But suffice it to note for our purposes here that abortion is triply condemned by the natural law: again, it involves a deliberate turning of the reproductive process away from its natural end; it manifests an extraordinary degree of personal moral corruption insofar as it follows from a will to override the protective maternal and/or paternal instincts nature has put into us; and it violates the right to life that every innocent human being has by nature.

Now there is much more to the story than this, and people used to living in the post-"sexual revolution" era immediately raise all sorts of objections. Andrew Sullivan, for example, in his book *The Conservative Soul*, criticizes me for implying that a bodily organ or natural capacity can have only one "core" function.[10] But neither I nor any other natural law theorist I know of has denied, or need deny given natural law theory, that such organs and capacities can have many functions. The function of the penis, for example, is not only to get semen into the vagina, but also to urinate. Nor is there any particular need for natural law theory purposes to identify which of these is the "core" function, as long as there is no obstacle to fulfilling both of them; and men obviously have no difficulty both urinating and copulating. The point is unaffected by the fact that it is not possible to do both of these things at once, since there is nothing in natural law theory that has the absurd implication that if you currently have both an urge to urinate and an urge to make love to your wife, then you had better find a way to do both at the same time unless you can determine which is the "core" function. For the theory doesn't necessarily require that you follow any such urge immediately or even at all; it requires at most only that, when you do follow such an urge, you do so in a way that does not frustrate the natural end of the capacity in question. (If you're wondering, my advice in the present case would be to think about baseball for a few minutes so that you can go urinate first.)

Another common objection is: "Wouldn't natural law theory entail that sterile people cannot marry?" No, not necessarily. For if someone is sterile through no fault of his own, *he* has not done anything to interfere with nature's purposes. And even a sterile married couple cannot, according to natural law theory, allow their own sexual encounters to culminate in anything other than ejaculation into the vagina. That procreation would not result anyway is irrelevant: The point is not to do something *oneself* that interferes with natural processes. And of course, a sterile couple's "experimentation" with various outré sexual acts will inevitably tend to corrupt their perception of its meaning, which is primarily procreative but secondarily (as ancillary to its procreative purpose) to unite husband and wife in mutual affection, *not* to provide a kind of built-in entertainment apparatus. Finally, if someone married a sterile person *precisely as a means* of avoiding procreation, natural law theory *would* condemn this as immoral.

One also frequently hears objections along the lines of "Wouldn't this theory entail such absurdities as that it is immoral to prop up a table with one's leg, or to get a hysterectomy to save a woman's life, or to clean the earwax out of one's ears?" No, no, and no. Natural law theory does not condemn using a natural capacity or organ *other than* for its natural function, but only using it in a manner *contrary to* its natural function, frustrating its natural end. Hence holding a table up with one's leg, or holding nails in one's teeth , does not frustrate the walking and chewing functions of legs and teeth, especially since nature obviously does not intend for us to be walking and eating at every single moment. But having one's leg amputated to make some sort of bizarre political statement, or throwing up one's food so as not to gain weight *would* frustrate nature's purposes and thus be condemned by natural law theory as immoral. Amputating a leg or removing other organs to save a person's life, though, would not be ruled out by natural law theory, since these organs and their functions are metaphysically subordinate to the overall purpose of sustaining the life and activities of the organism as a whole, and can thus be sacrificed if this is the only way to prevent the loss of that life. Finally, as long as the earwax is able to perform its natural function of protecting the ear canal, there is nothing immoral in cleaning away the excess. And even the over-enthusiastic Q-Tip user is not committing some major sin, but at worst acting contrary to wisdom in a very minor way (as even your doctor will tell you). Natural law theory does not entail that every frustration of nature's purposes is a serious moral failing. Where certain natural functions concern only some minor aspect of human life, a frustration of nature's purposes might be at worst a minor lapse in a virtue like prudence. But where they concern the maintenance of the species itself, and the material and spiritual well being of children, women, and men – as they do where sex is concerned – acting contrary to them cannot fail to be of serious moral significance.

The $64 question in recent years, of course, is: "Does natural law theory entail that homosexuals can't marry?" And the answer is that they *can* marry. But of course, what that means, as a matter of conceptual necessity, is that they can marry *someone of the opposite sex*. What they *can't* do is marry *each other*, no more than a hetero sexual could marry someone of the same sex, and no more than a person could "marry" a goldfish, or a can of motor oil, or his own left foot. For the metaphysics underlying natural law theory entails that marriage is, not by human definition, but as an *objective metaphysical fact* determined by its final cause, inherently procreative, and thus inherently heterosexual. There is no such thing as "same-sex marriage" any more than there are round squares. Indeed, there is really no such thing as "sex" outside the context of sexual intercourse between a man and woman. Sodomy (whether homosexual or heterosexual) no more counts as "sex" than puking up a Quarter Pounder counts as eating; and far from "hating" or "fearing" sex, traditionally minded married couples who have lots of children may be the only people really having much genuine sex at all these days. No legislature or opinion poll could possibly change these facts, any more than they could repeal the law of gravity or the Pythagorean theorem. And any "law" that attempted such an impossibility would be absolutely null and utterly void, a joke at best and a straightforward assault on the very foundations of morality at worst. For if "same-sex marriage" is not contrary to nature, than nothing is; and if nothing is contrary to nature, then (as we will see) there can be no grounds whatsoever for moral judgment.

Obviously, such views are bound to regarded as shocking and offensive to many today. It is important to remember, though, that the understanding of sex I've been describing is, this or that detail aside, pretty much the understanding all human beings have had until very recently, and probably still do have outside the modern secular West. Even contemporary evolutionary psychologists would endorse much of it as a factual description of why natural selection favored certain biological and behavioral characteristics, and why the institutions of marriage and family have been as they have been for most of human history, even if these theorists would not endorse the *moral* claims I've made or wish to preserve the traditional arrangements in modern times. It is worth noting too that in the Western world, not only homosexual behavior, premarital sex, and the like, but even contraception between married people was widely condemned until very recently. Sigmund Freud himself noted matter-of-factly that:

> [I]t is a characteristic common to all the perversions that in them reproduction as an aim is put aside. This is actually the criterion by which we judge whether a sexual activity is perverse – if it departs from reproduction in its aims and pursues the attainment of gratification independently.[11]

Every Christian denomination officially taught against contraception until the 1930s, when the Anglicans first started to allow it. And even the secular *Washington Post* fretted at the time that this would lead to the collapse of traditional sexual morality.[12] (They don't make the liberal media like they used to.) For once the *Post* was right: It *did* lead to just the consequences they predicted, even if these consequences have now come to be labeled "progress." The New Atheists and other secularists like to play the rhetorical game of pointing to some currently unpopular traditional moral or religious proposition and saying "See what these crazies believe? How can anyone take them seriously?" But of course, secularist views were once widely unpopular too, and still are in many quarters, and yet we're not supposed to count this as evidence against them. Well, you can't have it both ways. If a view's unpopularity is irrelevant in the one case, it is irrelevant in the other as well. It might be that, as secularists claim, what most people have believed about religion and sexual morality for most of human history was wrong; but it might be the case instead – and indeed is the case, given the arguments we've been examining – that what they believed was right, and that the current state of secular opinion on these matters is evidence not of progress but of steep decline and extreme decadence.

There is much more that could be said. For example, when worked out thoroughly, the natural law approach to sexual morality can be seen to entail that polygamy and divorce, while historically permitted within some otherwise conservative religious contexts, are suboptimal at best and in practice usually positively immoral. As I have said, the subject requires a book of its own, at least given the extreme depravity into which modern civilization has fallen from a natural law point of view. But what has been said already suffices to show that whatever quibbles one might have over the details, the main outlines of traditional sexual morality are *obviously* rationally justifiable, even unavoidable, if one assumes the truth of a broadly Aristotelian metaphysics. One can be forgiven for suspecting that that is one reason (if admittedly not the only one) why contemporary philosophers and other intellectuals refuse to reconsider their rejection of that metaphysics. A prominent philosopher of mind once assured me that if Aristotle's metaphysics really does have such conservative moral implications, that would be reason enough to reject it. And that is the way many secular academics think these days: Their egalitarian liberalism is the axis around which everything else turns, and all of metaphysics, epistemology, and even science itself, when it seems to touch on moral or religious questions, must be judged by reference to how well they conform to this standard. (Ask former Harvard president Larry Summers, whose suggestion that it is at least possible that there are innate intellectual differences between the sexes led to calls for his resignation.) These people already "know" that anyone who disagrees with them must be ignorant and bigoted; don't bother them with arguments to the contrary, which, they have foreordained, can only be exercises in the rationalization of prejudice. Yet their own "research" into moral questions is not a disinterested pursuit of truth, but an exercise in liberal apologetics, with the main conclusions determined in advance. As in so many other ways, they have become exactly what they claim to despise.

Now, notice that at no point so far in my exposition of natural law theory in general or its approach to sexual morality in particular have I appealed to scripture, or traditional religious teaching, or even to a purely philosophical notion of God. As this indicates, the tedious secularist allegation that opposition to abortion, "same-sex marriage," and the like can only rest on "faith," or an appeal to divine revelation, is pure fiction. Traditional morality does not rest on arbitrary divine commands backed by the threat of punishment, but rather on the systematic analysis of human nature entailed by classical philosophy. Plato's and Aristotle's condemnation of homosexuality was not based on the Bible, after all, but on their respective rationally grounded systems of metaphysics and ethics.

Does that mean that God is irrelevant to natural law theory? Not at all. For while what has been said so far has required no reference to Him, it remains true that, as we saw in our discussion of the soul, man's overarching end is to know God, and he has an immortal soul that gives him a destiny beyond this earthly life. Furthermore, since God is the First Cause of the world and the one who ultimately orders things to their ends, He is the Author of the natural law, even if knowledge of the grounds and content of that law can largely be had without reference to Him. Obedience to the natural law is thus obedience to God. These are just facts, knowable through pure reason, and thus there is no reason why inquiry into our moral duties should not take account of them. Indeed, it must take account of them, for at least two reasons. First of all, since knowing God is our highest end, our moral duties include, first and foremost, religious duties: duties to pursue knowledge of God, to honor Him as our Creator and the giver of the moral law, to teach our children to do the same, and so forth. These duties are not some optional extra tacked on to a rationally based system of morality; they are integral to such a system.

Second, without keeping in mind that our ultimate destiny is an eternal one and that knowing God is our natural end or purpose (even if it is left to us, as beings with free will, to decide whether to pursue and realize that end), our understanding of our lives in the here and now, including our understanding of morality, becomes massively distorted. This life, in both its good and bad aspects, takes on an exaggerated importance. Worldly pleasures and projects become overvalued. Difficult moral obligations, which seem bearable in light of the prospect of an eternal reward, come to seem impossible to live up to when our horizons are this-worldly. Harms and injustices suffered in this life, patiently endured when one sees beyond it to the next life, suddenly become unendurable. This is one reason secularists are often totally obsessed with politics and prone to utopian fantasies. They do not see any hope for a world beyond this one – even if only because they often don't want to see it – and thus insist that heaven, or some reasonable facsimile, simply *must* be possible here and now if only we hit upon the right socio-economic-political structures. That this is a sheer delusion is obvious to anyone who takes a cold look at the experience of the last few centuries; and yet the "progressive" secularist has difficulty parting with it, seeing as he has already given up religion and would have nothing left at all if he also gave up what I have called his counter-religion. Dawkins is an especially pathetic example of this mindset. Asked in an interview what the world might be like if children were raised without religion, he answered: "It would be paradise on earth . . . a world ruled by enlightened rationality . . . a much better chance of no more war . . . less hatred . . . ," indeed even "less waste of time . . ."[13] And he thinks *religious* people are credulous? Post-National Socialism, post-Communism, even post-Great Society, a belief that "paradise on earth" is possible is hardly *less* mad than any theological doctrine. That Dawkins is capable of spouting such tosh should be enough to discredit him with all serious people, including serious atheists.

Faith, reason, and evil

This brings us to the problem of evil, about which I need say only a little. For while that problem is beyond question of the utmost difficulty and seriousness from the point of view of practical human life, as a defense of atheism, the "argument from evil" is completely worthless. This is where faith of a sort at long last enters our discussion, though not in the way secularists think it would. For faith, properly understood, does not contradict reason in the least; indeed, in the present context it is nothing less than the will to keep one's mind fixed precisely on what reason has discovered to it.

Let us digress for a moment, then, and elaborate on the nature of faith and its relationship to reason, argument, and evidence; then we'll return to the problem of evil. Aquinas famously characterized the sorts of arguments we've been examining so far as *praeambula fidei* or "preambles of faith." What did he mean by this?

The arguments we've been examining, if successful, show that pure reason can reveal to us that there is a God, that we have immortal souls, and that there is a natural moral law. These claims are, of course, elements in the teaching of the main monotheistic religions. But those religions also go beyond these elements, and claim access to further knowledge about God, the destiny of the human soul, and the content of our moral duties, which derive from a revelation from God. Does belief in such a revelation go beyond reason? Is this where faith comes in? The answer, again, is no . . . or at least, not necessarily. For the claim that a divine revelation has occurred is something for which the monotheistic religions typically claim there is evidence, and that evidence takes the form of a miracle, a suspension of the natural order that cannot be explained in any way other than divine intervention in the normal course of events. Christianity, for example, not only claims that Jesus Christ was God Incarnate and that what He taught therefore has divine authority; it also claims that He was resurrected from the dead, and that this incomparable miracle authenticates His teaching. Indeed, Christianity lays everything on this line. As St. Paul famously put it, "if Christ has not been raised, then our preaching is in vain and your faith is in vain."[14] If the story of Jesus's resurrection is true, then you must become a Christian; if it is false, then Christianity itself is false, and should be rejected.

But the mainstream Christian tradition has also always claimed that the resurrection of Jesus Christ is a historical event the reality of which can be established through rational argument. Indeed, the philosophical arguments we've been examining so far play a role in the case for Jesus's resurrection. For that case can only be properly understood once it has already been established that there is a God and that human beings have immortal souls. Given that God exists and that He sustains the world and the causal laws governing it in being at every moment, we know that there is a power capable of producing a miracle, that is, a suspension of those causal laws. Given that human beings have immortal souls, we know that the death of a person's body is not necessarily the annihilation of the person himself; for if some power were able to bring the matter of the person's body together again with his soul, the person would then come back to life. To establish the existence of God and the immortality of the soul through philosophical arguments is therefore to establish the realistic possibility of the sort of miracle on which Christianity rests its claim to a divine revelation.

The case for the resurrection of Christ doesn't exist in a vacuum, then; it presupposes this philosophical background. For without that background in place, the historical evidence for Christ's resurrection might seem inconclusive at best, since any miracle will obviously seem less likely a priori if you don't already know that there is a God who might produce one. But when interpreted *in light of* that background, as it should be, the evidence for Christ's resurrection can be seen to be overwhelming. That, at any rate, is what the mainstream Christian theological tradition has always claimed. And if it is overwhelming, then there are by the same token conclusive rational grounds for believing that what Christ taught was true, in which case the key doctrines of Christianity are rationally justified. The overall chain of argument, then, goes something like this: Pure reason proves through philosophical arguments that there is a God and that we have immortal souls. This by itself entails that a miracle like a resurrection from the dead is possible. Now the historical evidence that Jesus Christ was in fact resurrected from the dead is overwhelming when interpreted in light of that background knowledge. Hence pure reason also shows that Jesus really was raised from the dead. But Jesus claimed to be divine, and claimed that the authority of His teachings would be confirmed by His being resurrected. So the fact that He was resurrected provides divine authentication of His claims. Hence reason shows that He really was divine. But He was also obviously distinct from the Father to whom He prayed and the Holy Spirit whom He sent. Since this entails the doctrine of the Trinity, reason shows that doctrine must be true as well. And so forth. At every step, evidence and rational argumentation – not "blind faith" or a "will to believe" – are taken to justify our acceptance of certain teachings. Of course some of those teachings are taken on the basis of authority, but the point is that the trustworthiness of that authority is something that, it is claimed, can be established by reason. We can know that such-and-such a teaching was true because Christ taught it; we can know that He is an authority to be trusted because His miraculous resurrection puts a divine seal of approval on what He said, including His claim to be divine, and a divine being cannot be in error; we can know that He really was resurrected because of such-and-such historical evidence together with our background knowledge that God exists and that the soul is immortal; we can know that God exists and that the soul is immortal because of such-and-such philosophical proofs; and so on. Every link in the chain is supported by argument.

Please keep in mind that I am not actually *giving* any of the arguments for the resurrection of Christ or for Christianity just now. So don't say, "Oh how silly, I can spot a thousand holes in that case!" I *wasn't trying to make* the case; that would take a book of its own.[15] All I am interested in doing here is sketching out the general strategy that Christian theology has traditionally used in justifying its doctrinal claims, and the point of doing so is to understand where faith fits into the picture. For notice that at no point in the strategy just described has it been mentioned. So how *does* it come into play? This way. Suppose you know through purely rational arguments that there is a God, that He raised Jesus Christ from the dead, and therefore that Christ really is divine, as He claimed to be, so that anything He taught must be true; in other words, suppose that the general strategy just sketched can be successfully fleshed out. Then it follows that *if you are rational* you will believe anything Christ taught; indeed, *if you are rational* you will believe it even if it is something that you could not possibly have come to know in any other way, and even if it is something highly counterintuitive and difficult to understand. For reason will have told you that Christ is infallible, and therefore cannot be wrong in anything He teaches. In short, reason tells you to have *faith* in what Christ teaches, because He is divine. And that is at bottom what faith is from the point of view of traditional Christian theology: belief in what God has revealed because if God has revealed it it cannot be in error; but where the claim that He revealed it is itself something that is known on the basis of reason. Faith doesn't conflict with reason, then; it is founded on reason and completes reason.

Now of course Christianity does not teach that every believer must be able to make some fancy philosophical case for the existence of God, the resurrection of Christ, and all the rest. Most people probably could not even understand the arguments. Their belief is based on what they have been taught by some authority – the Church, or theologians or philosophers, say – and in that sense it is based on faith rather than reason. But that is just an elliptical way of saying that it is not *directly* based on rational arguments, even though it *is indirectly* based on them. For on the traditional Christian understanding of things, the authorities in question, or some of them anyway, must have and do have the arguments needed. We find an exact parallel in science. The man in the street who believes that $E = mc^2$ probably couldn't give you an interesting defense of his belief if his life depended on it. He believes it because his high school physics teacher told him about it, say, or because he heard it mentioned on an episode of *Star Trek*. Of course, a writer for *Star Trek* probably couldn't give a much better defense either – he was just citing some general background scientific knowledge in the same way the original man in the street was – and even the high school physics teacher wouldn't do so well defending it against a smart enough skeptic who knew the physics literature. You'd have to go to a university physics department, say, if you're going to find someone who can give a really solid explanation and defense, and even then some of those people are going to be more articulate and better informed than others. Most people who believe that $E = mc^2$, and who believe almost any other widely known and generally accepted scientific proposition, do so on the basis of faith in exactly the sense in question here. They believe it, in other words, on the authority of those from whom they learned it. Everyone acknowledges that this is perfectly legitimate; indeed, there is no way we could know much of interest at all if we weren't able to appeal to various authorities. But if this is legitimate in other aspects of life, there is nothing per se wrong with it in religion.

It is also true that certain doctrines are held within Christianity to be "mysteries." But this doesn't mean that they are inherently irrational and must be accepted on "blind faith." It means instead that, while they are in themselves perfectly rational and coherent, our intellects are too limited to grasp them very deeply, so that they could not have been arrived at by unaided reason and require divine revelation. And that they have in fact been divinely revealed is something that it is claimed we *can* know through reason. So, even with theological mysteries, though reason cannot directly arrive at them on its own, it can do so indirectly. Your three-year-old child could not possibly discover by himself that people cannot breathe on the moon, say, or that too much candy and junk food will be bad for him in the long run. Indeed, he might not even be able to understand how these things could be true when you tell him. Still, he does know from experience that you are trustworthy, and so he believes them. He has faith that these "mysteries" are true, and it is perfectly rational for him to have it; indeed it would be irrational for him not to have it. But that is exactly the sense in which Christianity claims we ought to have faith in the mysteries it teaches, precisely because (it is claimed) we can know through reason that these mysteries have been revealed.

This is the sense, then, in which the sorts of arguments we've been examining are "preambles to faith." They set the stage for faith by giving it a rational basis, making it analogous to the sort of faith everyone – including secularists – has in authorities (parents, scientists, experts in various other fields) which they have a rational basis for believing are trustworthy. And this understanding of faith has, as I have said, been the mainstream one in the history of Christianity. The First Vatican Council famously decreed that the existence of God could be known with certainty through "the natural light of human reason," and anathematized anyone who dissented from this judgment. Aquinas and the other great figures of the Scholastic tradition had also condemned the view that God's existence could not be proved. Of course, secularists would ridicule such statements as an attempt to settle a philosophical question by dogmatic fiat. But what they fail to realize is that the point of these condemnations was to distance Christianity from the sort of irrationalism and fideism that would make religious belief out to be a purely subjective or emotional affair, cut off from any grounding in objective fact and rational argument. I do not doubt that there are and have been Christians and people of other religions whose theory and/or practice does not fit this understanding. But I do not speak for them, and neither did Aquinas and the other great thinkers of the Western religious tradition. And if the "New Atheists" are serious about making a rational case for atheism, then, as I have said, they should be taking on the best representatives of the opposing point of view – not blabbering on for hundreds of pages about the dangers of "faith" as an irrational will to believe something in the face of all evidence, when this is an attitude that the mainstream Christian theological tradition has itself always condemned. Why they insist on looking for debating partners at madrasahs and revival tent meetings, rather than at a cathedral or a *quodlibet*, is beyond me, unless it is precisely so as to avoid having to pick on someone their own size.

The New Atheists emphasize, after all, that they cannot to be expected to defend everything that has been done in the name of atheism. Hence Dawkins, Harris, and Hitchens, with practiced dudgeon, distance themselves from Stalin, Mao, Pol Pot, and other Communist mass murderers – devout atheists all – on the grounds that people so obviously wicked and irrational surely cannot be representative of "real" secularism. To admit otherwise, you see, would be to explode the myth of the "paradise on earth" Dawkins says would result from keeping children innocent of religious instruction – a "right" that Stalin and Co. were only too willing to guarantee to their citizens, in spades. His learning worn about as lightly as a sledge hammer at Kolyma, Hitchens employs, against Paley's "design argument," one of those "half-remembered scraps of Popperism" David Stove said were always burbling out of the mouths of scientists who think they know something about philosophy.[16] Hitchens is no scientist, but he did take a degree in

Philosophy, Politics, and Economics at Oxford forty years ago, where, presumably, he came upon Karl Popper's dictum that "a theory that is unfalsifiable is to that extent a weak one."[17] It never occurs to him that by refusing to allow even one of the 100 million corpses produced by Communism to count as evidence against the moral claims of atheism, he makes his own position far more "unfalsifiable" than anything Paley ever said (since, after all, the latter did allow that it was at least *possible* that organisms could have arisen through impersonal processes). But then, that is the Christopher Hitchens recipe for Serious Journalism: one part real knowledge, one part filibuster, one part sheer bluff. Click "Save," email it to Graydon, down the last bit of Scotch, and you're done for the night. How *can* you go wrong?

And yet these same New Atheists insist that snake-handlers in Kentucky, suicide bombers on the West Bank, and Cardinal Newman in his study, simply must be lumped together into some amorphous whole called "religion," and the idiocies and crimes of some put on the account of the others. It's the by–now-familiar shtick: Heads I win, tales you lose. Simplistic thinking is bad except when New Atheists do it. Progressively minded people are always educated, informed , and open-minded, unless the subject is religion. Etc., etc., etc. Well, it should be clear enough by now that I am not defending, and would not defend, everything that goes by the name of "religion." If the arguments we've been examining are correct, then the true religion, whatever it is, is obviously going to be a monotheistic one. That narrows things down considerably. Now as I have said, making the case for Christianity specifically is beyond the scope of this book, which is about "natural theology" (i.e. knowledge of God that can be ours via unaided reason) rather than "revealed theology" (knowledge of God based on a divine revelation). But the reader will not be surprised to learn that that is where I think the truth lies. And if a monotheistic religion's claim to be founded on a divine revelation is going to be at all credible, that claim is going to have to rest on a very dramatic miracle; there simply is no other plausible way in which an alleged revelation might be verified. The resurrection surely counts as such a miracle, for there are no plausible natural means by which a dead man could come back to life. What does Islam have to match this?

Muhammad's "miracle," the Muslims tell us, is the Qur'an itself. This is, shall we say, rather anticlimactic, especially given that the contents of the Qur'an can be quite easily accounted for in terms of borrowings from Jewish and Christian sources. Jewish miracle claims are going to be the ones familiar from the Old Testament – Moses's miracles, for example – but Christians accept those too, so even if their historicity were verified, they could not make the case for Judaism over against Christianity specifically. Moreover, the direct eyewitness evidence for these miracle stories is more controversial than the evidence surrounding the resurrection. All things considered, then, the one purportedly revealed monotheistic religion which can appeal to a single decisive miracle in its favor is Christianity. Establish that the resurrection really occurred, and you will have proven that Christianity is true; show that it did not occur, and you will, as St. Paul himself affirms, have disproved Christianity. There is no other world religion that opens itself up to rational evaluation so crisply and clearly.

In any event, now that we have a fix on the relationship between faith and reason, we can turn once again to the problem of evil. The atheist says that if God exists, He would, being all-powerful and all-good, prevent the suffering we see around us; yet suffering persists; therefore God does not exist. I have said that this argument is worthless. The question has been hashed over to death by philosophers and theologians, and there is much that could be said.[18] But Aquinas, as he so often does, gets to the nub of the matter. The first premise of the atheist's argument is simply false, or at least unjustifiable – that is to say, there is no reason whatever to think that an all-powerful and all-good God would prevent the suffering we see around us – for it is "part of the infinite goodness of God, that He should allow evil to exist, *and out of it to produce good.*"[19] If God can bring out of the evils that we actually experience a good that is far greater than what would have existed without them, then of course He would allow those evils. But God is *infinite* in power, knowledge, and all the rest – Pure Actuality, Being Itself, Goodness Itself, and so forth, as we have seen – and, since human beings have immortal souls, so that our lives in the here-and-now are but a trivial blink of the eye compared to the eternity we are to enter, there is no limit to the good result that might be made in the next life out of even the worst evils we suffer in this one. For even the worst evils we suffer are finite. Therefore there is every reason to think that God can and will bring out of the sufferings of this life a good that so overshadows them that this life will be seen in retrospect to have been worth it.

We are familiar with small-scale analogues to this from everyday life. Suppose your child is trying to learn how to play the violin. This will require much practice, and thus a sacrifice of time that could be spent playing. It will also require hours of frustration and boredom, some pain and discomfort as he gets used to keeping his arms and head in an awkward position for prolonged periods of time and builds up calluses on his fingers, and possibly humiliation when at recitals and the like he makes serious mistakes in his playing or sees how much better other students are than he is. He may often want to give it up, and keeping him from doing so may require not only encouragement but also occasional punishments for failures to practice every day. On bad days he might almost hate you for what you're putting him through. But eventually he becomes very good indeed, and the frustration he once felt disappears entirely. He might even forget about it almost completely, and if he is a normal, sane human being he certainly will never hold it against you or think the suffering he once thought was unbearable is even worth thinking about now. Indeed, if anything, his accomplishment will have the value for him that it does precisely because he had to suffer for it. In hindsight, he might well say that he wouldn't have had it any other way. Such examples could be multiplied indefinitely.

Of course, I am not claiming that the relatively minor suffering in question is comparable to the death of a child, or bone cancer, or Auschwitz. But then, neither could the relatively minor joy of being a great violinist compare to the beatific vision. Indeed, even the greatest horror we can imagine in this life pales in insignificance before the beatific vision. To quote St. Paul once again, "the sufferings of this present time are not worth comparing with the glory that is to be revealed to us."[20] To be sure, the atheist might well retort that he doesn't believe there is a beatific vision, much less a God. He may say that he can't imagine anything in the next life that might outweigh the worst suffering present in this one. But that brings me to the reason why I say that the argument from evil is worthless. For the only way the atheist can make it plausible to say that nothing could outweigh Auschwitz, etc., is if he supposes that there is no God and thus no beatific vision. But if he's *supposing* that there is no God, then in presenting his argument from evil he's simply *arguing in a circle*, assuming the very thing he's trying to prove, and thus not proving it at all. In effect he's saying: "There is no God, because look at all this suffering that couldn't possibly be outweighed by any good. How do I know there's no good that could outweigh it? Oh, because there is no God." If you think that's a good argument, you need a logic course.

Note also the double standard implied to the extent that the atheist rests his case on the claim that he "can't imagine" anything that might outweigh the sufferings of this life. For if some creationist says he "can't imagine" how an eyeball could have evolved (or whatever), Dawkins and Co. reply, quite reasonably, that the limits of one person's imagination don't necessarily correspond to the limits of reality. Yet when the shoe is on the other foot, we're supposed to take the limits of Dawkins's imagination, or Hitchens's, as an infallible guide to what an infinite First Cause or Supreme Intelligence is capable of doing vis-à-vis bringing good out of evil. If anything, the limits of our imagination are far, *far* less relevant to understanding what a First Cause who is Being Itself and the Supreme Intelligence might bring about by way of good for a creature with an immortal soul than they are relevant to understanding the potentials inherent in a finite impersonal process like natural selection operating on finite living things.

The bottom line is this. Reason itself, as I have argued, shows us that there is a First Cause who is Being Itself, Goodness Itself, all-powerful, all-knowing, and all the rest, and it also shows us that we have immortal souls. Hence reason tells us that there is a God who created us for a destiny beyond this life and who is fully capable of guaranteeing that the good we attain in the next life outweighs the evil we suffer in this one to such an extent that the latter, however awful from our present point of view, will come to seem "not worth comparing" to the former, and indeed if anything will even be seen to have been worth having gone through from the point of view of eternity. And therefore, reason itself tells us that there is simply no reason to believe that even the worst possible sufferings of this life constitute any evidence whatsoever against the existence of God. Nevertheless, since we are finite beings, it can be very hard to keep this in mind when faced with severe suffering. The arguments of philosophers and theologians, however logically impeccable, seem cruelly abstract and cold when compared to the agony of the parents of a raped and murdered child. But then, reason *is* abstract and cold. Atheists are always telling us how we need soberly to follow it where it leads us, even if it were to break our hearts by telling us that there is no hope for cosmic justice, no hope for seeing lost loved ones ever again, no hope for a life beyond this one. Then, when a Thomas Aquinas reassures us that in fact no matter how bad things get in this life, reason assures us that God can set it right, they feign outrage at such cold-hearted logicality. Some people just can't take yes for an answer.

In any event, it is precisely because of the abstraction and coldness of reason that a kind of faith is needed where evil is concerned. Not because faith is emotional. Faith is *not* emotional; it is rather an act of the will. And again, not because faith contradicts reason, for it doesn't. Rather, faith in God in the face of evil is nothing less than the will to *follow* reason's lead when emotion might incline us to doubt. The intensity of the pain one feels can make him want to shake his fist at God, like Job. Yet reason says that that pain is part of an overall plan which we cannot yet fathom, but one in which God can bring out of that pain a good compared to which it will pale in insignificance. Hence reason tells us: have faith in God. We will not always be able to understand what that plan is, or how this or that particular instance of suffering fits into it. We have some general clues here and there – for instance, the fact that certain goods, like patience, forgiveness, and self-sacrifice, cannot be had without certain evils. But we don't know the details. And yet, why should we *expect* to know them? If there is a God of the sort the arguments I've described point to, and if the soul's ultimate destiny surpasses the cares of this life in the way its immortality implies, then these matters are so far beyond our ordinary experience that it would be extremely surprising if we *could* fully understand them. Again, the atheist will of course dismiss all of this as falsehood added to falsehood. The point, though, is that he cannot do so and at the same time have his "argument from evil" against the existence of God, for if that argument *assumes* that all these claims are false, then it simply begs the question against the theist, and thus fails to prove anything. It is all attitude, and no substance.

Aquinas tells us that faith is a supernatural gift. For from the point of view of Christian theology, at least, whatever reasons might lead us to belief in God and in what He has revealed, divine grace, acting in the interests of our salvation, is its ultimate cause. And here again, if I might be forgiven for saying so, Christianity has an edge over its monotheistic competitors. For if we have reason to trust in God in the face of suffering, how much more ought we to trust in a God who so loves us that He became flesh, to suffer with us, and for us?

But this is, as I say, a book about natural rather than revealed theology. And we have seen that given the metaphysical picture of the world handed on to us by the Greeks, and especially Aristotle, a powerful case (at the very least) can be made for the existence of God, the immortality of the soul, and the natural law conception of morality. But of course, modern philosophers rejected that metaphysical picture; and the gradual working out of the implications of this move is, I maintain, the reason why God, the soul, and the natural law have come into the disrepute they have among contemporary intellectuals. (One likes to think that if a resurrected Descartes were told "You bastard! You gave us Richard Dawkins!" he would repair to a confessional immediately.) What remains to be seen, then, is why the early modern thinkers made this transition, why their reasons for doing so were no good, and why a return to classical philosophy – and thus the religious conclusions that follow from it – is rationally unavoidable.

5. Descent of the Modernists

You might expect that, given his lofty status as the very "father of modern philosophy," René Descartes (1596–1650) would, like Plato, be the subject of an apocryphal tale or two. If so, you'd be right; and as with Plato, the content of one such tale reflects something deep about the thinker's ideas. The fanciful story of Plato's divine pedigree calls to mind the heavenly character of the world of Forms he took to be the highest reality, from which our souls descended and to which they would return. A legend about Descartes that began to circulate about a century after his death is possibly even weirder, and at least as indicative. It is said that he used to travel with a life-size, and extremely life-like, mechanical female doll, which he named Francine after his late illegitimate daughter, and which he would keep in a trunk next to him while he slept. The captain of a ship Descartes was on, terrified upon seeing the robot sit up when he opened the trunk out of curiosity, dragged it to the deck and threw it overboard.[1]

Why would such an odd story come to be told about Descartes? As it happens, Descartes had a view of the soul which was in some respects like Plato's. But his overall conception of human nature was decidedly mechanical, insofar as he took the human body and brain to be composed of nothing more than purposeless material components operating, like clockwork, according to blind physical laws. If the father of modern philosophy is falsely said to have made a robotic copy of his daughter, his contemporary intellectual descendents – who have largely abandoned his notion of the soul but kept his mechanistic conception of the body – would, as we will see, make "robots" of us all. That his philosophy was seen even in his own day to have these implications is no doubt the reason why the legend in question gained currency.

Pre-birth of the modern

To understand the revolution in thought associated with Descartes, however, we need to go back before his time, and indeed before the rise of "modern philosophy" in general, to the work of medieval writers like John Duns Scotus (c. 1266–1308) and William of Ockham (c. 1287–1347), who, though Scholastics, rejected Aquinas's synthesis of Aristotelianism and Christian theology. Their reasons for doing so anticipate certain key themes of modern philosophy, and in ways that make evident how, far from constituting an advance of reason, these themes tend inexorably toward reason's undoing. Certainly they led to the undoing of the Scholastic tradition, which had reached its apex in Aquinas's thought. (To be cute about it – or at least as "cute" as Aristotelianism gets – you might say that much of modern philosophy and its disastrous consequences were contained in these writers "eminently" if not "formally.")[2]

Both Scotus and Ockham denied the possibility of the sort of knowledge of God Aquinas claimed could be had through reason, and on a superficial reading this might seem to peg them as forerunners of New Atheist scientism. I know this because Christopher Hitchens is a superficial reader, and proves it by chatting up Ockham as a kind of heroic proto-rationalist, bravely pushing "true science" as far as it could go in those dark days before *Discover* magazine and PBS's *Nova* made its wonders available to both the knowledge-hungry masses and journalists writing for deadlines.[3] Predictably, he makes a big deal, in this connection, out of Ockham's razor – the principle that we ought not to multiply entities beyond necessity – which proves, I guess, that he read E.D. Hirsch's *Dictionary of Cultural Literacy* back in the '80s. This great breakthrough, Hitchens tells us, made possible the abandonment of the superfluous appeal to God as First Cause, which superfluity we are presumably expected to believe was beyond the capacity of a man like Thomas Aquinas to see. Except that Aquinas – again, rather famously to people who've actually read Aquinas, but don't let *that* stop the balls-out self-confidence of a Dawkins or Hitchens – explicitly considers this "superfluity" objection to theism and shows in the Five Ways that God's existence is (for reasons some of which we've examined) *necessarily entailed* by the very existence of change, causation, final causality, etc., and thus is not a matter of "hypothesis," redundant or otherwise. And except that "Ockham's" famous principle was more or less already stated by medieval predecessors like Petrus Aureolus and – wait for it – Thomas Aquinas himself, *precisely in the course of considering the "superfluity" objection.*[4] Indeed, even *Aristotle* had formulated a version of it *precisely in the course of arguing for an Unmoved Mover.*[5] Oops. Better hope Hirsch gets all that into the next edition, Hitch.

The motivation for Scotus's skepticism was an excessive emphasis (as Thomists see it) on God's will over His intellect. Aquinas, in Scotus's estimation, makes God and His actions too comprehensible, too rational, too open to our puny philosophical investigations. So radically free is God's will, in Scotus's view, that we simply cannot deduce from the natural order either His intentions or any necessary features of the things He created, since He might have created them in any number of ways, as His inscrutable will directed. Ockham pushes this emphasis on the divine will even further, holding that God could by fiat have made morally obligatory all sorts of things that are actually immoral; for example, had He wanted to, He could even have decided to command us to hate Him, in which case this is what would be good for us to do. Thus are we brought by Ockham to the idea that morality rests on completely arbitrary divine commands rather than rationally ascertainable human nature (Aquinas's preferred theory). We are also brought to the conclusion that we ought to look to faith rather than reason for knowledge of God's nature, since (in Ockham's view, but again contrary to Aquinas's) there is nothing in creation that can give us such knowledge. Hitchens is welcome to believe that such fideism is an advance for human reason if he wants to, but if I were him I wouldn't tell the editors of *Free Inquiry* (a "secular humanist" fanzine for which he sometimes writes, presumably for love rather than money), lest they boot him out of their pages for sounding too much like Pat Robertson.

Ockham is often described as a nominalist; in fact he was a conceptualist, which is bad enough (recall our discussion in Chapter 2). For Ockham, there are no true universals, essences, or natures in the objective world, only particular individual things. Universals or essences exist in the mind alone. Hence there can be no such thing as a shared human nature, and thus no basis in human nature for a rational system of ethics. This, together with his emphasis on God's absolute power and inscrutable will, underlie Ockham's turn to faith as the only possible source of moral knowledge. They also underlie his denial that we can demonstrate the existence of causal connections between things. For if things have no shared essences, and God could have made anything follow upon anything else, then we simply cannot know with certainty that causes of type A will always be followed by effects of type B. In praising Ockham's views on causation (as he does) Hitchens effectively commends him for combining a demonstrably false metaphysical theory (conceptualism) with a theological premise (about God's will and power) that Hitchens himself rejects. Truly inscrutable are the ways of the Hitch; he is a riddle, inside an enigma, wrapped in a cocktail napkin.

Or maybe not. For the reason he praises Ockham here is because he thinks Ockham's view undermines the possibility of tracing causes back to a First Cause. And that may well be true (though Ockham's own attitude toward philosophical arguments for God's existence was more complicated than Hitchens lets on). But not only is Ockham's view based on premises Hitchens himself either wouldn't accept or shouldn't accept; it has further implications that Hitchens *couldn't* accept. The alert reader will have noticed that the view in question sounds, at least in part, like David Hume's; and skepticism about the possibility of our knowing objective causal connections between things, whether inspired by Hume or Ockham, notoriously threatens not only cosmological arguments for God's existence, but the very possibility of science. For if there are no shared essences, and if we cannot get behind the appearances of things to their underlying causal bases, then molecules and quarks, gravitation and electromagnetism go the way of the First Cause, and science follows theology onto the scrap heap. This is, I dare say, an extremely well-known problem for Humean theories of causation (and thus for views, like Ockham's, which are similar), though of course no such problem – for either cosmological arguments or for science – faces the Aristotelian and Thomistic views of causation we looked at in Chapters 2 and 3. Hitchens assures us that theists "have consistently failed to overcome [Ockham's] objection [to a First Cause]." In fact, as we have seen, it was overcome long before Ockham was born. What Hitchens should have written is: "I wouldn't know the difference between conceptualism and realism, essentially and accidentally ordered causal series, Aristotle and Hume, etc., *even if* I were intellectually honest; but then, neither will the book reviewer at the *New York Times*, so who cares?"

As the comparison with Hume indicates, views like Ockham's prefigured themes that would come to define modern philosophy, and modern civilization more generally. The idea that only particular individual things exist and share no universal natures in common naturally led in the political sphere to the conclusion that human beings are not related by natural bonds of community, but are "atomistic individuals" who unite into society only by contract. As we have seen, it also undermined the possibility of deriving morality from human nature. Meanwhile, Scotus's and Ockham's tendency toward voluntarism (i.e. their emphasis on will over intellect), and the related idea that morality derives from arbitrary divine commands, became secularized in the notion that all law rests ultimately on the sheer will of a sovereign, rather than in a rationally ascertainable natural order. Combine these themes and you are not far from Thomas Hobbes's view that man's "natural" condition is to be at war with his fellowman, and that this unhappy situation can be remedied only by agreeing to submit to the will of an absolute ruler.

As has been noted by the Protestant theologian Paul Tillich (who was not exactly Captain Orthodoxy himself), Ockham's pulverization of all reality into a collection of unrelated individuals also had a tendency to turn God into merely one individual among others (albeit a grand and remote one).[6] He is, on this conception, no longer Pure Being, pervading and sustaining the world at every moment, but merely a superhuman external spectator, arranging things from outside. What I described earlier as Aquinas's "grade 3" conception of God is thereby replaced by a more anthropomorphic "grade 2" conception, opening the door to the follies of Paley and the crude straw man of village-atheist polemic. And given that the existence of a "grade 2" God is far less philosophically defensible than a "grade 3" God, faith becomes more central to religion and reason recedes, which in turn leads to skepticism about the possibility of giving religion a rational foundation at all.

Ockhamite views also prepared the way for modern philosophy in another way. As we have seen, Aristotelian metaphysics involves a number of complex distinctions which require for their expression an equally complex technical vocabulary; and this complexity only grew as Aquinas and other Aristotelian Scholastic philosophers of the Middle Ages developed Aristotle's views further. This is unfortunate for the student of philosophy, but unavoidable given that the real world just is, Aristotelians would say, as complex as the vocabulary needed to describe it. But suppose that we interpreted this vocabulary in terms of a nominalist or conceptualist metaphysics, rather than a realist one. Then all those complicated technicalities would reflect, not objective reality, but only our subjective ideas or the way we decided to use words. The Scholastic philosophy that inherited this terminology would come to seem an exercise in mere wordplay and irrelevant hair-splitting, rather than a serious investigation of the real world. And that is exactly what happened as views like Ockham's started to proliferate within Scholasticism. The early modern philosophers who rejected Aristotle and his Scholastic successors as mere sophists did not realize that the version of Aristotelianism they were familiar with was not the real McCoy, but only a version corrupted by nominalism – the very same nominalism many of them would come to endorse themselves.

Thoroughly modern metaphysics

But this was not the main reason why the moderns rejected Scholastic Aristotelianism. To understand that, we need to understand the relationship between modern philosophy and modern science; and the connection is not what it is often assumed to be.[7] The usual story is that modern scientific discoveries refuted Aristotelianism, putting philosophers in a position of having to find something new to replace it. But modern science did *not* refute "Aristotelianism," if this is meant to refer to Aristotle's thought as a whole. To be sure, it did disprove certain *scientific* theories that had been accepted by Aristotle and his successors, such as the view that the earth stood at the center of the solar system, and that the planets are embedded in a series of concentric spheres surrounding the earth. But these theories are completely independent of Aristotle's *metaphysical* ideas, such as the distinction between actuality and potentiality, the doctrine of the four causes, hylomorphism, and so forth. And even where Aristotelian metaphysical ideas were frequently expressed in terms of outdated scientific assumptions, the ideas can easily be restated in different terms. For example, it was often said by Aristotelians that the Unmoved Mover keeps the world in motion by moving the outermost heavenly sphere – a natural assumption to make if one assumes that there are such things as heavenly spheres. But that it turns out that there are no such spheres doesn't show there is no Unmoved Mover after all, for the argument for the Unmoved Mover does not rest on Aristotle's mistaken astronomy, but rather on the distinction between actuality and potentiality. And this distinction is metaphysical, not scientific (in the modern sense of "scientific"). That is to say, it is a description of reality that is more general and basic than any scientific theory, resting as it does on facts (about change) that science itself takes for granted. Hence it is valid *whatever* the empirical scientific facts turn out to be; and (to repeat what was said earlier) while that doesn't mean that it cannot be subjected to rational evaluation or criticism, such criticism can only come from some alternative metaphysical theory, not from empirical science.

This is no desperate ex post facto attempt to salvage an otherwise indefensible worldview. For one thing, Aristotelian metaphysical ideas are, as I keep saying and as will be established by the end of the next chapter, unavoidable, whether the early modern philosophers thought so or not. For another, the distinction I am making, between metaphysical ideas and scientific ones, is just an obvious one to make. As noted before, empirical science must take many things for granted, such as the existence of patterns of cause and effect. Thus, while it might be able to establish whether some *particular* causal relationship exists, it cannot possibly establish whether *causation as such* is real or not, given that its method presupposes its existence. Nor, at the most general level and for the same reasons, can it tell us *what* causation per se is or what kinds of causation exist. And so on for notions like actuality, potentiality, substance, attribute, form, and so on. Empirical science of its very nature cannot give us the full story about these matters; but metaphysics just is the rational investigation of them. Hence metaphysics is obviously different from empirical science.

Moreover, medieval Aristotelians themselves made the distinction in question even before the rise of modern science; it wasn't forced on them by embarrassing empirical discoveries. As always, Aquinas affords us a clear example. Far from insisting dogmatically that the Ptolemaic astronomy accepted in his day must be correct, he acknowledged that "the suppositions that these astronomers have invented need not necessarily be true; for perhaps the phenomena of the stars are explicable on some other plan not yet discovered by men" and that the case made in its defense "falls short of a convincing proof, for possibly the phenomena might be explained on some other supposition."[8] Nor is the Galileo incident, of which most people know only a caricature, evidence of Scholastic intransigence. Cardinal Bellarmine conceded at the time that if there were real proof of Copernicus's view that the sun was at the center of the solar system and that the earth moves around it, the Church would have to acknowledge that the common interpretation of certain biblical passages was mistaken. Galileo's difficulty arose, *not* because he advocated Copernican views – he had done so for years with the knowledge and approval of the Church, and even the warm encouragement of Pope Urban VIII and several other churchmen – but rather because he rashly insisted on treating them as more than hypothetical, as having been *proved* when they had not, at the time, been proved at all. Indeed, some of Galileo's own arguments, it is now known, were seriously flawed. While it turns out that his conclusions were correct anyway, and while some of the decisions made by churchmen in dealing with him might be questioned, the fact remains that it was Galileo, and not the Church, who dogmatically went beyond the evidence then available, and that his popular image as a heroic martyr for science is only slightly more grounded in fact than the story of Washington and the cherry tree.[9]

The point, in any case and to repeat, is that modern science did absolutely nothing to refute Aristotle's metaphysics. So why was it abandoned? And what, then, *was* the connection with modern science? As we have seen, if the general Aristotelian-Thomistic-Scholastic picture of the world is correct, then reason itself tells us that the highest kind of life is one devoted to the contemplation and service of God, that the goal of our lives here and now ought to be to prepare for the next life, and that to the extent God wants us to concern ourselves with earthly affairs, it is largely to build families (preferably with lots of children) and to find our fulfillment in sacrificing our petty desires and selfish interests for the sake of their well being. These conclusions of natural theology and natural law theory also lay the foundation for revealed theology (in the manner sketched in the previous chapter); and as things worked out in the later Middle Ages, the end result was both a complex intellectual system in which Aristotelian categories had been more or less officially incorporated into the warp and woof of Christian thought, and a social order that was (in theory if not always in practice) deferential to ecclesiastical authority and other-worldly in its orientation. Needless to say, all of this rather takes the fun out of things for people who think a *really* grand society is one that extends the franchise to anyone with a pulse, celebrates quirky new ideas, makes it easy for you to divorce your wife if you get bored with her, and provides lots of cheap consumer goods.

But it is not only contemporary secularist progressives who regard this traditional worldview with horror; many early modern thinkers did too. Consider that by the time Bacon, Hobbes, Descartes, et al. were writing, Martin Luther had already greatly extended Ockham's individualist tendencies in religion and politics, replacing not only ecclesiastical authority but also (what he regarded as) the stifling and unbiblical system of Aristotelian Scholasticism with the primacy of individual conscience. In his defense of divorce, he had (together with Henry VIII) inaugurated a revolution in social mores, undermining one of the traditional bulwarks of the stability of the family. John Calvin's brand of Protestantism had replaced the traditional emphasis on the spiritual dangers of wealth and benefits of poverty with a new affirmation of industry, thrift, and acquisition as Christian virtues. Intentionally or not, the Reformation thus ushered in a new worldliness the practical results of which – increased wealth and a new sense of individual freedom – led to a desire for more of the same. At the same time, its fragmentation of Christianity into hostile camps and the bloody conflicts to which this gave rise made religion come to seem a dangerous source of social unrest; and its pitting of faith and the Bible against reason and philosophy increasingly made religion come to seem rationally unfounded as well. So, while the ancients pursued wisdom and virtue for their own sakes, and the medievals applied ancient learning to shoring up the claims of religion and directing man toward his destiny in the hereafter, the moderns, naturally enough given the new cultural climate that shaped their values and perceptions, sought to reorient intellectual endeavor to improving man's lot in this life, and to defusing post-Reformation religious tensions by sowing a general skepticism about the possibility of attaining much in the way of religious knowledge, so that there'd be little left to fight over. Hence Bacon's conception of a new science that would give us mastery over nature, the promise of new technologies, and hope for making this world a fitting habitation for man. Hence Locke's aim of drawing definite limits to what was strictly knowable where religion was concerned, so as to put all conflicting creedal claims on an equally low epistemic footing and thereby to lay the predicate for his doctrine of religious toleration.

"And what is wrong with all that?" many readers will ask. Well, there might be nothing at all wrong with it; and then again, there might be something very deeply wrong with it. But the point for now is not to determine whether this project was good or bad, but rather to emphasize that to a very great extent it was *a desire to further the project*, and not an actual refutation of Aristotle, that moved modern thinkers away from his metaphysics. The agenda determined the arguments rather than the other way around. In particular, it determined a new conception of what science could and should be: not a search for the ultimate causes and meaning of things (as Aristotle and the Scholastics understood it) but rather a means of increasing "human utility and power" through the "mechanical arts" or technology (Bacon), and of making us "masters and possessors of nature" (Descartes).[10] Usefulness would replace wisdom, and pampering the body in this life would push aside preparing the soul for the next. Hence modern science, far from refuting Aristotle's metaphysics, was simply *defined* in such a way that nothing that smacked of Aristotelian formal and final causes and the like *would be allowed to count* as truly "scientific." There was no "discovery" here; there was only stipulation, an insistence on forcing every object of scientific investigation into a non-Aristotelian Procrustean bed, and – if necessary – simply denying the existence of anything that couldn't be wedged in. For the Aristotelian Scholastic categories led, in the view of thinkers like Locke, to a dangerous "dogmatism" in religious and philosophical matters. (In other words, if we accept these categories, we'll have to admit that the entire Scholastic system is more or less rationally unavoidable.) And in the Baconian view, they distract us from the one thing needful. (In other words, if Aristotle is right, then we'll end up spending more time contemplating first principles and the state of our souls and less time thinking up new gadgets.) While the early modern philosophers and their contemporary successors quibble over this or that argument of Aristotle, Aquinas, and Co., then, what they *really* don't like are *the conclusions*. Admit formal and final causes into the world, and at once you are stuck – *rationally* stuck – with God, the soul, and the natural law. The modern, liberal, secular project becomes a non-starter. So, "reason" must be redefined in a way that makes these conclusions impossible, or at least severely weakened. The classical metaphysical categories, especially Aristotelian and Thomistic ones, must be banished from science and philosophy altogether, by fiat. The game must be rigged so that Aristotle and St. Thomas cannot even get onto the field; then, centuries later, the successors of the early moderns, quite pleased with the results of their handiwork and not too concerned with how it was achieved, can pretend that this refusal even to play the game counted as a "victory."

You don't have to take my word for it. As philosopher Pierre Manent has put it, for the early modern philosophers, "in order to escape decisively from the power of the singular religious institution of the Church, one had to renounce thinking of human life in terms of its good or end" and the "'pagan' [i.e. classical Greek] idea that nature is naturally legislative."[11] Hence "it is the teaching of Aristotle, which was essentially adopted by Catholic doctrine, that Descartes, Hobbes, Spinoza, and Locke will implacably destroy."[12] In the same vein, intellectual historian Mark Lilla has recently noted that Hobbes's materialism had a "political end," namely "the dismantling of Christendom's theological-political complex," toward which end "the whole of Aristotle would have to be scrapped, along with the shelves of medieval commentary on him."[13] The eminent 20th-century philosopher Gilbert Ryle once asked, "Why is it that although nearly every youthful student of philosophy both can and does in about his second essay refute Locke's entire Theory of Knowledge, yet Locke made a bigger difference to the whole intellectual climate of mankind than anyone had done since Aristotle?"[14] And his answer is that Locke's conclusions – epistemological modesty in religion and the like, coupled with a doctrine of toleration of different opinions over such matters – have been found congenial and useful despite the notorious badness of Locke's central arguments *for* those conclusions. The philosopher and historian of science E.A. Burtt, in his classic study of *The Metaphysical Foundations of Modern Physical Science*, concludes that "wishful thinking" lay behind the belief of the early moderns that all the phenomena previously explained in Aristotelian terms could be readily accommodated by a new science in which formal and final causes were replaced by entirely quantifiable properties of the kind suitable for prediction and control of nature, and subsequent technological application. "The sources of distraction [from this ambition] simply had to be denied or removed," and

> any solution of the ultimate questions which continued to pop up, however superficial and inconsistent, that served to quiet the situation, to give a tolerably plausible response to their questionings in the categories they were now familiar with, and above all to open before them a free field for their fuller mathematical exploitation of nature, tended to be readily accepted and tucked away in their minds with uncritical confidence.[15]

Lilla, Ryle, Burtt, and (to some extent) Manent, it should be noted, are sympathetic with this modern project themselves, even as they acknowledge that it has often been sustained more by ideological commitment than dispassionate argument. This parallels the acknowledgment by contemporary writers like Nagel and Lewontin (quoted in Chapter 1) that the naturalistic interpretation of science to which they are committed is less an independently motivated philosophical position than an attempt to prevent a "divine foot" from getting in the door.

Whatever the philosophical deficiencies of this project, it has undeniably been a smashing PR triumph. We all "know" it was right, because it *won out*, and like good students of Francis Bacon we think that practical success is all that means anything. (Let the Aristotelians, always fussing over logic, worry about the circularity involved in such reasoning.) Plus it has, as promised, given us lots of neat-o gizmos with which to while away our pointless lives now that purpose has been utterly banished from the world by naturalistic diktat. And make no mistake, that is *exactly* what naturalism does, built as it is on the "Mechanical Philosophy" (as it was called) that the early moderns put in place of Aristotelianism. The historical development of this new philosophy was complex, but the basic idea was this: There are no formal or final causes in the natural world, or at least none that we can know about; there are only material and efficient ones, and even then only material and efficient causes of a sort Aristotle would not have recognized. In particular, matter is to be understood, not as the correlate of form, but rather as comprised of unobservable particles having only mathematically quantifiable features. Cause and effect relations have nothing to do with any powers inherent in things nor any directedness toward ends or goals, but merely with regularities of the sort enshrined in "laws of nature." Particles can be arranged in relatively simple ways –for example into atoms and molecules, as we would now say – or in very complex ways – into rocks, trees, human bodies, planets, and galaxies, for instance. But either way, the resulting objects are nothing over and above the particles that compose them. The "laws of nature" describe the ways in which the particles behave whether in more simple arrangements or more complex ones. And that is simply all there is to material reality: meaningless physical particles interacting according to meaningless laws of nature. The ordinary objects of our experience do not have their own individual "forms" in Aristotle's sense, because there is ultimately nothing over and above the particles that make them up, and the particles are all governed by exactly the same laws of nature. There are no "final causes" either, because none of the behavior of the particles is oriented to any goal or purpose. They simply regularly bang into one another in such-and-such ways, so that sometimes the result is this sort of object or event and sometimes it's that sort; and that's it.

Well, there *is* a little more to the story than that, to be sure. But that's enough to convey the anti-Aristotelian flavor of the "Mechanical Philosophy"; and there is, at bottom, precious little that is *essential* to it other than its anti-Aristotelianism. The original idea was that the interactions between particles were as "mechanical" as the interactions of the parts of a clock, everything being reducible to one thing literally pushing against another. That didn't last long, for it is simply impossible to explain everything that happens in the material world on such a crude model, and as Newton's theory of gravitation, Maxwell's theory of electromagnetism, and quantum mechanics all show, physical science has only moved further and further away from this original understanding of what "mechanism" amounts to. As the philosopher William Hasker has noted, there is by now really nothing more *left* to the idea of a "mechanical" picture of the world than the mere denial of Aristotelian final causes or teleology.[16] This underlines the point that the modern understanding of science is defined more by an animus against Aristotelian Scholasticism than by any positive content; and it parallels, incidentally (though by no means accidentally), the point made in Chapter 1 that secularism is less a positive vision of the world than a mere animus against religion.

Animus, attitude, agenda, but little in the way of argument. That, I have suggested, is what lay behind the intellectual revolution that displaced the classical philosophy of Plato and Augustine, and especially of Aristotle and Aquinas, and enthroned the modern philosophy of Bacon, Hobbes, Descartes, Locke, Hume, and all the rest. But "little" is not "nothing," and there were some arguments, though none of them very impressive. The undeniable success of the quantificational approach to the study of the natural world, and especially the technological achievements it has made possible, might seem an obvious retroactive justification of this revolution. But there are three reasons why such an argument in favor of the moderns over the Scholastics is no good. First of all, it blames the Aristotelian tradition for failing to achieve something it was not, for the most part, trying to achieve in the first place. Classical and medieval philosophy and science aimed at wisdom and understanding, not the prediction and control of nature. The latter may have its place, but on the classical view it was not considered of

fundamental importance. Second, that an emphasis on the mathematically quantifiable aspects of nature has had dramatic technological consequences does not show that there are no other aspects
of nature; in particular, it does not show that there are no formal
and final causes. You might as well say that the fact that Beethoven,
though deaf, was possibly the greatest composer in the history of
music, demonstrates that there is no such thing as sound. Third,
some late Scholastic thinkers *did* in fact begin to give the quantifiable aspects of nature greater emphasis than their predecessors had;
in fact, the work of Galileo and company built on that of these
Scholastics.[17] And it is not as if the subsequent findings of modern
science cannot be incorporated within an Aristotelian framework.
What Aristotelianism rules out is not these findings, but only a
purely mechanistic or naturalistic interpretation of these findings.[18]

A particularly famous criticism of Aristotelian Scholasticism by
early modern philosophers is enshrined in Molière's joke about the
doctor who pretends to explain why opium causes sleep by saying
that it has a "dormitive power." The reason this is supposed to be
funny is that since "dormitive power" just means "a power to cause
sleep," the doctor's answer amounts to saying "opium causes sleep
because it has a power to cause sleep"; and this, it is said, is a mere
tautology, and therefore explains nothing at all. (A real knee-slap-
per, no?) In general (so the objection continues) Aristotelian
Scholasticism, in positing inherent causal powers, forms, and final
causes of various sorts, merely peddles empty phrases of this sort
instead of genuine explanations. The trouble with this objection,
though, is that the statement in question, while admittedly not terribly informative considered all by itself, is *not* a tautology; it does
have substantial content, even if that content is minimal. To say
"opium causes sleep because it causes sleep" *would* be a tautology.
But the statement in question says more than that. It says that
opium has a *power* to cause sleep; that is to say, it says that the fact
that sleep follows the ingestion of opium is not a mere accidental
feature of this or that sample of opium, but derives from something
in the very nature of opium as such. That this claim is by no means
trivial or tautological is evidenced by the fact that the early modern
philosophers rejected it as *false*. They didn't say, "Sure, opium has a
power to cause sleep, but that doesn't tell us anything" (which is

what they should have said if it really were a tautology). Rather, they said, "Opium does *not* have such a power, because there *are no* inherent powers, forms, etc."[19] Moreover, they couldn't very well dismiss the appeal to powers and the like as tautological on the grounds that such an appeal has only minimal content, because their own alternative proposal, when it too is considered all by itself, *also* has minimal content: To say "Opium causes sleep because the chemical structure of opium is such that, when ingested, sleep results" is hardly more informative than "Opium causes sleep because it has a power to cause sleep." If the former statement is not a tautology – and it isn't – then the latter isn't either.[20]

Of course, the critic of Scholasticism is going to say, "But the reference to chemical structure isn't *supposed* to be a complete explanation all by itself; it's just a starting point, and detailed empirical investigation into the specific chemical properties of opium would be needed in order to give a fully satisfying explanation." And that is perfectly true. But exactly the same thing is true of the Scholastic appeal to forms, powers, final causes, etc. Such appeals are *not supposed* to be the whole story. What they are intended to do, rather, is to point out that whatever the specific *empirical* details about opium turn out to be, the fundamental *metaphysical* reality is that these details are just the mechanism by which opium manifests the inherent powers it has *qua* opium, powers that a thing has to have if it is going to have any causal efficacy at all. This is perfectly consistent with, and indeed is (from an Aristotelian point of view) the only way properly to understand, the results of modern chemistry: The empirical chemical facts as now known are nothing other than a specification of the material cause underlying the formal and final causes that define the essence of opium. As elsewhere, the "critique" of Aristotelianism here rests on an unjustified double standard coupled with a failure to distinguish metaphysical issues from empirical ones.

The empiricist John Locke presented some equally bad objections to the Scholastic doctrine of forms and powers, dramatically manifesting thereby his own inherent power of generating exasperatingly muddleheaded arguments, already famously evident from the rest of his philosophical oeuvre. He tells us, for example, that the existence of "monsters" and "changelings" – severely deformed or mentally retarded human beings, such as the "Elephant Man" or Dustin Hoffman's character in *Rain Man* – shows that there are no hard and fast forms, essences, or species in the natural world, and that Aristotelians would, implausibly, either have to assign such creatures to a form or species of their own or deny that they belonged to any species at all. But as should be obvious from what we've said about this issue already, realists about universals, including Aristotelians, wouldn't say, and wouldn't have to say, either of these things. They would say instead that to instantiate a form or universal *imperfectly* is not to fail to instantiate it *at all*. Deformed and mentally retarded human beings are just that – human beings who happen to be deformed and retarded – not members of another species or of no species, just as a copy of the Mona Lisa you buy at a museum gift shop is still a copy of the Mona Lisa even if it gets torn or you spill coffee on it.

Similarly, Locke's further claim, that the fact that a human being might lose his memory, ability to reason, or various body parts while remaining a human being shows that things have no essential properties, simply ignores the Aristotelian distinction between various levels of actuality and potentiality. What makes a human being a rational animal, on the Aristotelian view, is not that he or she actually does or can exercise rationality at some point or other, but rather that an inherent potential for the exercise of rationality is actually in every human organism in a sense in which it is not in a turnip, or a dog, or a skin cell. This is obvious from the fact that a mature and undamaged human being actually reasons, whereas even a mature and undamaged turnip, dog, or skin cell does not and cannot reason. And yet an immature or damaged human being is still a human being, which entails that it has the form of a human being and thus the potentials inherent in that form, whether or not they are ever actualized. This, as we saw earlier, is why a fetus or a Terri Schiavo counts as a rational animal just as much as you or I do. Again, that something isn't a *paradigmatic* instantiation of some form doesn't entail that it isn't an instantiation at all. And as long as a fetus or a deformed or mentally retarded person is, biologically, a living creature of the species *homo sapiens*, it counts metaphysically as an instantiation (however imperfect) of the form or universal "rational animal." Locke would no doubt object to categories like actuality and potentiality no less than to the (related) notions of forms and final causes, but to try to shore up his "argument" against Aristotelianism by dismissing such categories would simply be to beg the question against it.

As we'll see, this is only the beginning of Locke's many sins against philosophy. And yet he is one of the most important figures in the early modern anti-Aristotelian revolution – and arguably the *quintessential* modern philosopher, insofar as now-prevailing Western attitudes about scientific rationality, religious toleration, government by consent, and individual rights owe more to Locke than to any other thinker. As has been noted, the generally acknowledged feebleness of his arguments has not led many to want to reconsider his conclusions, precisely because those conclusions have become so deeply embedded in the Western liberal consciousness that it is simply taken for granted that they *must* be defensible somehow, whether or not Locke himself was able to pull it off. The currently popular dodge among Locke scholars is to propose that the value of his philosophy lies in the whole rather than in any of the parts. That is to say, whatever the defects of Locke's various particular arguments for his philosophical system, the main case in its favor is that considered as a systematic totality it constitutes an alternative to Scholasticism that accounts equally well for all the "evidence" while avoiding Scholasticism's alleged difficulties, so that it should be preferred to Scholasticism on grounds of simplicity. And this seems to be the standard contemporary attitude toward the early moderns in general: Maybe their various particular arguments were bad, but the overall metaphysical position they left us with – in particular, a "mechanical" conception of the world devoid of formal and final causes – nevertheless turns out to account just as well for all the "facts" as the older Aristotelian view did, but in a more parsimonious way. So, though they got the details wrong, in the end they were right anyway, given Ockham's razor (or "Ockham's" razor, I guess I should say). The main objection to Aristotelian Scholasticism is that we just don't *need* it.

As I argue in my book-length study of Locke (which is creatively titled *Locke*), one rather serious problem with this sort of argument is that it is blatantly question-begging. For what *count* as the "facts" or "evidence" that a philosophical system ought to be able to account for is itself partly what is in dispute between Aristotelians and moderns. From the point of view of the mainstream tradition in classical philosophy, that universals are real is itself (and for the reasons discussed in Chapter 2) just a demonstrable fact, and the only question that remains is what *kind* of realist one is going to be, Platonic, Aristotelian, or Scholastic. The same thing is true for final causes. These are not "hypothetical entities" or "theoretical postulates" designed to "explain" such-and-such empirical evidence à la molecules, atoms, and quarks; they are rather unavoidable metaphysical realities whose existence is a necessary precondition of there being any "empirical evidence" at all. So to say that a theory which denies formal and final causes is a more "parsimonious" way to "account for" the "empirical evidence" is to follow Bacon and the contemporary naturalistic scientism that derives from him in *assuming*, without *showing*, that all rational argumentation involves a kind of probabilistic empirical theorizing, and never a metaphysical demonstration. As with Dawkins's crude misreading of Aquinas as if he were Paley, it is an attempt to rig the debate by framing it in the very terms that are in question.

But even if we granted the moderns their question-begging scientism, their case against Aristotelian Scholasticism would utterly fail, for two reasons. First, the modern "mechanistic" understanding of the natural world has led to problems, paradoxes, and absurdities that are far more egregious than anything the Scholastics were ever accused of. Second, Aristotelian formal and final causes are simply unavoidable if we are to make sense of modern science and reason themselves. Our final chapter will develop this second theme; the remainder of this chapter will explore the first.

Inventing the mind-body problem

Whatever Locke's significance, it is Descartes who is, as I have said, generally regarded as the "father" of modern philosophy, and for good reason. He was certainly a man of very great brilliance, and his contributions to the new science were, in his own day, at least as influential as his philosophical system. And yet it is the latter for which he is now best known, and Descartes's successors within philosophy down to the present day have directly or indirectly tended to define their positions either in Descartes's terms, broadly understood, or (more commonly, especially as the centuries have worn on) in reaction against him. One way or the other, Descartes effectively set the agenda; hence his claim to paternity. One reason, I think, is this. Though Descartes was not the first modern philosopher full stop, he *was* the first to make the modern philosophical project seem like something other than an exercise in sheer madness. These days we are used to philosophers and other intellectuals saying all sorts of preposterous and/or evil things as a matter of course: that the human mind is a kind of computer program; that all facts are "socially constructed"; that a man can "marry" another man; that abortion and sometimes even infanticide are perfectly justifiable; that bestiality is just a matter of taste; and so forth. But the early moderns, despite the weakening of their intellectual immune systems caused by Ockhamism, by the new individualism and worldliness, by the wars of religion, etc., were for the most part inoculated by the residual moral and intellectual heritage of medieval Christianity against accepting too much craziness, at least all at once and in an undiluted form. Hobbes's thoroughgoing materialism was acknowledged to be destructive not only of religion as such (and not just the hated Scholastic variety) but of reason itself; and his moral and political philosophy was widely recognized for the obscenity that it is. And though Bacon's overall program was enthusiastically endorsed, his own philosophical defense of it was far from thoroughly worked out, and seemed (given his anti-Aristotelian denigration of our natural, unreformed intellectual powers) to threaten to lead to skepticism. There was a need for someone to provide the modern philosophical project with a plausible systematic philosophical articulation, and in a way that would not break *too* radically with the past. Enter Descartes.

By all appearances a sincere Catholic, Descartes's hostility was, in theory anyway, directed only against the Scholastic framework in which the Christian tradition had come to be embedded, not against that tradition itself. And though he rejects Aristotle's philosophy (and thus by implication Aquinas's too) there are some affinities between his thought and that of Plato and Augustine. In particular, a decidedly Platonic-Augustinian conception of the soul plays a central role in Descartes's system, and by no means in an ad hoc or insincere fashion. Quite the opposite, in fact, as *something like* Descartes's modern twist on Plato's conception of the soul follows more or less automatically if (a) you want to replace the Aristotelian account of the natural world with the "Mechanical Philosophy" or some contemporary approximation to it, but (b) you also do not want to end up a thoroughgoing immoralist and irrationalist of the Nietzschean sort, for whom the 17th century was not ready, and who even today likes to disguise himself in scientific and moralistic clothing. The meaning and purpose that Descartes, like other moderns, banishes from the material world is given by him a new and exclusive home in the human mind, conceived of as a non-physical or immaterial substance existing independently of the human body and brain; and there is no other home it *could* have, given a mechanistic-cum-materialistic conception of nature. But with such a redoubt secured, it might seem possible to stave off the disaster that is (as we shall see) otherwise inevitable once one denies the reality of formal and final causes: the complete undermining of the possibility both of moral evaluation and of reason itself. Reason and morality, though devoid of a foundation in the natural order, could purportedly be grounded instead in the nature of the human soul, as Descartes re-conceives it: not as the form of the body (à la Aristotle's and Aquinas's hylomorphism) but as a kind of substance or object in its own right, albeit an imperceptible one – a "ghost in the machine" of the human body, as Gilbert Ryle famously lampooned it, whose unseen presence keeps at least one small portion of reality, the human world, from being totally swallowed up by the blind and impersonal forces the Mechanical Philosophy took to govern the rest of the universe.

Unfortunately, this strategy failed dismally, and partly because of its inherent connection to that *most* distinctively modern of philosophical tendencies, Descartes's introduction of which would all by itself merit him his status as the father of modern philosophy: *subjectivism*, the idea that all that we can know directly and with certainty are *the contents of our own minds*, and that if we can know anything else, it is only on the basis of what we know of our own minds, and even then only indirectly and with less certainty. To be

sure, this emphasis on the primacy of subjective human consciousness kept at bay the cold and inhuman conception of the world otherwise entailed by the Mechanical Philosophy. But it also tended
inevitably to cut the human mind off from contact with objective
reality, and when combined with the mechanistic conception of
nature, with the moderns' tendency toward voluntarism and anti-
realism (whether in its nominalist or conceptualist form), and with
the radical individualism and this-worldliness that has ever-
increasingly permeated Western civilization since the 16th century,
the result could not fail to be an unprecedented moral and intellectual catastrophe.

Here is how it all happened. (Brace yourself for some unavoidable technicalities and abstractions here and there.) Remember that
according to the Mechanical Philosophy, there are no formal and
final causes in the natural world – no fixed natures or essences of
things, no inherent powers or substantial forms, and no purposiveness or goal-directedness. There are only blind laws of nature governing the behavior of inherently meaningless and purposeless
physical particles or the like; everything in the material world, no
matter how complex, somehow boils down to this sort of thing. But
of course, many things certainly *appear* to have essences, natures,
and powers, and to act in accordance with some purpose or goal;
that is what common sense would say, anyway. For example, opium
certainly *seems* to have an inherent power to cause sleep; common
sense wouldn't say that there's nothing more going on here than a
regular or "law-like" correlation between ingesting something with
opium's chemical structure and then falling asleep. It certainly
seems to common sense to be true to say that the purpose of the
heart is to pump blood, and that having this purpose is part of its
nature or essence. And so forth. But the moderns write all of this off
as mere projection. Hume famously holds that when the mind perceives that events of type A are frequently followed by events of
type B, it forms an expectation of B whenever encountering A, and
this expectation is projected onto the world as an objective necessary connection between A and B. But in fact there is, he claims, no
reason to think there is any such connection at all; the "necessity" is
all in us, not in the world, an invention of the mind itself. You
expect opium to make you sleepy; but as far as the objective facts

are concerned, opium could in theory literally turn you into a frog (or whatever) rather than make you sleepy. Similarly, Locke held that the essences we take things to have or the species we take them to fall into are also creations of the human mind, something more invented than discovered. And while this sort of view had always been a hard sell when applied to the biological realm (where the objective reality of essences and final causes seems hard to deny), Darwin would, centuries later, finally give the mechanistic conception of nature some apparent biological credibility by arguing that species are fluid rather than fixed and that the appearance of purpose can be accounted for in entirely purposeless terms. It isn't that hearts have the function or final cause of pumping blood; it is rather (to truncate the story considerably) that creatures without hearts, and thus without circulating blood, died out and creatures with hearts survived. And so on for every other biological attribute. Goal-directedness even in the world of living things is in this view an illusion, a projection of the human mind. In reality (so Darwinians claim) there are only the blind and purposeless forces of mutation and natural selection, whose results only *seem* as if they furthered some natural goal or end.

This sort of view is also exemplified by the famous distinction between primary and secondary qualities developed by early modern thinkers like Galileo, Descartes, and Locke. The Mechanical Philosophy wants to say that heat, cold, redness, greenness, tastes, odors, and the like are, like everything else (it claims), somehow reducible to the motions (or whatever) of material particles. Yet there is a serious and well-known difficulty with this view. One and the same apple – composed, like everything else, of nothing more than material particles interacting according to laws of nature – can look red to one observer and grey to another who is color blind. It will taste sweet to someone with a normal gustatory apparatus, but not to someone whose tongue is burned or otherwise damaged. One and the same bucket of room-temperature water will feel warm to someone whose hand has been soaking in ice water, and cool to someone whose hand has been soaking in hot water. And so on for other sensible qualities. This sort of messiness is unwelcome if, like the advocates of the Mechanical Philosophy, your aim is to show that every feature of the natural world can be quantified,

described in terms of exceptionless laws, and thereby made suscep-
tible of prediction, control, and technological application.

The solution was to hold that material objects have both "primary" and "secondary" qualities. Primary qualities include solidity, extension, figure, motion, number and the like, and in particular
any quality that can be mathematically quantified and which does
not vary in any way from observer to observer. Secondary qualities
include colors, sounds, tastes, odors, and so forth, and an object's
having them amounts to nothing more than a tendency to cause us
to have certain sensations. So, for example, when we observe an
apple or a bucket of water, we perceive the former as having a certain length, width, and depth, and also a certain color; and we perceive the water in the bucket as swirling around in it, and also as
being warm. Now according to the view in question, the length,
width, depth, and swirling motion are primary qualities, and there
really is something in the objects themselves that "resembles" our
perceptions of them (as Locke put it). But while there is also something in the objects that causes our perceptions of redness and
warmth, there is nothing in the objects that resembles our perceptions of these secondary qualities. In other words, if by "redness"
you mean the tendency of an object to absorb certain wavelengths
of light and reflect others, and to cause us to have certain sensations
thereby, than the apple is certainly red. But if by "redness" you
mean what common sense means by it – the character of the sensation itself, the appearance the apple presents to a person with normal vision, as opposed to a color blind person – then the "redness"
is *not* in the apple, but *only in the mind of the observer*. If by "warmth"
you mean the motion of the molecules making up the water, then
the warmth really is in the water. But if instead by "warmth" you
mean (as common sense does) the way the water feels when you put
your hand in it, the warmth is *not* in the water, but *only in the mind
of the observer*. And so on for all other colors, tactile sensations,
tastes, odors, and the like. Objectively, according to the Mechanical
Philosophy, there are just colorless, odorless, tasteless particles in
motion. Color, odor, taste and the like *as we experience them* do not
exist in the objective world, but only in our minds. Color, odor, taste,
etc., can be said to exist objectively only if they are *redefined* in terms
of the quantifiable properties of particles and collections of particles.

Now this automatically entails a mind-body dualism of the sort Descartes was famously committed to. For if sensible qualities as we experience them do not exist in the external material world, then they do not exist even in the brain and nervous system either, for these are, according to the Mechanical Philosophy, made up like everything else in the natural world of nothing more than colorless, odorless, tasteless particles governed by exceptionless laws of nature. And if these qualities *do* exist in *the mind* – and there is nowhere else for them to exist, according to the Mechanical Philosophy – then the mind *necessarily* cannot be material, or at the very least not wholly material, since these sensible qualities themselves cannot be material. The mind must instead be something like the soul as conceived of by Plato, an immaterial or non-physical substance existing apart from the body and brain. There are thus two realms, the material world (including the human body and brain) whose nature is as the Mechanical Philosophy describes it, governed by the laws of physics, chemistry, etc., and the mind or the soul, which is neither governed by physical laws nor locatable in space. Apart from the mind, the body is a purely mechanical system, no more conscious than any other machine, and no less subject to the purposeless laws of nature.

Any reader familiar with the currently trendy field of "consciousness studies" might recognize in all of this the origins of what have come to be known as "qualia," a technical term for the characteristic features of a conscious experience that determine "what it's like" to have it. For example, what it's like to see red is different from what it's like to see green; what it's like to feel warmth is different from what it's like to feel cold; what it's like to taste coffee is different from what it's like to taste cheese; and so on. That which gives each of these experiences its distinctive character is what is meant by its "quale" (the singular form of "qualia"), and more or less corresponds to what the early modern philosophers took to be the purely subjective ideas that secondary qualities produce in our minds, and to which nothing in the objective physical world corresponds even though the mind erroneously projects these qualities or "qualia" (redness as it appears to us, warmth as it appears to us, etc.) onto that world. The focus of the current debate among philosophers, neuroscientists, and others over whether and how consciousness can be explained in a "naturalistic" way is the question of whether qualia in particular can be so explained. A sensation of redness is obviously very different from a sensation of greenness, and even more radically different from a sensation of coolness or the experience of tasting coffee or hearing a sound. Yet one cluster of neurons firing seems qualitatively pretty much like any other, and certainly very different from any of these sensations. For this reason (and many others) it is hard to see how any sensation could be reduced to or explained in terms of nothing but the firing of neurons.[21] While various positions have been taken on this issue, it is probably fair to say that the field is mainly divided between those theorists who think it is obvious that qualia cannot be explained naturalistically and those who think it is obvious that they can be, and each side finds it difficult to take the other seriously.

Predictably, the latter, "naturalistic" or materialist side tends to characterize the former as unscientific and engaged in wishful thinking, desperate to find some aspect of human nature that won't succumb to the relentless advance of scientific reductionism the way everything else has. (This despite the fact that most of the best-known critics of attempts to explain qualia and consciousness in materialistic terms – such as David Chalmers, Frank Jackson, Colin McGinn, Thomas Nagel, and John Searle – are irreligious, and in some cases positively hostile to religion.) Precisely because everything else has succumbed to materialistic explanation (so the objection continues) this hope for a special and irreducible feature of human nature is surely doomed. For why should one little aspect of reality, the human mind, be uniquely resistant to scientific explanation?

It is hard to know whether this sort of rhetoric owes more to ignorance or more to intellectual dishonesty, but when one considers that Daniel Dennett is one of its main purveyors, it is tempting to throw up one hands and say "both"; it would certainly fit his modus operandi vis-à-vis religion. In any event, there is a very good reason why the human mind alone should be uniquely resistant to "scientific explanation," if that is understood in a mechanistic-cum-materialistic sense; and it is precisely an understanding of the history of science, rather than some desperate attempt to avoid its implications, that reveals why. As Nagel especially has emphasized, and as our discussion to this point indicates, the standard conception of "scientific method" from the time of the early advocates of the Mechanical Philosophy down to the present day has taken science to be in the business of stripping away the subjective appearances of things – those features that vary from perceiver to perceiver – and re-describing the world entirely in terms of what remains invariant from perceiver to perceiver, and especially in terms of what can be mathematically quantified.[22] Whatever does not fit this model is treated as a mere projection of the mind rather than a genuine feature of objective physical reality. The physical world, on this understanding, *just is* whatever exists independently of any mind or conscious experience or subjective mental representation. Now while this method can be applied to all sorts of phenomena, there is one phenomenon to which it quite obviously *cannot* possibly be applied even in principle, and that is the mind itself. It is one thing to explain heat "naturalistically" or in materialistic terms by stripping away and ignoring its appearance – the way heat feels to us when we experience it – and redefining it as molecular motion. It is quite another thing to propose "explaining" *the feeling of heat itself* in a way that strips away and ignores its subjective, mind-dependent appearance and redefines it in terms of objectively quantifiable properties (of the firing of neurons or whatever). For in this case the phenomenon to be explained *just is*, of its very nature, subjective or mind-dependent, so that it cannot coherently be "explained" in a way that strips away or ignores the subjective appearance of the phenomenon to be explained. This would not be to "explain" the phenomenon at all, but just to ignore it or implicitly deny its existence. But "qualia" just are, by definition, these subjective or mind-dependent features, while "matter" or "physical reality" just is whatever exists independently of any mind or subjective point of view. Hence it is in principle impossible to "explain" qualia in purely material or physical terms, and any materialist attempt at such an "explanation" is really just a disguised denial of their very existence, and thus of the existence of conscious experience itself.

Far from being a desperate attempt to avoid the implications of modern science, then, dualism appears to follow necessarily from modern scientific method itself. For the reason science has "explained" almost everything other than the mind is *precisely because everything that doesn't fit the mechanistic model has been swept under the rug of the mind, treated as a mere projection.* Since the mind's role has been from the get-go to serve as a holding tank for everything that can't be assimilated to the reductionistic method, it cannot fail to be uniquely resistant to such explanation. Materialist rhetoric of the sort described above is thus a shell game. It is like confidently asserting, after one has cleaned an entire house only by sweeping all the dirt in it under a certain rug, that the gigantic dirt pile that now exists under that rug can easily be dealt with using the same method. Obviously that is the one method that cannot possibly be used to deal with the dirt; analogously, mechanistic-cum-materialistic reduction is the one method that cannot possibly be used to explain qualia.

The early modern philosophers and scientists who made this move of stripping away the appearances of things and relocating them into the mind generally realized that it had these dualistic implications. Descartes is only the best-known example. Locke (under the influence of the now less well-known Ralph Cudworth) was another, and though he was less certain that this entailed that the mind as a whole is a non-physical substance or independently existing object, he was clear that what we now call "qualia" are necessarily irreducible to and inexplicable in terms of physical properties of any sort, whether or not they somehow inhere in a physical organ like the brain.[23] This move was part and parcel of the rejection of Aristotelian formal causes, since redness, warmth, and the like, considered as they appear to our senses, are just *forms* of a kind that are particularly difficult to redefine in entirely quantifiable terms per the imperatives of the Mechanical Philosophy, and thus must (unlike motion, extension, etc.) be removed from its account of the physical world entirely.

But it is the denial of final causes that most clearly poses an absolutely insurmountable obstacle to any attempt to explain the mind in purely material terms. Final causality is about goal-directedness, orientation toward an end that need not exist. Hence the acorn has the oak as its final cause, and this remains true even though the oak does not yet exist and (if the acorn never has a chance to grow into it) may never exist. Hence each kind of efficient cause is, on an Aristotelian account, ordered to or directed toward its specific kind of effect or effects. But the human mind manifests final causality more obviously than anything else. It intends or plans actions and outcomes that do not yet exist and may never exist, but remain directed toward those actions and outcomes all the same. More generally, even where purposes and actions are not in question, the mind is characterized by what philosophers call "intentionality" (from the Latin *intendere*, to point to or aim at): it is directed toward or represents things beyond itself. For example, you can think about rocks and trees, dogs and cats, circles and squares, planets and galaxies, molecules and atoms, and in doing so your mind is, as it were, "directed toward" them or "pointing beyond itself" to them. Notice that this is so even if you have no intention of doing anything (e.g. of picking up a certain rock, petting a certain dog, or whatever). You might be simply contemplating them. ("Intentionality" is a more general phenomenon than the having of intentions to act in this or that way.) It is also so even if the things in question do not exist. You could be thinking about something that doesn't exist anymore (the World Trade Center), never existed at all (unicorns), or never will exist (a perpetual motion machine). Intentionality is regarded by many as the defining feature of the mind, the "mark of the mental," as the 19th-century philosopher Franz Brentano famously characterized it. And it should be obvious that it is simply a *conceptual impossibility* that it should ever be explained in terms of or reduced to anything material, at least as matter is understood by the advocates of the Mechanical Philosophy and their contemporary naturalistic descendents: material systems, the latter tell us, are utterly devoid of final causality; but the mind is the clearest paradigm of final causality; hence the mind cannot possibly be any kind of material system, including the brain. As Peter Geach once wrote, "When we hear of some new attempt to explain reasoning or language or choice naturalistically, we ought to react as if we were told that someone had squared the circle or proved the square root of 2 to be rational. Only the mildest curiosity is in order – how well has the fallacy been concealed?"[24]

I will have much more to say about this in the final chapter of this book, but it should be evident already why those who confidently assert that the human mind is destined to succumb to materialistic explanation manifest thereby, not any genuine under-standing of either the human mind or of science, but merely their own cluelessness. Descartes's dualism was no pre-scientific holdover; it was nothing less than the logical outcome of modern science, inevitable given the new anti-Aristotelian conception of the material world contemporary materialists hold in common with Descartes. Indeed, as prominent materialist philosophers of mind like Jerry Fodor and Joseph Levine have acknowledged, there is very little if any clear content to the materialist's idea of "matter" other than the denial that paradigmatically mental properties like intentionality and qualia can count as irreducibly material.[25] We find here a parallel to secularism – which, as we have seen, has no positive content but is merely a rejection of religion – and to mech-anism – which, as we have also seen, ultimately has no non-nego-tiable positive content, but consists in the mere denial of Aristotelian formal and final causes. And once the move in question is made, it becomes difficult even to make sense of the idea that "everything that exists is material," at least if "everything" is sup-posed to include the mind. Talk of "reducing" mind to matter or "explaining" the former in terms of the latter disguises what is real-ly an attempt to eliminate from our conception of the world every-thing that is essential to mind and to replace it with a materialistic-cum-mechanistic substitute. A "materialist explanation of the mind" is thus like a "secularist explanation of God" or a "mechanis-tic explanation of formal and final causes." Secularism doesn't "explain" God, but denies that He exists; mechanism doesn't "explain" formal and final causes, but denies that they exist; and materialism ultimately doesn't "explain" the mind at all, but implicitly denies that it exists. ("Eliminative materialism" makes this denial explicit rather than implicit. It is sometimes character-ized as an "extreme" form of materialism, but it is more accurately described as an "honest" or "consistent" form of materialism. It is also insane, and a *reductio ad absurdum* of the entire materialist proj-ect. But more on this later.)

Unless one simply denies the existence of the human mind, then, Descartes's mind-body dualism, or something like it, is inevitable, given the conception of the material world bequeathed to us by the Mechanical Philosophy. But I hasten to emphasize that

I do not say this by way of endorsement of Descartes's dualism. For while that theory is certainly less mad than materialism is, it faces grave and notorious difficulties of its own, and once again the problem stems directly from the abandonment of Aristotelianism. Recall that for Aristotle and Aquinas, the human soul is the form of a living human body, and its relation to the body is therefore to be understood as one instance among many others of "formal causation": just as the form of a rubber ball is that essence or nature which makes the parcel of rubber a ball rather a stick or a doorstop, and the form of a tree is just that essence or nature that makes the matter of the tree into a tree rather than a rock or an animal, so too is the soul just the form, essence, or nature that makes the matter of the body into a living human body rather than a tree, rock, or ball. In other words, the soul-body connection is no different from the form-matter relationship existing everywhere else in nature. But Descartes rejects formal and final causes, and thus cannot explain the connection between soul and body in these terms. He thinks of the soul not as a form – merely one component of a complete substance – but as a kind of substance or complete object in its own right, only immaterial rather than material. Its relationship to the body must therefore be understood in terms of what Aristotle called "efficient causation" rather than formal causation. And, especially given that even Aristotle's notion of efficient causation was severely attenuated by the moderns in the ways described earlier, this seems to imply that we are now somehow supposed to think of the soul's relationship to the body on the model of one billiard ball knocking into another.

This could not fail to make Descartes's conception of the soul seem utterly mysterious to his successors. The body and brain, like other physical objects, have length, width, depth, mass, and the other properties the Mechanical Philosophy ascribes to matter. But the soul, Descartes tells us, has none of these things. So how can they possibly get into any sort of cause-and-effect relationship with each other? Not through physical contact, obviously. Moreover, the law of the conservation of energy entails that the amount of energy in the physical universe is constant. But for the mind as understood in Descartes's sense to have any causal influence on the body, it would surely have to transfer energy into the physical universe;

and for the body to have a causal influence on the soul, it would have to transfer energy out of the physical universe. Hence the notion of souls and bodies interacting seems, if understood Descartes's way, to violate the laws of physics. Far from making for a simpler picture of reality, Descartes's abandonment of formal causes leads to paradox: it both entails that physical objects cause in us sensations of redness, greenness, warmth, coolness, etc., that are immaterial and have no resemblance to the physical things themselves, and also that there is no way in which such a causal connection could possibly exist consistent with the laws of physics.

It gets worse. In Descartes's view, what science describes, what it is about, is the physical world external to the mind. But science *itself* takes place, as it were, *within* the mind, consisting as it ultimately does of thoughts, concepts, theories, and the like (defined by their intentionality) developed on the basis of sensory evidence (defined by their sensory qualities or qualia). And given the impossibility of causal interaction between the mind and the physical world, it follows that there is no way for the scientific enterprise to get in any sort of contact with the very reality it is supposed to be studying. The Mechanical Philosophy thus entails a picture of science that ultimately makes science impossible.

Or it would do, anyway, if Descartes and other early modern philosophers hadn't brought God in to save the day. How so? Given the gap between the mind and the world just described, it is theoretically possible that the material world is totally different from the way it appears to the senses; indeed (as Descartes famously illustrates in his image of an all-powerful demon who has put into his mind the illusion that there is a material world outside it) it is even theoretically possible that there is no material world at all. And if our senses are untrustworthy and there is no material world, then arguments of the sort Aquinas uses to argue for God's existence – all of which begin with premises about the material world known through the senses – are unavailable. Hence Descartes does not use them. He appeals instead to arguments like the famous "ontological argument" of the medieval philosopher St. Anselm, which tries to demonstrate God's existence from premises that do not depend on sensory experience at all, but proceed, like a geometrical proof, from self-evident first principles. (To give a brief and oversimplified summary, the argument holds that since God, if there is one, would by definition have to be the greatest possible being, and a thing is greater if it exists in reality than if it does not, it follows that God must exist in reality. Otherwise He just wouldn't be the *greatest possible* being, which He must be by definition.) Then, having proved (he thinks) the existence of God, he appeals to God's goodness to guarantee that He made our senses to be reliable so that we can trust what they tell us when we use them to carry out our scientific investigations. Problem solved.

Or maybe not. The ontological argument, and other related arguments used by Descartes, are important and interesting, certainly far more so than ignoramuses like Dawkins and Dennett let on in their embarrassingly ill-informed dismissals of Anselm. Still, even philosophers who believe that God's existence can be demonstrated have tended to reject it – including Aquinas, who held that we could only know the truth of the ontological argument's key premise (concerning what God is by definition) if we had a direct knowledge of the divine essence, which we do not, which is why our knowledge of God must be indirect, based on our knowledge of His effects. Writers like Locke do defend something like Aquinas's argument for a First Cause, but his empiricism is ultimately incompatible with the (Aristotelian) understanding of causation that underwrites that argument, as we saw when considering Hume. And then there is Paley's flat-footed "design argument" and its successors, which, as we have seen, open themselves up to relentless pummeling by conceding the mechanistic premises of their atheistic opponents. Ironically, the Mechanical Philosophy (in this and other ways, as we shall see) made a direct appeal to God *more* necessary than it had been in the Scholastic view (which does not appeal to God to safeguard the possibility of knowledge, committed as it is to an Aristotelian understanding of causation on which the connection between the mind and the world is not especially problematic). At the same time it effectively undermined the possibility of arguing for His existence, at least on the sorts of grounds favored by thinkers like Aristotle and Aquinas.

Without God to solve the "interaction problem" vis-à-vis mind and body, it became increasingly tempting to try somehow to reduce mind to matter, so that the problem of explaining how they get in contact with one another would disappear. And yet the whole idea of reducing mind to matter is incoherent, especially given the conceptions of both mind and matter entailed by the Mechanical Philosophy. (For reasons only some of which we've seen. We'll look at some others later, and I discuss the whole field of philosophy of mind in much greater detail in my book *Philosophy of Mind*. I'm a wizard with the creative book titles, no?) Thus was invented the famous "mind-body problem": It seems that mind cannot possibly be reduced to matter; and yet it also seems that the mind could not possibly interact with the material world in the way it does if it was not itself material. How to resolve this paradox? That's the problem. It has appeared to some philosophers to be unsolvable; and it *is* unsolvable if one clings pathologically (as contemporary philosophers do) to the mechanistic assumptions that created the problem in the first place. The only way to solve it is to return to the Aristotelian-Thomistic conception of the soul as the form of the body, having certain immaterial operations but nevertheless "interacting" with the material world as a *formal* rather than an efficient cause.

Universal acid

The mind-body problem is only the beginning of sorrows. A thousand other weeds have sprouted in the soil fertilized by the works of Bacon, Hobbes, Descartes, Locke, Hume, and Co., and they are very poisonous ones indeed. Like the mind-body problem, they are commonly referred to as "traditional" problems of philosophy, but also like that problem, they are in fact, for the most part, of relatively recent vintage, arising only as a result of the moderns' rejection of key classical, and especially Aristotelian, metaphysical categories. Here are some examples.

A. The problem of skepticism: Recall that in the Aristotelian conception of the soul, when the intellect knows something outside it, one and the same form exists both in the intellect and the thing known. For example, when you perceive or think about triangles, the very same essence or nature – triangularity – that exists in actual triangles also exists in your mind. A kind of union between the mind and its object occurs by virtue of their sharing a form, nature, or essence that is irreducible to either of them. This is what makes knowledge possible: there is no gap between the form as it exists in the mind and as it exists in the object, because these are the same form.

But the moderns rejected formal causation, and with it this picture of knowledge. There is for them no question of one and the same form or essence coming to exist in both mind and reality. Rather, there exist in the mind various "representations" of external objects, whose relationship to those objects is analogous to the way a painting or photograph pictures something, or perhaps to the way words and sentences describe or refer to something. The "mental representation" is one particular thing, and its object is another particular thing of an entirely different type, there being no common universal form or nature shared between them. Knowledge involves a causal relationship between these two particular things, where the kind of causation in question is efficient causation rather than formal causation – again, think of one billiard ball knocking into another. The mind knows the object represented when the "mental representation" is caused "in the right way."

One problem with this is that we need some explanation of how a "mental representation" comes to be a *representation* in the first place – that is, how it comes to have "intentionality" – and for reasons alluded to above (and to be explored in more detail in the next chapter), there is no way this can be explained on a mechanistic-cum-materialistic conception of the world. But there is also a notorious problem of explaining how we could possibly know, even in principle, whether our "mental representations" *have* in fact been caused by the things they purportedly represent. For example, you take yourself to be reading this book– that is how your mind "represents" the world to you right now – but how do you know that this "representation" is really being caused by a book, by light from the book striking your retinas, etc.? Maybe it is being caused instead by mad scientists who have your brain hooked up to a supercomputer which is running a virtual-reality program, feeding into your brain a non-stop series of hallucinations that are indistinguishable from reality, as in movies like *The Matrix* and *Vanilla Sky*. Indeed, maybe that is what your entire life has been, unbeknown to you. There seems to be no way even in principle to rule this possibility out. For a painting or photograph will look the same whether or not the things it represents are real; and by the same token, any "mental representation" would also "look" the same whether or not the things it represents are real.

The modern metaphysical picture entailed by mechanism, especially when conjoined with nominalism, thus opens up an unbridgeable "gap" between mind and reality.[26] There are in this view only diverse particular things, and no universals; and they are related by chains of efficient causes, not by formal or final causality. Why some of these things should faithfully "represent" others (or even "represent" anything at all, but let that pass for now) becomes totally mysterious. They have no shared formal causes to unite them. Nor can any appeal to efficient causation help, especially when, as in modern philosophy, it is detached from final causality. For there is no end- or goal-directedness in any cause on the modern view, and thus no reason for it to be ordered to the production of one effect rather than another. Causes and effects become, as Hume put it, "loose and separate," anything being in principle capable of producing anything else. Hence there can be no reason to suppose that a particular "mental representation" has to have been generated by some particular cause, not even by the thing it is a representation of.[27]

One sorry byproduct of all of this is that generations of hapless Philosophy 101 students have come to think that philosophy is fundamentally about wondering whether the table in front of you really exists. And this sort of radical skepticism about the mind's capacity to know the world outside it really does become a serious theoretical problem when one takes the standard modern philosophical assumptions for granted. Of course, few people are inclined to take such skeptical doubts seriously in practical life. But many people *are* inclined to take seriously the relativist view that all belief systems are "socially constructed" and that none of them represents reality more accurately than any other. This view too rests on the modern assumption that knowledge involves a system of "representations" which can in principle float entirely free of the reality they purportedly represent. The difference between the man who thinks he can't know whether the table in front of him really exists and the man who thinks that science is no more objectively true than voodoo, is just that the first man is considering the possibility that the "representations" in his own individual mind might not match up to reality, and the second is considering the possibility that the "representations" which comprise a complex belief system shared by many minds might not match up to reality. Relativism is thus on all fours with skepticism about our ability to know whether tables, chairs, etc., are real. Defenders of science rightly condemn relativism, but few of them realize that the modern philosophical assumptions they are themselves typically committed to, and in terms of which they interpret the results of empirical science, are precisely what lead to skepticism and relativism in the first place.

B. The problem of induction: Relativism is hardly the only challenge to empirical science opened up by the anti-Aristotelian philosophical assumptions that most modern philosophers (and most modern scientists too, in their philosophical moments) take for granted. As noted already, when formal and final causality are abandoned, causes and effects become "loose and separate," and there is no objective reason why any cause should produce such-and-such an effect or range of effects, or why any effect should have been produced by such-and-such a cause. Thus we are led into the famous "problem of induction": How can we know that what we haven't observed is like what we have observed? How can we know that the future will resemble the past? If we can't know these things, then science is obviously impossible, since it is in the business of describing the world in general (both the observed and unobserved portions) and making predictions on the basis of that description. But if things have no shared forms or essences (formal causality) and nothing intrinsically points beyond itself toward anything else (final causality), then, to repeat, how can we possibly infer from the things we observe to the things we don't, or from the past and present to the future?

That, at any rate, is the "problem of induction" as Hume left us with it. (Once again we see that a so-called "traditional problem of philosophy" goes back only to the early moderns, who, unlike the ancients and medieval, *created* problems rather than solved them.) The 20th-century philosopher Nelson Goodman famously posed a related puzzle, which goes roughly like this. Let us say that something is "grue" if it has been observed to be green before a certain time (say January 1, 2010), and observed to be blue after that time. Now emeralds are obviously green, and we suppose that they will still be green when 2010 arrives. But why do we not assume instead that they are grue, and thus will be blue after 2010? After all, the evidence we have so far for their being green is also evidence that they are grue. The puzzle is notoriously difficult to solve; and I submit that without the acknowledgment that things have formal and final causes (for example, that greenness is part of the form or essence of emeralds and that causal processes like those which produce emeralds are ordered toward a definite range of outcomes) it cannot be solved. It is no surprise that it should have been discovered by Goodman, who was one of the foremost nominalists in 20th century philosophy.

C. *Personal identity*: A human being, in the Aristotelian-Thomistic view, is a composite of form and matter, the soul just being the form of the matter of the body. Now any material thing is bound to fail perfectly to instantiate its form in some respect or other. An oak tree might be stunted in its growth due to disease or to some external circumstance, but it is still an oak, for it still has the form of an oak and not of some other kind of thing, even if it does not instantiate that form perfectly. (Recall the analogy with a painting, which might still be a portrait of the Mona Lisa even if it becomes scratched up and torn.) A human being is no different. He may lose or even be born without a certain limb, say, but he is still a human being, since he still has the form of a human being even if he doesn't instantiate it perfectly. Specifically, a human being has the form of a rational animal, even if (due to brain damage, say) he fails perfectly to instantiate that form. Hence Terri Schiavo, as I have said, was still a rational animal even though given her condition she could no longer exercise her capacity for rationality. But a rational animal just is a kind of *person*; hence Terri Schiavo was still a person, with all the rights any person has, including a right to be provided by those in whose care she was with the normal means of sustenance any human being needs, i.e. food and water.

That, at any rate, follows from an Aristotelian-Thomistic conception of human nature. But suppose one abandons this conception, as the early modern philosophers did. Then we get something called the "problem of personal identity" (yet another "traditional" problem of philosophy which is really entirely modern); and we also get, after several centuries of gradually following out the logical implications of this abandonment, a circumstance where an obscenely large number of Terri Schiavo's fellow human beings could get themselves to believe that starving her to death wouldn't constitute murder.

If there are no formal causes, then the soul is not the form of the body, not a principle of unity that ensures that a person remains the same person throughout all the changes he undergoes as he gains, loses, and rearranges his various component parts. All that exist are the parts themselves, and though they may form a more or less stable configuration, even this stability cannot provide a clear principle of unity given that in the absence of final causes none of the component parts is inherently ordered toward the functioning of the whole of which it is a component. All of this remains true whether one thinks (as Descartes did) that one of the parts in question is an immaterial one, or supposes instead (as materialists do) that they are all material.

In Descartes's case, this leads inevitably to a complete dissociation of persons from their bodies. For the soul, in his view, is not the form of the body but an independent substance in its own right, imperceptible to the senses and only contingently – and as we have seen, utterly mysteriously – related to the body. Moreover, the soul is the real person, being that which has what is most distinctive of persons, their capacity for rationality. So, man is no longer a rational *animal* on Descartes's view, but rather an immaterial "thing that thinks," his rationality divorced from his animal aspects. Accordingly, being imperceptible, a person's soul – and thus, strictly speaking, the person himself – disappears from the world of the senses. All we ever observe or can observe are people's bodies, not their souls, not *them*. How we can ever know whether other minds or persons even exist at all thus becomes problematic.

Locke rejected Descartes's belief in an immaterial substance and instead identified a person with his stream of consciousness, though he too dissociated persons from their bodies. For you to continue to exist tomorrow or next year is not in his view for an immaterial substance or even a body to persist from now until then, but rather just for someone then existing to be able to remember doing what you are doing now; and that person might, in theory anyway, even be someone in another body from the one you are in now, if somehow your consciousness "jumps" from one body to another. (Various qualifications have to be added to this to make it remotely plausible, but that is the basic idea.) Other theorists focused instead on the body itself as the key to personal identity, holding that a person continues to exist as long as his body does, or at least as long as some crucial part of it (such as the brain) does. Yet others have held that some combination of psychological elements (memories, personality traits, and the like) and bodily ones constitutes a person and that they must all persist together for the person himself to persist.

The history of these developments is complicated, but as materialism and naturalism have driven Descartes's belief in immaterial substance off the philosophical stage, one result of modern philosophical thinking about the nature of personal identity has been a tendency toward skepticism about the very concept of a person. This has been facilitated by an obsessive focus on various bizarre scenarios that views like Locke's seem to make possible at least in theory. For example, suppose that everything about your mind is (as many materialists assume) somehow encoded in your brain, and that by scanning your brain a sufficiently powerful computer could "read off" the contents of your mind. Then we can imagine that your consciousness could be "downloaded" by this computer, after your death, into a new brain and body cloned from yours. In such a case, Locke would say, you would continue to exist in a new form, since the person that wakes up in this new body would have all your memories, and thus would just be you. But now suppose that *two* new bodies are cloned and the computer "downloads" your consciousness into each of them. Which one would be you? Locke's theory would seem to imply that both of them would be. But that can't be right. For suppose one of these clones kills the other. If they were literally the same person, it would follow that one and the same person would be both dead and alive at the same time. Indeed, it would follow that one and the same person both successfully committed suicide (since the one clone killed "himself," i.e. the other clone) and survived his suicide attempt (since the clone who did the killing is still alive).

That is just the beginning of the paradoxes. Suppose instead that half of your brain is surgically removed, preserved alive in some kind of nutrient bath, and stored in a vault somewhere. Suppose also that you survive this operation and remain capable of some measure of consciousness, however impaired. No doubt Locke would say that you, as a person, still exist. Now suppose that the other half of your brain is eventually taken from the vault and transplanted in some other person's body, and that the person who wakes up from this operation has many of your memories and personality traits. Would this person in some sense be you too? Locke might have a hard time answering, though as we've seen it would seem absurd to suggest that one and the same person can exist in two places at the same time. But other theorists would say that since this person doesn't have your original body – you still have it, even if half of your brain has been taken from it – you as you exist now are still far more closely continuous with your original self than he is, and that this is enough to show that you and you alone can claim to be the person you were before your operation. This other person only has certain parts of you (even if some of them are memories and the like) but that doesn't make him you. On this sort of view, it is only that later person who is the "closest continuer" of the original person who counts as that person. So far, so good. But now suppose that you die and this person who had received part of your brain and your memories survives. Then, suddenly, *he would* now be the "closest continuer" of the person who existed before your operation; in which case the theory would have to say that he now *is* you – even though he wasn't you just a few moments before!

Paradoxes like these have led contemporary philosophers like Derek Parfit to conclude that there really is no such thing as a "person" or a "self" as traditionally understood.[28] There are only various degrees of physical and psychological continuity between earlier and later stages of what we call "persons," but no such thing as a single abiding self which persists throughout the changes. When there is a very high degree of continuity, as there usually is in everyday circumstances, we say that "the same person" persists from moment to moment. When there is a lower degree of continuity, or when several later persons seem continuous in various respects with earlier persons (as in the bizarre thought experiments described above) we are not sure whether to say that "the same person" continues to exist or not. Either way, all that exist objectively are the various continuities and discontinuities, and whether to count these as the persistence or disappearance of a certain "person" or "self" is ultimately a matter of convention. This sort of conclusion is inevitable once we abandoned formal and final causes. If there is in the natural order no single unifying principle, no form or final cause, that unifies the various parts of a thing into a systematic whole, then *objectively* there are just the "loose and separate" parts themselves, and our classifying them as together constituting a "person" (or as constituting anything else for that matter) reflects our interests rather than any natural order of things.

Consider also that if there are no forms or essences, then there is nothing to constitute a power or capacity of thought or awareness that persists even when (due to brain damage or the like) a certain person has no way of exercising that power or capacity. There is just this or that individual episode of thought or awareness, or some continuous stream of thought or awareness. Nor, given the rejection of final causes, are these episodes ordered toward any ultimate end or goal, supernatural or otherwise; they have no purpose beyond themselves. Hence, if they have any value at all, it is only the value we give them.

The inevitable result of these various lines of thought is that it is only actual *episodes* of thought or consciousness that matter for determining when a person can be said to exist, and not any inherent *powers or capacities* for thought or consciousness, for (given the denial of formal causes) there are no such things. Moreover, the value of these episodes derives from us, not from any natural end or goal, since (given the denial of Aristotelian final causes) there are no such things as natural ends or goals either. And if we suppose there is no life beyond this one, then whatever value these episodes have must be entirely this-worldly. Furthermore, whether some entity in which these episodes of thought or consciousness take place counts as a "person" or not is ultimately a matter of convention, of how we decide to apply the word "person." The upshot is that nothing that does not in fact manifest any episodes of thought or consciousness – such as fetuses or people in "persistent vegetative states" – can plausibly count as a person; or at least, we have every reason (on this view) to adjust our usage of "person" so that it does not cover them. And even if fetuses and PVS patients did have any such episodes, those episodes would be unlikely to be of much value; certainly fetuses and PVS patients themselves would not be capable of valuing them, and these episodes have no intrinsic value, since (again, on this view) nothing does. Moreover, people in great pain or otherwise incapable of enjoyable episodes of thought or consciousness can have no reason to value even the episodes of thought or consciousness of which they are capable; nor (if we suppose naturalism) is there any life beyond this one by reference to which these unpleasant episodes might in some way be redeemed. On the other hand, if certain non-human animals have more pleasurable states of consciousness than fetuses and PVS patients do, then maybe (so this mad line of thought continues further) we ought to afford some of them the moral status we afford to healthy and fully formed human beings. Thus is the way opened to the moral justification of killing unborn children and starving crippled women to death, while saving whales and promoting vegetarianism. And it all began with the abandonment of Aristotle by professing Christians like Descartes and Locke.

D. Free will: Unlike some of these other problems we are considering, the question of free will predates the rise of modern philosophy, but it became much more problematic afterward. In an Aristotelian-Thomistic analysis, the relationship between a choice and the action it results in can be understood as an instance of formal-cum-final causation.[29] The matter or "material cause" of the action is the sequence of neural firing patterns, muscular movements, and the like by means of which the action is carried out. The formal and final causes of the action – that which gives intelligible structure to the movements – is just the soul considered as a kind of form, and in particular the activities of thinking and willing that are distinctive of the soul's intellective and volitional powers. The action is free precisely because it has this as its form, rather than having the form, say, of an involuntary muscular spasm. Nor are the intellect and will themselves determined by such things as physical law, because they exist as parts of the realm of formal and final causes, not material and efficient ones.

But when formal and final causes are chucked out, intellect and will, if not themselves denied outright, must be assimilated either to Descartes's immaterial substance or to the realm of the meaningless, purposeless chains of efficient causation between material elements recognized by the Mechanical Philosophy. To take Descartes's route entails, as we have seen, making human action as unintelligible as mind-body causation is on his account. To take the materialist route entails more or less denying free will outright, unless it is simply redefined so that any action that flows from our desires counts as "free," even if those desires were themselves determined by forces outside our control (a theory known as "compatibilism" since it alleges that free will and determinism are compatible). Intellect and will are no longer formal and final causes (given that there are no such things) but rather efficient causes, reducible, like everything else (so it is claimed), to arrangements of material elements operating according to impersonal laws of nature. Hence human behavior differs in degree but not in kind from the behavior of billiard balls and soap suds. It is more complicated, but no less determined by blind physical forces. In how he acts as well as in what he is made of, man becomes, for the moderns, a machine, a "robot" like the pseudo-Francine of Cartesian legend, made of flesh and blood rather than steel and plastic but still every bit as material and mechanical.

E. Natural rights: How can such a creature be governed by a natural moral law, or be said to have natural rights? Well, he can't be; but that didn't stop some early moderns from trying vainly to show otherwise. Take the latter topic, natural rights, first. You will not find the notion in Aristotle or Aquinas, certainly not explicitly.[30] But later Scholastic thinkers did develop the idea that human beings have certain rights by nature and not just by legal convention, and as indicated in Chapter 4, this does seem to follow from any natural law theory based on Aristotelian formal and final causes. If every man has, by virtue of having the same form or nature, the same ultimate natural end (God) and various subsidiary natural ends (those associated with natural capacities like reason, procreation, and so forth), then they have the same basic moral obligations under natural law. But no one can fulfill his obligations if others may interfere with this fulfillment as they wish. Hence the same natural law that enjoins certain obligations on all of us also entails that we must not be interfered with in fulfilling them; in short, it entails that we have a *right* not to be interfered with in this way, and this is a natural right insofar as it is entailed by the natural law. This entails in turn various specific rights, such as the right an innocent man has not to be killed or maimed, since his life and his faculties were given to him by nature for the purpose of realizing various natural ends.

Now, what becomes of natural rights if there are no formal or final causes, and thus no universal human nature nor any natural ends or purposes by reference to which rights get their point? Hobbes is the most clear-sighted about this: In the state of nature, he says – "nature" being understood now in the mechanist sense, not the Aristotelian one – everyone has the "right" to do anything he wants, including killing, stealing from, and otherwise harming others; that is to say, no one has any rights at all in the *moral* sense of the term, for there is no moral law, but only an amoral universal permissiveness. Morality has to be invented by us in order to stave off the nightmarish social chaos this would entail. Locke, to the credit of his heart if not his head, will have none of this. There is a natural law even in the state of nature, he insists. Its source is God's ownership of us. Since God created us, we are His property, and thus anyone who harms another human being in his life, liberty, and possessions effectively violates God's property rights. Strictly speaking, then, it is not we who have any rights over ourselves, but rather God who has all the rights. In a derivative sense, though, we can be said to have natural rights. For example, since, in order to respect God's property, I am obligated not to harm you, it is *as if* you had a right not to be killed, maimed, enslaved, or stolen from. Hence talk of natural rights can serve as a useful shorthand for our obligations as stewards of what belongs to God.

As with Descartes's account of knowledge, God now takes center stage in a way He had not in the Aristotelian-Thomistic tradition. In that tradition, appeal to formal and final causes can all by itself take us very far in determining the grounds and content of morality. Since Locke rejects this metaphysical grounding, though, he has no choice but to go straight to God to find any plausible source of moral obligation. Unfortunately, he also effectively undermines the possibility of carrying out this strategy successfully. For one thing, Locke's empiricist theory of knowledge is, as Hume would later show, incompatible with the notion of causation underlying arguments for God as a first cause of the world (the only sort of argument Locke himself seems to put any stock in). For another thing, even an appeal to God cannot solve the problem Locke's rejection of Aristotle has made for him. To know how to respect God's property, we need to know what counts as misuse or destruction of that property. Does picking and eating an apple count as misuse or destruction of God's property? Or chopping down a tree to build a house? Presumably not, and in fact these are for Locke paradigm cases of using the resources God gave us in line with His purposes. Famously, he develops an entire theory of property on the idea that we can acquire something by mixing our labor with the resources God has given us. The trouble is that we need to know what counts as "mixing" labor rather than wasting it, what counts as using something in line with God's purposes rather than frustrating those purposes, and so forth. And short of appeal to a divine revelation – which would turn Locke's theory into a theological one rather than a natural law theory – there is no plausible way to know these things if there are no final causes in nature.

As always with the moderns, it gets worse. Locke is a conceptualist; he thinks universals exist only in the mind, having no basis in objective reality. Forms or essences are made by man, not determined by nature. But as Jeremy Waldron has pointed out, in that case Locke seems effectively to undermine his claim that human beings have equal rights.[31] For as with every other form, essence, or nature, the form, essence, or nature of *human beings too* would have to be man-made, on Locke's account. And if you say that every human being has various natural rights which cannot be overridden by any other human being or government, but then go on to say that what *counts* as a human being in the first place is ultimately a matter of human convention, then you have made natural rights claims utterly vacuous. "Every human being has natural rights which we can't take away." Hooray! "But we get to decide who is a human being and who isn't." Oh. The modern elements in

Locke's philosophy inevitably destroy the more traditional ones. He takes back with his left hand what he has given with his right. And this pattern has continued for roughly three centuries. As the consequences of the moderns' rejection of classical metaphysics have been gradually drawn out, Western thought and Western culture have moved farther and farther away from what Western civilization, and indeed most human beings in every culture, had historically regarded as obvious moral truths.

F. Morality in general: Contemporary intellectuals would, of course, regard this as "progress." But that it is not progress is evident from the fact that the rejection of classical metaphysics undermines not only some particular moral code, but morality as such. At one level, this should be obvious. To deny that there are any formal or final causes in the natural world is implicitly to deny that there is any objective standard of goodness in that world either. If there is no such thing as a form or essence by reference to which a thing (including a person or an act) can be judged a better or worse specimen of its type, there is no sense to be made of its being objectively "good" or "bad" at all. If there is no natural end or point to a thing (again, including a person or an act) then there is nothing by reference to which it can be judged objectively "right" or "wrong."

Hume, always adept at drawing mad conclusions from mad premises, saw this, as did Hobbes. For the Humean, all value is subjective; that is to say, it exists only relative to the one doing the valuing. Reason, the "slave of the passions," can tell us what we must do to further the realization of whatever it is we value, and it can tell us whether the pursuit of some values would be consistent with the realization of others, but it cannot tell us what ultimate values we ought to have, since (in the absence of forms or essences of either a Platonic or Aristotelian sort) there just is nothing there in mind-independent reality for reason to grasp as an objective standard of goodness. Certain values tend to be widespread, and this generates the illusion that morality is objective, but of course, the fact that an illusion is widespread does not make it any less an illusion. And if those values should for whatever reason become less widespread, then all we can say is that what we count as morality has changed. It has not moved either farther away from what is objectively good or closer to it, for there is no such thing as objective goodness. The now-widespread horror of slavery cannot on this view be counted a moral advance, nor the widespread acceptance of fornication and homosexuality a moral regression. Objectively speaking, they are just different attitudes, and that's it. And should most people sincerely come to believe that it would be good to kill unwanted infants, or unwanted toddlers or teenagers, or unwanted old or sick people, or unwanted *anyone* for that matter – Jews, blacks, Catholics, Muslims, whomever – then that too, on this view, would simply be a different set of subjective moral evaluations, objectively neither better nor worse than any other.

Now Hume himself did think that many of the moral attitudes we have are somehow "natural" to us, and that even many of the ones that aren't are likely to arise in any culture given their utility in facilitating social life; he wasn't claiming that such attitudes are as arbitrary and ephemeral as fashions in clothing. But "natural" for a Humean cannot mean what it means in the mouth of a Plato, Aristotle, or Aquinas, but only the sort of thing an inheritor of the mechanistic picture of the world could possibly mean by it: "statistically common," or "conducive to inclusive fitness," or something equally devoid of normative force. And for that reason the Humean has nothing to say to the sociopath who simply happens not to share these attitudes, other than that he is not like most people. Nor does he really have anything to say to a group of sociopaths – Nazis, communists, jihadists, pro-choice activists, or whomever – who seek to remake society in their image, by social or genetic engineering, say. The Platonist, Aristotelian, or Thomist can say that such people are behaving in an inherently irrational and objectively wicked manner, given human nature. All the Humean can say is "Gee, hope they don't succeed."

Lots of people think more or less Hume's way these days, though they would like if possible to avoid making our horror of murder out to be *merely* a cultural prejudice, and they would really *really* like to count acceptance of fornication and homosexuality as an advance and not just a difference, which a consistent Humean has no business doing. This no doubt partially accounts for the resurgence of interest in Hobbes's moral theory, such as it is. Given the nastiness of the state of nature as Hobbes conceives of it – "solitary, poor, nasty, brutish, and short" and all that – he argues that rationally self-interested persons would agree to a social contract the terms of which would require renouncing the "right" to do whatever you feel like doing to the other parties to the agreement. For Hobbes it would also require submitting oneself to an absolutist government, and no one wants to defend this part of his theory today. But many are keen on his basic idea that morality consists in nothing other than whatever rules rationally self-interested persons would agree to following, as conducive to their "mutual advantage." We all benefit from not being killed; so a rule against murder would be accepted by all parties to the social contract. But lots of people want to have sex without the bother of getting married, so a rule against fornication is out. Etc., etc. A "lowest common denominator" system of morality follows pretty much automatically, and every social change in a "live and let live" direction can thereby be seen as a moral advance. So, you can indulge your every sensual appetite *and* still feel morally superior to those who disapprove of this. Ain't modern philosophy grand?

Obviously, though, this isn't morality at all, but just a non-aggression pact between self-interested bundles of impulse and willfulness, with the myriad petty Hitlers and Stalins who populate the Hobbesian jungle of today out, not for anything big like dividing up Poland, but only something simple and less messy – like, say, our agreeing to look the other way as they cheat on their wives, smoke dope, sodomize each other, or kill their unborn children. There would on this "contractarian" theory be nothing *in principle* wrong with kidnapping a child, raping and killing him, and dumping the body on his parents' lawn, if that's how you get your kicks; it's just that most people will hate you and hunt you down if you do this, so it's prudent to go along with a general policy that rules out that sort of high-jinks. Of course, this is a monstrous and evil way of looking at human life, so theorists who advocate it usually try to sweeten the pill by suggesting that since others will distrust anyone who seems insincere or too coldly calculating in his decision to abide by the social contract, a rationally self-interested person will cultivate a sensibility of valuing morality for its own sake, so that he will be *accurately* perceived as a reliably decent fellow. As the old joke has it, "sincerity is everything; if you can fake that, you've got it made." To which the contemporary kinder, gentler Hobbesian adds, "and if you can fake yourself out too, even better!" In recent years this is often spiced up with a trendy appeal to the "results" of "evolutionary psychology"; here as elsewhere, evolution is the talisman to wave if you want people just to shut up and accept what you're saying as "scientific."

Clearly, none of this is at all to the point, for even if it were true to say that it "pays" to pretend that there is such a thing as morality, and even if we were somehow hardwired by evolution to be inclined toward such pretense, that would not change the fact that, given a modern mechanistic-cum-materialistic view of the world, this would inevitably be *nothing more* than a pretense, with morality itself being an illusion. Moreover, while neo-Hobbesian theorists might find it easier to sleep at night believing their theory succeeds in propping up the few moral intuitions they've imbibed from what's left of Western Christian civilization, if it were ever to prevail in society at large the result would be disastrous. For our understanding of the grounds of morality can hardly fail to influence the seriousness with which we try to practice it. Here the natural law and divine command theories so despised by secularists must be admitted even by them to have an edge. Would you be more inclined rigorously to abide by policy X if you were truly convinced that God or nature unconditionally commands it, or if instead you were sure it was just something we feeble humans have cooked up because it is "mutually advantageous" (even if you don't see much advantage in following it yourself just now)? To ask this question is to answer it. However sincere the individual "contractarian" theorist might be in thinking that morality is entirely a human invention but one we're better off adhering to, if this attitude were ever to prevail in society at large, the result could not fail to be a widespread corruption of the moral sensibility. (The "if," of course, is meant facetiously: This attitude *has* largely prevailed, though by no means completely, which is why modern Western civilization is only *largely* a stinking cesspool, and not yet entirely one. Give the Humeans and contractarians time though.)

To be sure, there are other modern moral theories, but they inevitably collapse into mere riffs on the ones already considered. Classical utilitarianism, for example, famously regards morality as a matter of promoting "the greatest happiness for the greatest number." Nowadays the talk is all about "maximizing the satisfaction of preferences," or some other purportedly more precise substitute for happiness. Either way, the "happiness" or "preferences" in question are inevitably defined subjectively à la Hume, and it is notoriously difficult to explain *why* anyone should care about the happiness or preference satisfaction of the "greatest number" – as opposed to just his own, or that of some group he favors – without appealing to a "sentiment of generalized benevolence" or some such thing. But what happens if some people *don't* have this sentiment? We're back again to saying, "Well, they're just not like us, and we'd better make sure they don't win out." "Morality" becomes at best an assertion of the prevailing (and in principle ever-shifting) sensibilities of the majority, or at least of those with the loudest mouths. It has no ultimate basis in objective fact or in reason, but only in sentiment and existing custom.

This is, as I say, *inevitable* once one abandon's realism of the Platonic, Aristotelian, or Scholastic sort. Occasionally you'll find a clear-eyed liberal secularist who owns up to the fact, like Richard Rorty. But it is very hard for a liberal to maintain his smug pose of moral and rational superiority over traditional religious believers and other non-liberals if he admits that his ideals are just one set of ungrounded prejudices among others (though Rorty certainly gave it the old college try). And needless to say, smugness is half the fun of being a liberal (the other half being the tearing down of everything one's ancestors, and one's betters generally, worked so hard to build). So, many contemporary liberals prefer to look for inspiration to Immanuel Kant, the source of the main competing theory to utilitarianism in modern moral philosophy. Like the ancients and medievals, and unlike Hume, Kant sought to ground morality in reason rather than sentiment, though like Hume he rejected the classical metaphysics that underlay the ethical thinking of the ancients and medievals. Unsurprisingly, the result was totally unconvincing, or at least it would have been had Kant's writings not been so obscure that it is hard enough half the time to know what the hell he is saying, much less whether he's right or wrong about it.

Now Kant was not all bad. His views on sexual morality and

the death penalty, for example, are totally reactionary; that is to say, they are correct. They are for that reason a continual embarrassment to the thoroughly degenerate liberals of today, who would dearly like to quote him in favor of "freeing Mumia" and turning sodomy into a sacrament, if only they could. It is, I concede, hard to dislike a guy like that. But you should try anyway, because Kant was possibly a bigger disaster than Descartes and Hume put together, if only because he pretty much *was* Descartes and Hume put together, at least where metaphysics is concerned. Like Hume, he holds that what we think is knowledge of external physical reality is really just knowledge of the workings of our own minds themselves. This sounds like the rankest subjectivism, relativism, or skepticism, but Kant "saves" his position from this dire fate by holding that there is just something in the nature of reason itself that requires that we project onto the world the categories in terms of which we interpret it (such as causation); this is not just a contingent matter of "custom and habit" as Hume would have it, but a necessary feature of the structure of the mind, even if there is nothing in external reality that corresponds to those categories. This is supposed to soften Hume's position by marrying it to something like a "rationalism" of the sort represented by Descartes. But as we saw in Chapter 2, this sort of view (of which conceptualism and psychologism are variants) is simply incoherent.

Where morality is concerned, Kant's aim was to show that there is just something in the nature of reason itself that requires that we be moral, and that can reveal to us the content of our specific moral duties, yet without appealing to anything like human nature as it was understood by the ancients and medievals. The idea is summed up in his famous Categorical Imperative, the first formulation of which says that you should only follow a principle if you could will it to become a universal law binding on all rational beings. If you can't will this (so the argument goes), then it follows that there would be something inconsistent in following such a principle, and thus contrary to reason. Thus, reason, and not mere sentiment, can give us moral guidance. And while the Categorical Imperative as stated is purely formal, it gives us a test (so the argument continues) by means of which to evaluate any concrete principle and determine whether it is something we should follow. To take Kant's famous example, the principle "Break your promises when you might benefit from doing so" fails the test, since if everyone followed this rule, no one could trust others to keep their promises, and the whole institution of promising would soon disappear. Thus, you should never make a promise insincerely. End of story.

Or not. No one actually takes Kant's own way of understanding his theory seriously these days. For one thing, the Categorical Imperative is in fact a notoriously useless test for determining how one should act. Suppose you want to know whether to tell a lie on a certain occasion. "Tell a lie when you might benefit from doing so" isn't a rule that seems to pass Kant's test. But wouldn't "Tell a lie when it would lead to an overall good result" pass it? If so, then the Categorical Imperative gives conflicting results. Or suppose you've decided to give all your property to the poor, to forsake ever having a family or home of your own, and to devote the rest of your life ministering to the sick and dying in the streets of Calcutta or Kinshasa. Obviously, if *everyone* did this, the result would be a complete economic collapse, millions upon millions of more poor people, and indeed (if everyone gave up family life) the extinction of the human race. So would it be immoral for you to do it? Surely not. To patch up these problems with his theory, Kant would have to qualify his principle to such an extent, and make reference to so many concrete details of actual human life, that it would be obvious that there is no way he can derive morality from "reason alone," divorced from any account of human nature.

Moreover, the very idea that "reason alone," as Kant conceives of it, tells us to be moral, is sheer bluff. *Why* exactly should we believe that reason tells us to follow the Categorical Imperative – as opposed to being the "slave of the passions" (in Hume's sense) or following our rational self-interest (as Hobbes says)? Kant might respond that people like Hume and Hobbes simply misunderstand the essence or nature of reason, and if so he'd be absolutely right. But where does *Kant* of all people get off appealing to the nature or essence of reason, since his denial that we can know any objective essences or natures of things is if anything even more thoroughgoing than that of his predecessors? The whole Kantian project is a complete muddle from start to finish. (Again, see Chapter 2 for the executive summary.)

So, these days there isn't much Kant in the Kantianism of liberals who look to him as the great hero of the "Enlightenment." They still thrill to Kantian talk of "autonomy," the "dignity of persons" as "ends in themselves," and all the other gruesome fortune-cookie expressions of modern man's self-worship that we owe to this "catastrophic spider" (as Nietzsche so accurately summed up Kant). But their *arguments* for the ideas lying behind these slogans are not the sort Kant himself would put any stock in. Following John Rawls, they tend to see moral reasoning as an exercise in bringing our "moral intuitions" into "reflective equilibrium" by considering what principles the parties to a social contract would agree to follow, and where this contract scenario differs from Hobbes's by taking for granted that the parties already regard each other as having moral worth. In other words, the contract doesn't create morality, but rather merely expresses a deeper understanding of the "respect for persons" that already exists between the parties prior to the contract. "Well, OK," you might say, "but what justifies the key presupposition that people *really have* moral worth in the first place?" That, of course, is the $64 question. And the answer seems always to be just to repeat that these are "intuitions" we all have, or at least that all decent people have. And they're not mere desires or sentiments, you see, but somehow something more cognitive than that, though they're not cognitions of biological or other natural facts, and certainly not of anything like Aristotelian formal or final causes. Still, we are assured, they are "considered intuitions" (as the jargon has it), which, when you examine it, really boils down to little more than "intuitions we liberals find we still just have even after people try to talk us out of them." And what about people who don't share these intuitions? Well, you know, we'd just better make sure such people don't win out. In other words, we're back once again to a basically Humean-Hobbesian subjectivist account of morality, only the subjectivism is buried under heavy dollops of Kantian verbiage and obscurantist talk of "intuitions."

The bottom line is that by abandoning formal and final causes, modern philosophy *necessarily* denied itself any objective basis for morality. If nothing is objectively *for* anything – if nothing has any inherent goal, end, or purpose – then *reason* is not objectively "for" anything either, including the pursuit of the good. Hence there *cannot possibly* be any way of grounding morality rationally. And if there are no essences or forms in the sense affirmed by classical realists (whether Platonic, Aristotelian, or Scholastic), then there is no sense to be made of the good as an objective feature of reality anyway. The good becomes a function of our subjective preferences, desires, sentiments, or "intuitions," and reason is "for" whatever we want it to be for, which may or may not include the pursuit of what has traditionally been called "morality." *There is just nothing else for the good or for reason to be* if one follows the mechanistic line. Like causation, or free will, or knowledge, or the concept of a person, or the idea of natural human rights, morality in general becomes an illusion, a "projection" or convenient fiction at best, when one follows through consistently the implications of the moderns' anti-Aristotelian revolution. Indeed, insofar as personhood and free will are themselves necessary prerequisites to morality, the very possibility of a rational system of ethics is *triply* undermined by the moderns. Successfully grounding morality in reason requires putting oneself in the company of Plato, Aristotle, and Aquinas, and thus taking on board formal and final causes, immutable human nature, God, the soul, the natural law, the whole ball of wax. Awful luck, I know, for the sort of people who find the highest expression of human dignity in bathhouses, abortion clinics, and needle-exchange programs, but there it is.

Daniel Dennett once characterized Darwinism as a "universal acid" that eats through everything it touches, relentlessly undermining ancient philosophical ideas and commonsense assumptions alike.[32] As usual, Dennett gets no further than being half right, though in this case he does at least get that far. It is really the mechanistic-cum-naturalistic world picture of which Darwinism is merely a component that is the universal acid, and while Dennett's characterization was put forward in a triumphalist spirit, the truth is that the "acid" is so strong that it eats away, not only at the rational foundations of religion, but even things naturalists claim to value, such as morality. Secularists like the "New Atheists" fail to see this, for two reasons. First, they assume that the very existence of their own passionately held moral beliefs is sufficient evidence that atheism is compatible with morality. But it is no such thing. The question isn't whether an atheist has or can have various moral values or a morally decent character (apart from his irreligiousness, of course, which is, as we saw in the previous chapter, a very serious vice). Of course he can. The question is whether morality can be given an *objective rational foundation* on atheistic or naturalistic premises, and the answer is that it cannot. An atheist or naturalist can *believe* in morality – that is a psychological fact – but he *cannot* have a *rational justification* for his belief – that is a philosophical fact. For the premises required to ground morality also entail a theistic and generally non-naturalistic view of the world.

Secondly, secularists have so fallen in love with the idea of their own superior rationality and moral virtue that they simply cannot imagine that these things cannot be established on the metaphysical assumptions on which they've staked their ground. Well, fellas, get used to disappointment. For not only is morality (and thus your moralistic preening) impossible to justify on your own premises, but – for reasons we've hinted at and will explore in more detail in our final chapter – reason itself goes by the board as well.

Back to Plato's cave

The standard one-line summary of the Enlightenment goes like this: Because religion is based on blind faith, the founders of modern Western thought sought to free science and philosophy from its irrational embrace, to reduce or eliminate its influence on public life, and to re-orient even private life toward improving this world rather than preparing for an illusory afterlife. As we have seen, this has things almost precisely backwards. In fact the moderns didn't reject religion for resting on blind faith; it would be truer to say that they falsely accused it of resting on blind faith so that they could justify their rejection of it, and cooked up a new conception of what should count as "rational" in the hope of making the accusation stick. More precisely, their desire to re-orient human life toward this world and reduce the influence of religion led the early modern thinkers to abandon traditional philosophical categories and to re-define scientific method so that reason could no longer provide religion with the support it had always been understood to give it, at least not in any robust way. The groundwork for some of this was inadvertently laid by medieval thinkers like Ockham and by the

Protestant Reformation; and some early modern thinkers were less hostile to religion than others, and even wanted to preserve core elements of it. But the philosophical assumptions the modern thinkers all came to hold in common, and in particular their hostility to the key metaphysical doctrines of classical philosophy in general and Aristotelianism in particular, had an inherent tendency to undermine the traditional philosophical case for the existence of God, the immortality of the soul, and the natural law. Hence, while the rational credentials of religion are obvious and undeniable when one interprets it in classical and especially Aristotelian-Thomistic terms, they become highly problematic when looked at through modern philosophical lenses. And the moderns were able to insinuate that the latter lenses are the only ones now available by alleging that modern science has somehow "refuted" Aristotelian metaphysics. This falsehood transformed what was in reality merely a highly contingent, controversial, and problematic methodological stipulation into a "discovery," and made what was and is a dispute between rival metaphysical worldviews appear instead to be a "war between science and religion." Since any lie repeated long and loudly enough will come to seem the plain truth, the conventional wisdom about religion today is that it is and always has been without serious intellectual foundation, or at least any that is still viable. This myth is sustained by nothing more than rhetorical sleight of hand facilitated by a general ignorance of the history of ideas, even among philosophers, scientists, and other intellectuals, most of whom know nothing about what the medieval thinkers really said and thought, relying instead on potted caricatures having no more foundation in historical fact than the pious legends Parson Weems told about George Washington.

The costs of this centuries-long scam have been enormous. It has completely pulverized the intellectual foundations, not only of religion, but of any possible morality, and indeed of science itself (though this latter pulverization – discussed only in passing so far, but to be considered in more detail in our final chapter – often goes unnoticed precisely because it was done in the name of science). It has led to a debasement of man the most brutal realizations of which were National Socialism and Marxism, but which is evident too, albeit in a more subtle and seductive way, in the liberal West's

}222{

crass consumerism and 57 varieties of reductionistic psychology, from pop to Pinker. Whether you prefer your economic and Darwinian reductionism in jackboots (à la Stalin and Hitler) or pocket protectors and turtleneck sweaters (after the fashion of academic economists and evolutionary psychologists), human beings are in every case reduced to congeries of mechanical forces. As we will see, this vision is not only disgusting and dehumanizing, it is utterly incoherent. And it has been accompanied in the West by a now almost complete reversal of the system of morality outlined in Chapter 4, a system which, in its essentials anyway, the vast majority of human beings who have ever lived would have understood completely and taken for granted as obvious.

These results have come about slowly and gradually, over the course of centuries, precisely because they are so radically contrary to common sense that for much of the history of modernity most Western thinkers tried in vain to avoid or soften the implications of the new anti-Aristotelian philosophy. The twentieth century saw these implications reach full bloom, in the rise of the totalitarian political ideologies and in the "Great Disruption" in morals (as Francis Fukuyama has called it) just alluded to. The prevalence of abortion and the push for "same-sex marriage" are examples of the latter phenomenon emphasized by traditional religious believers, not because of any obsession with sex – as I have noted already, whatever obsession there is here is all on the side of liberals and secularists – but rather, I think, for reasons which are entirely rational given the classical philosophical worldview I have described in this book. One of them is that these practices are straightforward assaults on the family as it has traditionally been understood (the rationale of that understanding having been surveyed in Chapter 4), and thus on the core social institution and highest non-religious end of life in this world (subordinate though it is, like everything else in this life, to knowing God in the next world).

But an even deeper reason is that they constitute assaults on the very possibility of morality in a way that even murder and theft do not. Traditionally, sodomy has been classified together with murder, oppression of the poor, and defrauding a laborer of his wages as one of the four sins that "cry out to heaven for vengeance." Liberals and secularists find this mystifying, even mad. That is partly because of their tendency to reduce all morality to conflict resolution between self-interested preference satisfiers (or whatever), and partly because they have completely forgotten what it means for there to be a natural order, and the irreplaceable role the notion of such an order plays in understanding and justifying morality. Now it is without a doubt far worse to commit murder than to commit an act of sodomy; this is not in dispute. But murder is, in most cases anyway, essentially a horrifically unjust means of fulfilling what are otherwise innocuous and perfectly natural desires and impulses: anger, or jealousy, or the desire for some piece of property, for the love of a certain man or woman, or for justice itself. Sodomy, by contrast, flows from a positively *unnatural* desire, where "unnatural," it must always be remembered, is to be understood in the classical realist sense (Platonic, Aristotelian, or Scholastic). And abortion, unlike other forms of murder, adds to the injustice of that crime something even more gravely unnatural, namely the will to destroy one's own offspring. This, I submit, is why these practices have traditionally been regarded with such horror – not because they are by themselves the worst offenses, but because in their very unnaturalness they constitute an affront to the foundations of morality that even an ordinary murder does not. If there is no such thing as a natural order (again, in the classical realist sense) then there can be no basis for morality at all. But those who commit an act of sodomy or abortion seem to thumb their nose at the very idea of a natural order, to put themselves above and beyond it.

My aim here is not to catalogue the innumerable pathologies of contemporary Western society. Others have done so at length, and the pathologies in question are in any event blindingly obvious to anyone sympathetic to the classical philosophical worldview I've been describing in this book. Indeed, from such a traditional standpoint contemporary Western civilization, or at least its liberal-progressive "mainstream," cannot fail to seem a stinking cesspool of wickedness and irrationality. There was a time when even many liberals would have agreed with this judgment. Had you told a William Gladstone or even a John F. Kennedy that the liberalism of the future would be defined by abortion on demand and "same-sex marriage," and that its *avant-garde* would be contemplating infanticide, bestiality, and necrophilia, they would have thought you mad.

Certainly if you could have convinced them that this is the sort of thing to which their principles were leading, they would have been moved to do a serious rethink. But we are well past the time when slippery-slope arguments might be used to try to shock a liberal or a secularist out of his folly. You can no longer attempt the *reductio ad absurdum* with him, for he will now simply embrace with enthusiasm any absurdity that follows from his premises and thank you for suggesting it to him. He is well through the looking glass, his mind and his moral sensibility so thoroughly corrupted that to him it is obvious that black is white, up is down, sodomy is marriage, and scraping a fetus from its mother's womb is compassion. After a centuries-long climb up to the light that began with the ancient Greeks and culminated in the philosophy of Thomas Aquinas, modern man began a descent that has ended with the contemporary secularist lost once again in the bowels of Plato's cave, as blind as the pathetic denizens described in the *Republic* and as certain of his own rightness and of the madness and evil of those who would try to free him from his delusions.

In an article in *The Atlantic Monthly* in 1948, the then-eminent (if now largely forgotten) philosopher W.T. Stace – an empiricist who was not himself in sympathy with the Aristotelian-Scholastic philosophy I've been defending – said this about the moderns' decision to abandon that philosophy:

> The real turning point between the medieval age of faith and the modern age of unfaith came when the scientists of the seventeenth century turned their backs upon what used to be called "final causes". . . [belief in which] was not the invention of Christianity [but] was basic to the whole of Western civilization, whether in the ancient pagan world or in Christendom, from the time of Socrates to the rise of science in the seventeenth century. . . . They did this on the ground that inquiry into purposes is useless for what science aims at: namely, the prediction and control of events. . . . The conception of purpose in the world was ignored and frowned upon. *This, though silent and almost unnoticed, was the greatest revolution in human history, far outweighing in importance any of the political revolutions whose thunder has reverberated through the world. . . .* The world, according to this new picture, is purposeless, senseless, meaningless.

Nature is nothing but matter in motion. The motions of matter are governed, not by any purpose, but by blind forces and laws. . . . [But] if the scheme of things is purposeless and meaningless, then the life of man is purposeless and meaningless too. Everything is futile, all effort is in the end worthless. A man may, of course, still pursue disconnected ends, money, fame, art, science, and may gain pleasure from them. But his life is hollow at the center. Hence, the dissatisfied, disillusioned, restless, spirit of modern man. . . . Along with the ruin of the religious vision there went the ruin of moral principles and indeed of all values. . . . If our moral rules do not proceed from something outside us in the nature of the universe – whether we say it is God or simply the universe itself – then they must be our own inventions. Thus it came to be believed that moral rules must be merely an expression of our own likes and dislikes. But likes and dislikes are notoriously variable. What pleases one man, people or culture, displeases another. Therefore, morals are wholly relative.[33]

It was, in Stace's view, this purely *philosophical* revolution, and "neither the Copernican hypothesis nor any of Newton's or Galileo's particular discoveries" that was the "real cause" of the decline of religion and morality as it had traditionally been understood.[34] The argument of this book shows, I think, that Stace was right. But while as recently as the 1940s a mainstream intellectual writing in a mainstream liberal magazine could recognize that the source of modern man's radical shift in thinking about religion and morality was not science per se, but rather the early moderns' decision to replace one set of philosophical principles with another (highly contingent and challengeable) set, the contemporary intelligentsia has falsely come to regard reason, philosophy, and science *as such* to be at odds with religion and traditional morality. Whatever the reasons for this failure of philosophical and historical understanding – the hyper-specialization of contemporary academic life, the ahistorical approach Anglo-American analytic philosophers have traditionally taken toward their subject, the foolish neglect of the classical philosophical heritage by contemporary religious apologists eager to accommodate modern sensibilities – it has helped to afford the arguments of the New Atheists and other secularists a plausibility that is, however seemingly obvious, in fact wholly illusory.

The only possible remedy now left is to go back to first principles, for where ordinary commonsense judgments about what is real and what is right are concerned, there is almost no common ground left between religious believers and secularists. That is why we have had in this book to examine some fairly abstract philosophical ideas and arguments in such detail and at such length. In his abandonment of what most human beings who have ever lived, including most philosophers and scientists, have considered plain common sense with respect to matters of religion and morality, the contemporary secularist is like some paranoid autodidact who has just read Descartes's *Meditations* and seriously wonders whether he is dreaming right now, or trapped in *The Matrix* like Keanu Reeves. The man with traditional moral and religious beliefs, by contrast, is like the average person who finds such far-fetched doubts preposterous and not worth taking seriously, whether or not he has any answer to the skeptic who challenges him. Such a man, who continues to believe what his senses tell him even if he has no fancy reason for doing so, is sane; and the man who seriously doubts his senses, on the basis of what he takes to be solid rational arguments, is insane, despite his superficial rationalism. To be sure, it can be shown, through complex rational arguments, that the skeptic is wrong and the senses trustworthy. But even in the absence of such arguments, the average person is justified in dismissing the skeptic, and the skeptic is *not* justified in doubting his senses. Similarly, the ordinary religious believer is, I submit, perfectly justified in continuing to believe as he always has whether or not he has any sophisticated answer to charlatans like the New Atheists. Being asked to justify one's belief that there are purposes in the world and that a divine intelligence has put them there, or that sodomy is unnatural and therefore immoral, is like being asked to prove that you are now awake and not dreaming. You can humor such a request if you like, but the average person, at least, is under no obligation to do so, and can safely leave such eccentric worries to the philosophers. If an answer *is* to be given though, it cannot be one that rests on untutored common sense, as it could perhaps have been with earlier generations of secularists; for like a worm in an apple, the bad philosophy of the moderns, having been nibbling away for three or four centuries, has now thoroughly eaten its way through the secularist brain. The only thing that might patch up the hole, that might counteract this bad philosophy, is good philosophy.

We have already seen the essence of how this must go. When we get clear on the general metaphysical structure of reality – the distinction between actuality and potentiality, form and matter, final causality, and so forth (all of which are mere articulations or refinements of common sense, and thus on all fours with the ordinary man's belief in what his senses tell him) – we see that the existence of God, the immateriality and immortality of the soul, and the natural law conception of morality all follow. At the very least, it is very hard to avoid these conclusions once one grants the metaphysical premises in question. We have also looked at some of the arguments that support this general metaphysical picture, and noted some ways in which criticisms of it typically rest on caricatures and misunderstandings. Our final chapter completes the case by showing how that picture – and thus the religious consequences that follow from it – is *unavoidable* if we are to make sense of the one thing secularists and their critics still do have in common, at least rhetorically, namely, a commitment to reason and science.

6. Aristotle's Revenge

Pat burst in the door, having come straight from a frustrating faculty meeting. "She said 'Paul, don't speak to me, my serotonin levels have hit bottom, my brain is awash in glucocorticoids, my blood vessels are full of adrenaline, and if it weren't for my endogenous opiates I'd have driven the car into a tree on the way home. My dopamine levels need lifting. Pour me a Chardonnay, and I'll be down in a minute.'"[1]

When informed that this passage was taken from *The New Yorker*, the reader might naturally suppose it to be a caption from one of their famous cartoons, or perhaps an excerpt from a satirical fiction piece (though a satire of *what* exactly might be less clear – a couple preparing for a physiology exam or a spelling bee?) In fact, while you might well file this one under "self-satire, inadvertent," be sure to cross-reference it with "truth, stranger than fiction" and "absurd, nothing so much so that some philosopher hasn't said it." "Pat" and "Paul" are Patricia and Paul Churchland, two very real professors of philosophy at the University of California at San Diego, and their claim to fame and worthiness of a profile in the leading journal of urbane liberalism is their advocacy of "eliminative materialism," the theory that beliefs, desires, and other mental phenomena do not exist and ought to be eliminated from our description of human nature and replaced by concepts derived from neuroscience. Hence on this view, it is, strictly speaking, always *false* to say something like "I feel anxious," for "feelings" and "anxiety" are mental states, and there *are no* mental states according to eliminative materialism, only brain processes. What you should say, then, at least if you want to speak the literal scientific truth, is something like "My serotonin levels have hit bottom," etc.

How to lose your mind

If this doesn't sound utterly bizarre to you (at the *very* least), then you haven't understood it. The Churchlands are *not* saying that serotonin and dopamine levels, etc., *causally influence* feelings and moods, or that other neurological factors underlie other mental states and processes like remembering, desiring, believing, reasoning, and so forth. That would not be in the least bit new or noteworthy. They are saying instead that *there are no such things as* feelings, moods, remembering, desiring, believing, reasoning, etc. There is *only* what can be described in the technical jargon of neuroscience. In short, the mind as we think we know it *does not exist*; there is only the brain. Or rather, not as we "think" we know it, since there is (on this view) no such thing as *thinking*. Instead, our brains are just wired in such a way that we tend to make noises that sound like "I think that such-and-such" or "I feel so-and-so"; and the Churchlands just want us to stop talking that way, and instead to make other noises that sound like "The serotonin levels in my brain are . . ." (or whatever). Or rather, they don't "want" us to do this, since there is no such thing as *wanting* either (that's another would-be mental state); we should say instead that *their* brains are wired in such a way that they tend to make noises that sound like "There are no such things as mental states," etc.

As you can see, it is difficult to state this view clearly or consistently. (Actually, it is impossible to do so, as will become evident presently.) But the Churchlands give it their best shot. In fairness, they sometimes speak more cautiously, claiming only that eliminative materialism will *probably* turn out to be true, while acknowledging that we don't yet know enough about the brain entirely to replace our everyday ways of talking about our thoughts and feelings with descriptions couched in terms of neural firing patterns and brain chemistry. Still, they think we already know enough to go a long way in this direction, and in general to replace much of our commonsense understanding of the world around us with what they claim is a more accurate scientific description. For example, Paul Churchland confidently informs us that it is always false to say that people sitting around a fire "warm themselves next to [it] and gaze at the flickering flames." This is mere unscientific mumbo jumbo. The truth is rather that "they absorb some EM energy in the m range emitted by the highly exothermic oxidation reaction, and observe the turbulences in the thermally incandescent river of molecules forced upwards by the denser atmosphere surrounding."[2] When you get off a roller coaster, you shouldn't complain of a "feeling" of "dizziness" (at least if you don't want scientifically educated people to laugh at you, apparently); you should make reference instead to "a residual circulation of the inertial fluid in the semicircular canals of the inner ear."[3] And don't expect the Churchlands to feel your pain, for once again, "science" tells us that there isn't any such thing as "pain"; there are only "sundry modes of stimulation in our A-delta fibres and/or C-fibres (peripherally) , or in our thalamus and/or reticular formation (centrally)."[4] As the passage above indicates, the Churchlands apparently walk the walk themselves, and precisely by talking the talk, peppering their everyday conversations with allusions to the goings on in their nervous systems. The prurient reader might wonder what their pillow talk is like; no doubt it is not the sort of thing romance novelists or pornographers would find very marketable. (Paul Churchland does kindly relate that he and Pat have "exchanged a lot of oxytocin" over the years.[5] That's the kind of talk, apparently, that sweeps the gals off their feet down in San Diego.)

David Stove once said of people who seriously wonder whether the world fades out of existence when they stop looking at it, and spin around quickly every so often to see if they can catch it in the act of doing so, that "this may be good clean fun; and then again, it may be no fun, and bad, and unclean."[6] I can only assume, judging from the evangelical enthusiasm with which they peddle it in books and interviews, that the Churchlands find their own oddball philosophy great fun indeed. But that it is bad and unclean, indeed pathological, there can be no doubt. Not that we should be surprised that such people exist; for eliminative materialism is simply the last stop on the train leading away from Aristotelian final causes, the inevitable consequence of following out consistently a mechanistic-cum-materialistic picture of the world. But neither is it surprising that it is a minority view, even among materialists. Like liberals who say they support public schools but would never send their own children to one, most people who claim not to believe in teleology cannot bring themselves to put their money where their mouths are when their views threaten to affect them personally (and eliminative materialism, denying as it does that your thoughts, your mind, in effect *you*, exist at all, cuts pretty close to home). Unlike the Churchlands, they have sacrificed consistency, though they have also thereby preserved their sanity.

We'll return in a moment to the reasons why a consistently mechanistic worldview entails eliminative materialism. Let's first make it clear (if it isn't already) why the latter view is indeed insane. Note for starters that even if we could get through the day without using words like "think," "believe," "feel," "want," and the like, and instead made reference only to our serotonin levels and glucocorticoids (or whatever) – our every sentence sounding like something read aloud from a neurology textbook – this would not in the least entail a "conceptual revolution" of the sort the Churchlands so breathlessly look forward to, with the concept of mind entirely eliminated in favor of concepts drawn from brain science. When a forest ranger sees smoke rising over the hillside and shouts "Fire!" he has not "eliminated" the concept of smoke and replaced it with the concept of fire. When a journalist reports that "Washington threatened Libya with retaliation" though in fact it was the Secretary of State specifically who spoke of retaliation, he does not mean that the Secretary of State does not exist and only Washington does. And when a jilted lover tells us that his heart is broken, he hasn't thereby committed himself to the view that what failed romances really produce is not painful emotions but rather damaged body parts. In the first example, what we have is a case of *inference*: the ranger sees smoke and draws the conclusion that fire is present. In the second case, we have *metonymy*: the journalist refers to the U. S. government and its officials in a figurative way, by speaking of the city in which they are headquartered. In the third circumstance, we have a *semantic shift*: though it may have originated with a belief that the emotions associated with love have their seat in the heart, the expression "heartbreak" now has no connection at all with the organ that pumps blood, and refers only to the emotions associated with loss and grief.

The little soliloquy of Patricia Churchland's reported above surely reflects some or all of these phenomena, rather than anything close to a "replacement" of the concept of mind with concepts derived from neuroscience. Mrs. Churchland knows a lot about the brain; hence when she feels stress or anxiety, she *infers* that such-and-such is going on in her nervous system with respect to serotonin, adrenaline, etc., and reports it to her husband. She refers *metonymically* to her emotions by speaking of the neural events causally correlated with them. And perhaps as a result of years of indulging in this eccentric linguistic behavior, she so associates her innermost feelings with the brain processes associated with them that the words normally used to refer to the latter have in her usage subtly come to connote the former. There is really nothing here that differs in kind from the sort of behavior exhibited by a man who frequently grimaces, grabs his knee, and exclaims "Damn football injury!" His constant reference to the *cause* of his pain does not in the least show that he no longer thinks in terms of the pain itself, but only of the cause; and Mrs. Churchland's constant reference to her serotonin levels, C-fibres, and so forth doesn't show that *she* is anywhere near to "replacing" the concepts of anxiety and pain with the concepts of serotonin levels, C-fibre firings, etc. The only significant difference between the cases is that the ex-football player doesn't sound like a complete weirdo.

Of course, Mrs. Churchland might protest indignantly that she is in a better position than I am to know her own mind. But if so, she'd better think twice, for this move is, quite obviously, simply not open to an eliminative materialist (nor, come to think of it, is "thinking" twice or even just once). Not that such people have anything close to a grasp of the obvious. The commonsense objection to eliminative materialism is, after all, that it is just manifestly false, since the eliminative materialist himself (or herself, to revert to the politically correct pronoun in honor of Mrs. Churchland) has all sorts of thoughts, feelings, and other mental states, and even makes liberal use of mentalistic concepts in the course of stating the very eliminative materialist position that denies their validity. Hence the Churchlands constantly and casually refer to the "convictions" or "opinions" of the eliminative materialist, to what we do or do not "know" or "understand" about "memory" and "intelligence," to our "ideas" and "intuitions," etc., etc.[7] The eliminative materialist might retort that this is just loose talk that can easily be dropped if need be, but the problem goes far deeper than an occasional slip of the pen. The whole eliminative materialist enterprise is founded on the notion that science gives us the only accurate picture of reality. Yet science is in the business of making *assertions* about the world, developing *theories*, putting forward *explanations*, extending our *knowledge*, and so forth; and every one of these notions is utterly suffused with intentionality, which as we saw in the previous chapter is the central and defining feature of the mind. Insofar as an assertion, theory, explanation, or knowledge claim *represents*, *means*, *"points" to*, or is *"directed" toward* something beyond itself, it is every bit as "intentional" as the mind is, so that if the mind goes, science goes with it. Indeed, reason in general – another paradigmatically mental phenomenon – goes with it also, and thus so too does any rational argument anyone has ever given, *including any argument anyone has ever given or could give for eliminative materialism*. Worse, as Hilary Putnam points out, the very notion of *truth* would have to be abandoned by a consistent eliminative materialist, inextricably tied as it is to the idea of a claim, or belief, or thought that accurately represents reality.[8] As M.R. Bennett and P.M.S. Hacker put it, the eliminative materialist inevitably "saws off the branch on which he is seated."[9] In the name of reason, truth, and science, he destroys all reason, truth, and science.

Eliminative materialists sometimes acknowledge that this may well be, you know, a slight problem with their position. Their response is to shrug their shoulders and lament that we just don't yet have the resources even to state the theory in an adequate way, since the neuroscientists are still so far from completing their work of discovering all the physiological goings-on that underlie human behavior. But one fine day they'll be through, and then, well, just you wait. We'll no longer speak in terms of "truth," but rather in terms of what Churchland has called a "successor concept" that will replace truth (though by his own admission he has no idea what this "successor concept" will be).[10] We'll also have "successor concepts" to replace the concept of rationality and every other concept that science currently depends on. (Again, don't ask what those might be either, since even the Churchlands don't claim to know.) Presumably we'll also have to have a "successor concept" for *the concept of a concept*, since talk of "concepts" itself reeks of intentionality; or rather, I should say, we'll need a "successor something-or-other." Or maybe . . . well, let's not worry about it now. This Brave New World will be here eventually, and when it is, *then* all of us, including the Churchlands themselves, will finally know what the hell they're talking about.

Suppose someone told you that there might someday be a new form of addition according to which 2 and 2 would equal 23, admitted that this sounds like self-contradictory nonsense and that he has no way of explaining it coherently, but insisted that at some point in the future we might be able to understand it and even see that it is true. Would you take such a suggestion seriously even for a moment? Probably not; certainly you shouldn't. Given what addition is, we know that 2 and 2 can never make 23, and that's that. We needn't wait for some far-off day to find out, and anyone who says otherwise is a crackpot, unworthy of a moment's further notice. I submit that exactly the same thing is true of the Churchlands and other eliminative materialists, and for the same reasons. Given what science is, we know that to accept science is necessarily to accept the existence of theories, explanations, knowledge, truth, rationality, and the like, and *therefore* the existence of intentionality, and *therefore* the existence of minds. End of story. Whatever some future oddballs would be doing if they went around saying "2 + 2 = 23," we know it would *not* be arithmetic. And whatever some contemporary oddballs might be doing when they suggest that there might someday be a "science" that involved no theories, explanations, truth, rationality, or anything that smacked of intentionality or the mind, we know that they are not describing anything that could possibly count as science. The eliminative materialist worldview, which claims to base itself on science, is simply incoherent. Indeed, since it explicitly denies, on the basis of purportedly rational arguments, the very existence of rationality, truth, mind, etc. – in short, of everything constitutive of sanity – it is hardly much of an exaggeration to regard it as insane. To make such a judgment isn't to indulge in a gratuitous insult, but simply to take the eliminative materialist at his word.

The lump under the rug

Few materialists are eliminative materialists; it is very definitely a minority view, and most materialists are happy to acknowledge the obvious, viz. that the mind exists. What is interesting, though, is that few materialist critics of eliminative materialism will have any truck with the most obvious and decisive objection to the theory, namely that it is simply incoherent. William Hasker and Victor Reppert have put forward what I think is the correct diagnosis of this phenomenon, namely that materialists want to keep all their options open, even this most extreme one.[11] For there are, for reasons some of which we considered in the previous chapter, very serious problems with any attempt to explain the mind in purely material terms, and most materialists realize this. They hope and believe that these difficulties can be overcome, but in case this turns out to be impossible, they would rather deny that the mind exists at all than give up their materialism. Eliminative materialism thus serves as a last redoubt, a panic button or doomsday weapon they might want to deploy in case the dreaded menace of supernaturalism gets too close. Better for them to deny the mind – and with it rationality, truth, and science itself – than to admit the soul. Once again, the secularist manifests the very dogmatism of which he accuses the religious believer, and in rationalizing it is willing to contemplate absurdities of which no religious believer has ever dreamed.

But eliminative materialism *is* absurd and incoherent, and thus cannot be true. And as John Searle (who, as we have seen, is no religious believer) has argued, every form of materialism implicitly denies the existence of the mind, whether or not it intends to.[12] Thus, every form of materialism really entails eliminative materialism, and is thus as absurd, incoherent, and false as eliminative materialism is. We have already seen in the previous chapter the deep reason why this is so. The conception of matter that modern materialism inherited from the Mechanical Philosophy, since it strips of matter anything that might smack of Aristotelian formal and final causes, necessarily strips from it also anything like qualia and intentionality, and thus anything that could possibly count as mental. Scientific materialism "explains everything" in non-Aristotelian terms only by sweeping what doesn't fit the mechanistic model under the rug of the mind. And thus the only way to deal with the lump that remains, short of Descartes's dualism, is to throw out the rug, lump and all. Hence to say that matter, understood in mechanistic terms, is *all* that exists, is implicitly but necessarily to deny that the mind exists. Conversely, to acknowledge that both matter and mind exist is implicitly but necessarily to affirm either that something like Descartes's dualism is correct, or (if one wants to avoid the paradoxes inherent in Descartes's position) that something like Aristotle's view really is right after all, and that the moderns were wrong to abandon it in favor of mechanism.

And this brings us to a rich irony of historical proportions, yet one which goes almost entirely unnoticed. As I have said, most materialists would like to avoid eliminative materialism if they could. They have no problem, then, acknowledging the existence of reason, truth, beliefs, desires, or the mind and intentionality in general. At the same time, they are desperate to avoid anything that smacks of Descartes's dualism; and since, in the modern period, the mechanical conception of the natural world has unreflectively come to be taken for granted, so that Descartes's position has come to seem the only realistic alternative to materialism, these materialists tend to assume that if they can formulate and defend their position in a way that avoids dualism, they have thereby vindicated materialism. What they do not realize, however, is that many of their arguments can make sense *only if interpreted in Aristotelian terms, and in particular in terms of final causes.* Their arguments are ambiguous between a mechanistic reading and an Aristotelian one, and it is this ambiguity that gives them whatever plausibility they have. Yet they fail to see this ambiguity because of their general ignorance of the history of their subject, and in particular their ignorance of what thinkers in the Aristotelian tradition actually believed. While they dutifully parrot the general line that Aristotle and his Scholastic followers were all wrong and no longer worth taking seriously, they often inadvertently appeal to concepts that can make sense only if interpreted in a broadly Aristotelian way.

To see how this is so, keep in mind, first of all, that the usual objections to final causality are based on egregious misunderstandings, so that when contemporary materialists claim to reject final causes, what they are really objecting to is often something Aristotelians never believed in the first place. So, for example, to say that something has a final cause or is directed toward a certain end or goal is *not* necessarily to say that it consciously seeks to realize that goal. For Aristotelians, conscious goal-directedness in the natural world is limited to animals and human beings, and most of the final causality that exists in the world is totally unconscious. Furthermore, and contrary to another common misunderstanding, most final causality has nothing to do with a thing's having a "function" or "purpose" as those terms are usually understood (though function and purpose are indeed *one* kind of final causality). Thus it is no good to object that mountains or asteroids seem to serve no natural function or purpose, because Aristotelians *do not claim* that every object in the natural world necessarily serves some function. What they do claim is that everything in the world that serves as an efficient cause also exhibits final causality insofar as it is "directed toward" the production of some determinate range of effects. Thus (to repeat an earlier example) a match is "directed toward" the production of fire and heat rather than (say) frost or cold; that is the "goal" or "end" it "aims" at, even if it is never in fact struck. Final causality is that which makes efficient causality possible, the factor that grounds the necessary connection between causes and effects that is evident to common sense and which becomes problematic on a modern, mechanistic account of the material world.

Now let's consider the dominant materialist approach to explaining the mind in purely "naturalistic" terms, according to which the brain is a kind of digital computer and the mind is the "software" or "program" that is implemented on this "computer." The full story is rather complicated, and I examine it in more detail in my book *Philosophy of Mind*, to which I have alluded already and which you have, I hope, already purchased several copies of. But the basic idea is this: Individual thoughts are just physical symbols in the brain – like words or sentences, only encoded in the form of neural firing patterns, rather than in ink (as when you write a word or sentence), or sound waves (as when you speak it), or magnetic patterns on tape (as when you utter it into a tape recorder), or electrical current (as when you type it into a computer). Thinking – going from one thought to another – is just transitioning from one symbol in the brain to another according to the rules of an algorithm, in just the way a pocket calculator goes from "2" and "+" and "2" and "=" to "4" according to the rules of an algorithm, the difference between the calculator and the brain being a difference in degree but not in kind. The symbols get their meaning from the cause-and-effect relationships they bear to objects and events in the world outside the brain; hence such-and-such a brain process will count as a symbol meaning "There's a snake!" if it was caused by snakes affecting the sense organs of the speaker in such-and-such a way, and/or because it was hardwired into the brain by natural selection, since it got people to avoid snakes and this behavior was conducive to their survival. And that's it.Well, actually, that's *not* it; as I said, the story is much more complicated than that, and there are all sorts of details and qualifications that various theorists would add to it. Still, even when all the complications are taken account of, the story is utterly preposterous, and fails to hold water even for a moment, *at least if understood in terms of the modern mechanistic conception of the physical world.*

Here are some of the absurdities.[13] First of all, nothing counts as a "symbol" apart from some mind or group of minds which interprets and uses it as a symbol. For example, the words you're reading right now count as words at all only because English-language users so count them, given a series of historical accidents as a result of which "cat" is conventionally used to refer to cats, "dog" to dogs, and so on and so forth. In themselves and apart from these conventions, "dog," "cat," and the like are just meaningless squiggles of ink or meaningless noises. The same thing is true of every other physical symbol in whatever medium; for example, a drawing of a cat is also just a set of meaningless ink marks, and a computerized image of a cat a meaningless set of pixels, apart from someone who interprets them as cats. But then it is true also of any "symbols" purportedly encoded in the brain: By themselves they cannot fail to be nothing more than meaningless neural firing patterns (or whatever) until some mind *interprets* them as symbols standing for such-and-such objects or events. But obviously, until very recently it never so much as occurred to anyone to interpret brain events as symbols, even though (of course) we have been able to think for as long as human beings have existed. It follows that no brain events could have *been* symbols of any sort for all this time, in which case our thought processes were not the mere processing of symbols in the brain. More to the point, since the materialist's "computer model" of the mind tries to explain the mind in terms of symbols in the brain, but nothing counts as a symbol in the first place except when interpreted as such by a mind, the theory goes around in a circle and is simply incoherent. (The same incoherence afflicts Dawkins's and Dennett's ridiculous "meme" theory, by the way, since no brain process could count as a "meme" except when interpreted as such by some mind. Hence, since "memes" presuppose the existence of mind, they cannot explain the mind.)

As John Searle has argued, a related incoherence afflicts the suggestion that the brain works by running "algorithms" or "programs."[14] No physical system can possibly count as running an "algorithm" or "program" apart from some user who assigns a certain meaning to the inputs, outputs, and other states of the system. In the case of a pocket calculator, for example, you've got a mechanism which, in itself and considered merely in terms of its physical properties, can be described as displaying certain shapes on a screen whenever the pressing of certain buttons causes electrical current to flow through it in a certain pattern. That's it. What it does counts as generating *numbers*, and as *adding*, *subtracting*, *multiplying* them, etc., only relative to the intentions of the users who employ it for these tasks and the designers who created it for that very purpose. Any algorithm involves the manipulation of symbols according to rules, and (for reasons just noted) nothing counts as a symbol apart from some interpreter, and nothing could count as "following a rule" either unless it could at least in principle be conscious of doing so. For as Searle has emphasized, there is a difference between following a rule and behaving *as if* one were following a rule. Suppose someone tells me to follow the following algorithm: 1. Move from the front of the desk to the back of it and go to step 2; 2. Move from the back of the desk to the front and go back to step 1. If I comply, then I will begin circling the desk. Now suppose an earthquake knocks a marble off the desk and after hitting the floor it begins to circle the desk. The marble acts *as if* it were following the algorithm, but of course it isn't, while I really am following it. And the difference between us is that I am intentionally following the rules and the marble is not. Even if I forget what I am doing – say I get absorbed in a conversation while I'm circling the desk and no longer notice that I am doing so – my behavior still flows from my earlier intention and consciousness of having decided to follow the algorithm. Only what can be at least in principle conscious of following such rules can be said literally to follow an algorithm; everything else can behave only as if it were following one. At best, like a pocket calculator, it might be said to be following one in a derivative sense, insofar as its designers created it with that purpose in mind, though here too everything depends on their being something capable of consciously intending that an algorithm be followed.

Yet the algorithms purportedly being followed by processes in the brain are supposed to be totally unconscious even in principle. This, as Searle points out, is simply incoherent; such brain processes can no more be said to be following algorithms than the marble does. Nor can it coherently be said that these brain processes can count as running algorithms because we so interpret them. For the whole point of the appeal to unconscious algorithms was to identify those processes in the brain responsible for our thoughts, including our acts of interpretation. To "explain" thought in terms of algorithms and then to "explain" the algorithms themselves in terms of thought would once again be to go around in a circle.

Thirdly, the suggestion that the meaning of the symbols purportedly encoded in the brain derives from their causal connections with things in the external world is also incoherent. The idea is supposed to be that if objects of type A regularly cause brain events of type B, then brain events of type B will come to "represent" or "mean" objects of type A. Hence if the presence of cats is what regularly causes B, then B will come to mean or represent cats. (It is more complicated than this, but the complications don't matter for the point being made here.) As Karl Popper and Hilary Putnam have pointed out, a serious problem with this sort of theory (there are many others, for which again see my book *Philosophy of Mind*) is that it requires identifying certain points in a chain of causes and effects as having a privileged status, in particular as counting as "the beginning" of the chain and "the end" of the chain; yet objectively speaking, no points in the chain have any such status.[15] In the example at hand, the account requires treating the cat as A, the "beginning" of the causal chain – *the cat* per se, rather than the surface of the cat, or the fur of the cat, or the photons that travel from the cat, etc. – and treating some one particular brain state as B, the "end" of the causal chain – rather than treating the brain event immediately before or after it as the end, or the arrival of the photons at the eye as the end, or whatever. But objectively, apart from human interests and interpretation, there is just the ongoing causal flux: Light travels from the sun to the cat, bounces off the cat's fur and other visible parts, travels from there to our eyeballs, the rods and cones register the light followed by activity in the optic nerve, followed in turn by the firing of clusters of neurons in the brain, which is followed by the firing of other clusters, which is followed by the firing of other clusters, etc., which in turn leads to the flexing of muscles and movement toward the cat, which is followed by petting the cat, and so forth. And of course, the causal series extends further back before the light leaves the sun and further forward past the petting of the cat. Now, what makes anything in this series of events "the beginning" or "the end" of a series? The answer is that *we* pick out the cat specifically and some particular brain process specifically as being of interest, but in the objective physical world neither has any special status at all, being merely two links among others in a chain that extends before and after them indefinitely. In other words, it is only *relative to an interpreting mind* that a causal chain has such a beginning or end, in which case we cannot coherently appeal to the beginnings and ends of such chains in order to explain the mind. Yet again the materialist's account goes around in a vicious circle, implicitly presupposing the very phenomenon it is supposed to be explaining.

Finally, the materialist's "computer model" of the mind is incoherent in a fourth respect, insofar as it undermines the very possibility of rational argumentation, including any argument a materialist might want to give in support of his own theory. With a calculator, one symbol or set of symbols generates another entirely by virtue of the physical properties of the symbols; the meaning of the symbols plays no role whatsoever. Hence "2," "+," "2," and "=" generate "4" simply because the machine has been designed in such a way that the electrical impulses associated with the first set of symbols cause an impulse associated with the latter symbol, so that a "4" appears on the screen. The former symbols would generate this latter one whatever meaning we assigned to them, or even if they had no meaning at all. For example, if we took "2" to mean the number three, "+" to mean minus, and "4" to mean twenty-three, we would still get "4" on the screen after punching in "2," "+," "2," and "=," even though what the symbols "2 + 2 = 4" *now* mean is that three minus three equals twenty-three.

The same thing is supposed to be true of the way the brain transitions from one symbol to another; it is *only* the electrochemical properties of these purported symbols that are said to generate further symbols, and not the meaning associated with the symbols. (This is the whole point of the theory, for explaining everything in terms of electrochemical properties is supposed to show how thought can be a purely material process.) And that means that when we go from the thought that "All men are mortal" and the thought that "Socrates is a man" to the thought that "Socrates is mortal," the meanings of these thoughts play *no role whatsoever* in leading us from one to another; the symbols in the brain corresponding to the sentences "All men are mortal" and "Socrates is a man" would generate a symbol corresponding to the sentence "Socrates is mortal" even if the sentence "All men are mortal" meant that *it is raining in Cleveland*, the sentence "Socrates is a man" meant that *roast beef tastes good*, and the sentence "Socrates is mortal" meant that *Richard Dawkins is a Muslim*. So we would still say, "All men are mortal, and Socrates is a man, therefore Socrates is mortal," even if what those words really meant was *it is raining in Cleveland, and roast beef tastes good, therefore Richard Dawkins is a Muslim*.

The point is this. In the calculator example, we regard the calculator as reliably giving correct responses *only if* we suppose (what is obviously true in the ordinary case) that the symbol "2" means two, "+" means addition, "4" means four, and so forth; and if we assumed instead, for whatever reason, that the symbol "2" really meant three, "+" meant subtraction, and "4" meant twenty-three, we would *not* count the responses as correct. So even if the meaning of the symbols is not relevant to the physical operation of the machine, the meaning of the symbols *is* relevant, and crucially so, to whether we count the machine as actually giving arithmetically correct answers. Similarly, when we think it is rational to go from "All men are mortal" and "Socrates is a man" to "Socrates is mortal," that is only because we are assuming that these sentences have their usual meanings. If we assumed instead that they had the weird alternative meanings suggested above, we would *not* regard this chain of reasoning as rational at all, for it is obviously highly *ir*rational to argue that *it is raining in Cleveland, and roast beef tastes good, therefore Richard Dawkins is a Muslim.* Even if the meanings of the symbols purportedly encoded in the brain are not relevant to how one symbol generates another, the meanings of the symbols *would* be relevant, and crucially so, to whether this transition from symbol to symbol counts as *logical reasoning.*

One lesson of this is that since meaning is not at all relevant to how one symbol generates another according to the rules of an algorithm, but it is highly relevant to whether one thought logically follows from another thought, it follows that *logical thinking cannot be reduced to the algorithmic transition from one physical symbol to another.* Moreover, if the materialist nevertheless insists (as he must if he wants to provide a "naturalistic" "explanation" of thought) that such algorithmic transitions, embodied in electrochemical processes in the brain, are *all* that is going on when we go from one thought to another, it would follow that *the meanings of our thoughts, and thus the logical relationships between them (or lack thereof) have nothing whatsoever to do with why we draw the conclusions we do.* We would still think that "Socrates is mortal" follows from "All men are mortal" and "Socrates is a man" even if what this meant is something crazy like the claim that *Richard Dawkins is a Muslim* follows from *it is raining in Cleveland* and *roast beef tastes good.* In short, if the materialist's story is correct, then even if all our thought processes were totally irrational, and every argument we gave was completely fallacious, they would still *seem* like perfectly rational arguments to us. But in that case, we could never know whether any of our arguments or thought processes really are rational; however rational they *appear* to us, they might be completely insane. Hence, if materialism is true, no argument we ever give can be trusted – including arguments for materialism itself.

This line of argument is sometimes called the "argument from reason," and versions of it have been defended by such thinkers as C.S. Lewis, Karl Popper, Alvin Plantinga, and William Hasker.[16] And with it we see once again that materialism and naturalism, far from being the logical outcome of a rational investigation of the world, actually undermine the very possibility of rational inquiry. (This applies too, incidentally, to Dawkins's and Dennett's "meme" theory. If the competition between memes for survival is what, unbeknown to us, "really" determines all our thoughts, then we can have no confidence whatsoever that anything we believe, or any argument we ever give in defense of some claim we believe, is true or rationally compelling. For if the meme theory is correct, then our beliefs seem true to us, and our favored arguments seem correct, simply because they were the ones that happened for whatever reason to prevail in the struggle for "memetic" survival, not because they reflect objective reality.[17])

Now I have said that the materialist account of the mind is incoherent *at least given the conception of the physical world inherited from the Mechanical Philosophy*, which conception is explicitly or implicitly the materialist's "official" one. But suppose instead that we rejected this conception of the physical world and acknowledged that there are such things as Aristotelian formal and final causes. Then the "computational" model of the mind that I've been describing, whether or not one would find it of any value if given an Aristotelian reinterpretation (and I wouldn't), would at least no longer be flatly incoherent. For "unconscious rule-following" could now be understood as an instance of final causality. Just as the match is by its nature "directed toward" the production of fire and heat rather than some other sort of effect, and is so directed without being *conscious* of these specific effects as its "goal," so too might certain brain processes be naturally and unconsciously "directed toward" the production of others and ultimately toward the production of certain kinds of speech and behavior rather than others. In general, given final causality we could coherently pick out certain points as beginning and end states in a causal series, for this would just be a matter of identifying a certain cause as directed toward some particular effect as an "end" or "goal." And if some material features naturally "point" to others in this fashion, it at least wouldn't be flatly absurd to suggest that they could count as "symbols" that "mean" the things they "point" to. Unlike the mechanistic picture of reality, which completely drives purpose and meaning out from the material world and relocates it in the mind, the Aristotelian picture allows that there might be such a thing as genuine meaning, purpose or goal-directedness even in unconscious physical processes.

Thus, when materialists appeal to notions like "algorithms," "information processing," "computation" and the like in an attempt to give a "naturalistic" explanation of the mind, I suggest that their accounts sound at all plausible only because those concepts are unwittingly being understood in terms of something akin to Aristotelian final causes. Their ignorance of what final causality actually amounts to, and their dogmatic *rhetorical* allegiance to mechanism, keeps them from seeing this. But their common sense tells them that there really are purposes and meanings in the natural world, and couching their recognition of this fact in terms of "algorithms," "computation," etc., gives the illusion that this recognition is consistent with mechanism. When these confusions are exposed, it becomes clear that all the computer jargon is really doing very little work, and that either one sticks to a consistently mechanistic line, in which case the computer model is totally incoherent, or one explicitly acknowledges that there are final causes, in which case the computer jargon becomes otiose at best and confusing at worst, and it would be better just to return to a straightforwardly Aristotelian position.

Some materialists come very close to doing this. For example, David Armstrong suggests that his fellow materialists should look to the "dispositions" physical objects possess as instances of a kind of "proto-intentionality" or "pointing beyond themselves" toward certain specific outcomes, as when glass, being brittle, has a tendency toward shattering, specifically, even if it never in fact shatters.[18] What Armstrong and like-minded materialists fail to realize is that in taking this line they have more or less *returned to an Aristotelian conception of causality and abandoned mechanism.*

Such implicit neo-Aristotelianism is equally evident in the work of some contemporary philosophers concerned with the analysis of human action, such as G.F. Schueler and Scott Sehon.[19] Final causality seems even more obviously manifest in our actions and intentions than in other aspects of our mental lives: We act always for the sake of certain *ends, goals,* or *purposes.* Some philosophers have tried to show that this teleological or goal-directed element can be eliminated from our explanations of human actions, and that they can be described instead purely in terms of efficient causes. So, to take a stock example, it is said that an explanation like *Bob knocked over the glass of water for the purpose of distracting Fred* can be rephrased as *Bob had the intention of distracting Fred and this caused him to knock over the glass of water*, where the latter description eliminates the teleological element present in the first.[20] But as Schueler and Sehon argue, no such attempt at eliminating teleology can succeed. For consider the case where Bob's intention to knock over the glass makes him so nervous that his hand shakes uncontrollably and knocks over the glass before he otherwise would have. Then it is certainly true that *Bob had the intention of distracting Fred and this caused him to knock over the glass of water*, but it is *not* true that *Bob knocked over the glass of water for the purpose of distracting Fred*, for in this case he knocked over the glass not *for the purpose of* distracting Fred (even though he did want to do that at some point), but rather because he lost control of his hand. So the two descriptions are not equivalent at all. To salvage his reformulation, a materialist would have to stipulate that the intention in question can cause the resulting action only via bodily motions that the agent has guidance of or control over, rather than by involuntary shaking and the like; but the trouble with this is that "guidance" and "control" are *themselves* teleological notions – guidance or control is always guidance or control toward an end or goal – so that the analysis will not have truly eliminated teleology at all.[21] Hence it is simply impossible coherently to eliminate final causality or teleology from the explanation of human action. As Alfred North Whitehead once put it, "those who devote themselves to the purpose of proving that there is no purpose constitute an interesting subject for study."[22]

Irreducible teleology

The bottom line is this. Any materialist who argues: "Everything else has yielded to reductive materialistic explanation, so why should the mind be the only holdout?" thereby manifests only his own cluelessness. The mind cannot possibly fail to be a "holdout," indeed an *absolute barrier* to the reductive aspirations of materialism, precisely because it is the rug under which modern philosophers have historically swept everything that could not fit the mechanistic picture of the world. Descartes, Locke, and other early modern philosophers realized this, and that (rather than "ignorance of modern neuroscience" or any other such red herring) is the reason they were dualists. Dualism follows *necessarily* if one wants to maintain a mechanistic picture of the physical world while avoiding eliminative materialism. And the only way to avoid both dualism and eliminative materialism is to return to Aristotle.[23] That, in fact, is what some materialists have done, at least partially and without realizing it; but to follow through such a move consistently is just to cease to be a materialist.

Could it get any worse for materialism? Yes it can, and it does. For as it happens, the materialist's "everything else has yielded to reductive explanation" shtick isn't true anyway. As I have said several times in this book, the idea that modern science has eliminated final causes from our picture of the natural world is a myth, the statement of an agenda and a wish rather than an actual accomplishment. Human thought and action are the most obvious examples of phenomena that exhibit irreducible teleology, but they are far from the only ones. Indeed, final causality pervades the natural world from the level of complex biological organs all the way down to the simplest causal interactions at the microscopic level. And the greatest irony is that, not only have contemporary science and philosophy not shown otherwise, *they have if anything and despite themselves made the reality of irreducible teleology even more evident*. To see how this is so, let us examine three levels of physical reality in which final causality is unavoidable: biological phenomena, complex inorganic systems, and basic laws of nature.

A. Biological phenomena: The point of Darwinism is to complete the mechanistic revolution that began with Galileo, Descartes, Hobbes, Locke, et al., by eliminating teleology or final causality from biology. Yet contemporary Darwinian biologists, no less than their Aristotelian predecessors, constantly help themselves to teleological language in describing and explaining the phenomena with which they have to deal, and no one denies that it would be impossible for them to carry on their researches without it. They speak, for example, of the *function* of the heart, of what kidneys are *for*, of how gazelles jump up and down *in order to* signal predators, and in general of the *purpose, goal,* or *end* of such-and-such an organ or piece of behavior. Etienne Gilson's *From Aristotle to Darwin and Back Again* details how deeply teleological thinking has permeated evolutionary theory from the beginning, and David Stove's *Darwinian Fairytales* documents how central, and self-conscious, is its use in the work of prominent contemporary biologists like G.C. Williams and our good friend Richard Dawkins (whose "selfish gene" theory, with its talk of the ends or purposes of our genes, is teleological through and through).[24] Darwin himself once said that it is "difficult for any one who tries to make out the use of a structure to avoid the word purpose."[25] So what's the deal?

As Stove notes, while biologists who make use of such concepts surely realize that, for a Darwinian anyway, such use must always come "with an invisible promissory note attached . . . saying something like 'To be cashed at a later date in non-teleological terms,'" most of them have "issued so many of these promissory notes, that [they are] no longer conscious of their existence" and have "simply forgotten what teleological words *mean,* or else [have] forgotten the fact that they are not really available to Darwinians engaged in explaining adaptations."[26] However, some naturalistic philosophers have, to their credit, tried to pay off the debt accrued by their colleagues in biology by attempting an analysis of such teleological talk in non-teleological terms.[27] It is rather breathtaking – and, frankly, disgraceful – that Darwinian biologists themselves have done so little to try to deal with this rather glaring difficulty in their position. But perhaps that is for the best. For here, as in so many other instances where scientists' accomplishments in their own field give them delusions of competence in other domains, the issues are *conceptual and philosophical* in nature rather than empirical and scientific. And as C.D. Broad is reputed to have said (and as Dawkins's own worthless contributions to the debate over God's existence dramatically illustrate) "the nonsense written by philosophers on scientific matters is exceeded only by the nonsense written by scientists on philosophy."[28]

As it happens, though, the philosophers haven't done much better than the biologists would have – not because their philosophical acumen is less than that of the biologists, but because the task they are charged with is an impossibility, a fool's errand and time-waster if ever there was one. For it is, in essence, the task of showing how final causality is "really" just a kind of efficient causality – which, of course, it manifestly isn't. Final causality essentially involves goal-directedness, and efficient causality, at least as understood by materialists and naturalists, essentially does not, and never the twain shall meet (at least not short of a return to Aristotle). You might as well devote yourself to the "project" of showing how apples are "really" a kind of orange, or how circles are "really" a kind of square, or (for that matter) how mind is "really" a kind of matter. We have seen how the latter task inevitably ignores or even denies, rather than "explains," the existence of mind. Similarly, any attempt to "analyze" teleology in terms of efficient causes will inevitably simply ignore or deny the existence of teleology rather than explain it. If philosophers have any advantage over their scientific colleagues in this matter, it is only because they are, as Peter Geach might put it, able to "conceal the fallacy" more skillfully than mere biologists like Williams and Dawkins can manage.

Take the currently most popular strategy for "naturalizing" teleology, which is associated with the philosophers Ruth Millikan and (another old pal of ours) Daniel Dennett.[29] Here, as pretty much everywhere else according to some Darwinians, evolution itself solves every problem and wipes the tear from every eye. To say that the kidneys existing in such-and-such an organism have the "function" of purifying its blood amounts to something like this: Those ancestors of this organism who first developed kidneys (as a result of a random genetic mutation) tended to survive in greater numbers than those without kidneys, because their blood got purified; and this caused the gene for kidneys to get passed on to the organism in question and others like it. To say that an organ's function (now) is to do X is therefore shorthand for saying that it was selected for by evolution because its earliest ancestors did X. And there you go; we've thereby shown (or at least we will have with a few refinements and qualifications) that teleology is "reducible" to efficient causes after all. Another victory for naturalism, Enlightenment, secularism, and all-around niceness, and all made possible, as usual, through the intercession of St. Charles of the Galapagos.

Or at least it would be if it so obviously were not. One rather absurd implication of this theory is that you can't really know what the function of an organ is until you know something about its evolutionary history. But as Jerry Fodor has noted, "you don't have to know how hands (or hearts, or eyes, or livers) evolved to make a pretty shrewd guess about what they are for."[30] Another absurd implication is that nothing that didn't evolve could possibly have a biological function; indeed, the *first* kidneys, according to this theory, didn't have any function, because, being the result of a random genetic mutation, they hadn't been "selected for" by evolution. But (as, again, Fodor points out) given that it is at least theoretically possible that Darwin might have been wrong (as even the most diehard evolutionist would concede, though you can never be too sure), then if it turned out that kidneys did not evolve after all, it is hard to believe that this would show that they really serve no function.[31] Or consider "swampman," a creature familiar to those readers who like to peruse academic philosophy journals (all three of you).[32] Swampman, let's imagine, came about as a result of a freak accident in which lightning struck a pool of chemical waste in a swamp somewhere and produced a particle-for-particle duplicate of a living human being. Hence swampman walks, talks, and in every other way behaves just like you do. Now, do swampman's kidneys, eyes, ears, etc., have functions? Surely they do – the same functions that your kidneys, eyes, ears, etc., have. But the theory in question would have to deny that they have any function at all, given that swampman was not the product of natural selection.

The main problem with the theory in question, however, is the one emphasized by John Searle, namely that natural selection simply has nothing whatsoever to do with teleology or natural functions, and that that is indeed *the very point* of appeals to natural selection.[33] To say that such-and-such an organ was selected for by evolution is not to "analyze" or "explain" how it has the function it does, but rather to imply that it has no function at all but only seems to. It is, as noted above, to *eliminate* teleology. Hence any attempt to "reduce," "analyze," or "explain" teleology or function in Darwinian terms is simply muddleheaded, an exercise in changing the subject while pretending not to. Darwinians should, in Searle's view, stop trying incoherently to incorporate the idea of natural function into their account of the world, and recognize that biological phenomena are "entirely devoid of purpose or teleology" and that "teleological features are entirely in the mind of the observer."[34]

Sound advice, except that it is impossible to follow. As noted above, the concept of function is absolutely indispensable to ordinary biological research. (If you don't believe me, try giving an accurate and informative description of some organism and its various component parts that makes no reference whatsoever to function, purpose, or related notions.) You can say, if you want to, that in some particular context talk about functions is mere shorthand for talk about complex patterns of efficient causation, but in that case teleology will simply rear its head somewhere else instead. Indeed, it does so in Searle's own proposal: He says that the functions we see in biological organs are not really there objectively but exist only "relative to an observer who assigns a normative value to the causal processes."[35] But "assigning a normative value" is itself an instance of teleology or goal-directedness. In particular, it is an instance of the sort of teleology that essentially characterizes creatures with minds, and as we have seen, the human mind is the example *par excellence* of an irreducibly teleological phenomenon.

Dennett too sometimes speaks as if the functions we attribute to bodily organs and the like are not there intrinsically but derive from some other source, only for him this source isn't the human mind, but natural selection. This is also Dennett's way of giving a "naturalistic" "explanation" of the intentionality characteristic of human minds themselves: like other teleological phenomena, it ultimately derives, he says, from Mother Nature's "purposes" as manifested in the evolutionary process. The trouble with this, as should go without saying, is that if Dennett really means it when he says that "Mother Nature" has purposes and the like, he's either adopted a very peculiar religion indeed (since he would appear to be attributing something like godlike consciousness to nature) or conceding that Aristotle was right all along (if what he means is that there is real goal-directedness in nature, only it is unconscious). And in either case, he will thereby have abandoned naturalism rather than vindicated it. On the other hand, if (as is surely the case) he does *not* really mean that either "Mother Nature" in general or natural selection in particular has "purposes," but that this merely a figure of speech, then Mother Nature's "purposes" and "intentionality," being non-existent, cannot "explain" our intentionality, or biological functions, or indeed anything at all.[36]

It may be that Dennett intends for us to understand his talk of Mother Nature's purposes in terms of his notion of the "intentional stance," the idea that it is sometimes useful to treat an unthinking and unconscious complex physical system *as if* it had beliefs, desires, intentions, and other mental states, as when we say that a chess-playing computer "decided" to make such-and-such a move or that a burglar alarm set off by the cat "thinks" that an intruder is present, even though strictly speaking these things are incapable of deciding or thinking anything.[37] There are "real patterns" in such complex systems that cannot usefully be identified without using such mentalistic language (though in this case it is obvious that the reason for this is that human designers put such patterns into the physical systems in question). Similarly (Dennett seems to be saying) there are patterns in the natural order too that can best be identified by speaking of "purposes," "functions," and the like. Now I think he is absolutely right about that much. The trouble is that there is no way to interpret all of this as both genuinely explanatory and consistent with Dennett's naturalism. If he means that the purposes and functions we attribute to nature are not objectively there at all, but exist *only* relative to our interpretive act of taking the "intentional stance" toward them, then, again, he's essentially saying that nature's purposes are non-existent, in which case they cannot explain anything. All the "intentional stance" and "real patterns" stuff becomes nothing more than a rhetorical smokescreen. (Into the bargain, it also becomes incoherent, since if you say that our intentionality derives from Mother Nature's, and that Mother Nature's intentionality derives from our taking the "intentional stance" toward her, then you've gone around in a circle, since "taking a stance" toward something is itself a paradigm case of intentionality.) But if instead he is serious about there being "real patterns" in nature that cannot be described other than by talking of purposes and functions, then he has essentially *returned to an Aristotelian conception of final causality and thereby abandoned naturalism.*

The thing is, Dennett never comes out and tells us exactly what he does mean. And this fundamental ambiguity, which absolutely permeates his writings, is the source of whatever plausibility his position has. It is reasonable enough to say that nature "intends" this or that, or that natural phenomena have such-and-such "purposes" or "functions" – this is, after all, precisely why people have always been inclined to see Aristotelian final causes and/or divine design in the natural world – so the average reader doesn't bat an eye when Dennett uses this language. At the same time, Dennett never shuts up about what a hard-headed naturalist and Darwinian he is, and the whole point of naturalism and Darwinism is of course to reduce everything in the natural order to material elements governed by efficient causes. This combination generates the illusion that Dennett has somehow given a "naturalistic" account of purposes and functions. But the whole thing is a shell game. Like a perpetrator of that famous scam, who pretends to have placed a pea under one particular shell but in fact has rigged things so that he can at will make it disappear entirely or reappear under any one of them, Dennett pretends to have discovered function and purpose in natural selection, or in the "intentional stance," or in "real patterns," or under some other shell. In fact he has – like the Churchlands – eliminated them entirely, but disguises this fact by rhetorical sleight of hand. The philosopher Elizabeth Anscombe once famously judged David Hume a "mere – brilliant – sophist."[38] Mr. "Bright Stuff" can take pride in the fact that he is almost in Hume's rank as a philosopher, insofar as if you delete just the middle word in Anscombe's description of Hume, you get a dead-on summation of Daniel Dennett.

In any event, the contemporary biologist's absolute *favorite* place to relocate teleology while pretending it doesn't exist is not the human mind (*pace* Searle) and it is not Dennett's "Mother Nature" either; it is DNA. If there is one thing biologists gush over as much as natural selection, it is the discovery of this famous molecule and its structure – and for good reason, for it was a very great discovery indeed. And why was it so important? Because, we are constantly and rightly told, DNA contains the "information," "code," "instructions," "data," or "blueprint" required to build an organism; occasionally, given the current fad for computer jargon, one hears of "software," "programming," and the like too. Such language absolutely permeates biologists' descriptions of the function of DNA, and there is no way accurately to convey what DNA does without something like it. Notice, though, that every single one of these concepts, and others frequently used to describe the nature of DNA, smacks of the sort of intentionality or meaningfulness characteristic of human minds. DNA can serve as "information," "instructions," a "blueprint," or the like only if it means or represents something beyond itself the way a thought does (or the way language does, but as we've seen, the meaningfulness of language derives from that of thought). And as we have seen, computational concepts make sense only against the background of a user or interpreter who assigns a meaning to the symbols. But no one believes that DNA molecules literally have minds or consciously represent or think about anything at all, or that anyone is using them to "compute" with. So, what modern biology reveals to us is the existence of a physical structure that "points to" or "aims at" something beyond itself and yet is entirely unconscious. Where have we heard that before? Why, in Aristotle, of course. Moreover, as a "blueprint," what this structure points to or aims at specifically is the realization in an individual organism of a certain kind of structure or pattern definitive of the species – that is to say, the realization of a form or essence. "Modern" biology isn't so modern after all; the riffs are different, but underlying the jazzy hipster talk of "information" and "software" is the same old squaresville melody of Aristotelian final-cum-formal causality. Modern science, like all rebellious adolescents, has morphed into the father figure it once reviled.

Please note that this has nothing whatsoever to do with "irreducible complexity" or any of the other Paleyan red herrings familiar from the debate over "Intelligent Design," whose advocates foolishly concede the mechanistic assumptions of their opponents. The point is not that natural selection cannot explain this or that complex structure; the point is that whether or not it can explain such things, the biological presuppositions of natural selection unavoidably include teleological phenomena of the sort Darwin was supposed to have banished. Richard Dawkins himself bears witness to this fact, what with all his talk of genes as "selfish," "manipulative," and the like, since a gene can hardly be "selfish" or "manipulative" unless there is something in it like intentionality, purpose, or teleology. And if (as Dawkins himself insists) genes are not conscious, then what he is committing himself to, whether he realizes it or not, is unconscious teleology or final causality of the Aristotelian sort. To be sure, given that it is Dawkins that we are talking about, to some extent his "selfish gene" talk owes as much to muddleheadedness, the hope of selling books, etc., as to genuine scientific insight. Certainly the obsession with harrowing metaphors like "selfishness" and "manipulation," if not motivated by a desire to tart up an otherwise dull pop-science volume, reflects a dogmatic insistence on pushing "survival of the fittest" explanations as far as they can go (indeed, well beyond where they can go).[39] But if he is on to anything at all (and he is at least right about the bare idea that genes "aim at" certain outcomes beyond themselves), there is absolutely no way to convey it without using talk that implies intentionality or teleology. *Remove the teleological element in the description of DNA and genes and you strip them of everything that makes them explanatorily useful in biology.*

There is a tension, then, between biologists' "official" anti-Aristotelian position – reflexive and dogmatic, a prejudice picked up while in school and never seriously thought through – and their relentless use of teleological language in describing the phenomena with which they have to deal. The physicist Paul Davies – who is, like Fodor, Searle, and Stove, an irreligious evolutionist with no theological ax to grind – sums up this tension nicely:

> Concepts like information and software do not come from the natural sciences at all, but from communication theory . . . and involve qualifiers like context and mode of description – notions that are quite alien to the physicist's description of the world. Yet most scientists accept that informational concepts do legitimately apply to biological systems, and they cheerfully treat semantic information as if it were a natural quantity like energy. Unfortunately, "meaning" sounds perilously close to purpose, an utterly taboo subject in biology. So we are left with the contradiction that we need to apply concepts derived from purposeful human activities (communication, meaning, context, semantics) to biological processes that certainly appear purposeful, but are in fact not (or are not supposed to be). . . . [A]t the end of the day,

> human beings are products of nature, and if humans have
> purposes, then at some level purposefulness must arise
> from nature and therefore be inherent in nature. . . . Might
> purpose be a genuine property of nature right down to the
> cellular or even the subcellular level?[40]

Contemporary biology itself gives us every reason to conclude that
the answer to Davies's rhetorical question is "yes." There is only
one reason biologists refuse to accept that answer, and it has nothing whatsoever to do with either science or the follies of some
"Intelligent Design" theorists. It derives instead from the purely
philosophical assumption that the notion of final causality was
somehow "refuted" over three hundred years ago, an assumption
that we have seen is groundless and which is itself undermined by
the work of modern biologists themselves. As the biophysicist and
Nobel laureate Max Delbrück once wrote, if the Nobel Prize could
be awarded posthumously, "I think they should consider Aristotle
for the discovery of the principle implied in DNA," and "the reason
for the lack of appreciation, among scientists, of Aristotle's scheme
lies in our having been blinded for 300 years by the Newtonian
view of the world."[41] Paley is dead; and even if he weren't, who
cares? Aristotle lives.[42]

B. Complex inorganic systems: "Well, *maybe* he 'lives' in biology," you
might say, "but surely nowhere else!" *Everywhere* else, actually. The
examples we've looked at so far exhibit a certain pattern. Both in
science and in common sense, we pick out certain chains of cause
and effect (specifically of "efficient causation," as Aristotelians
would say) as having a unique significance, and this includes certain causal chains of particular interest to materialists trying to give
a "naturalistic" explanation of this or that. For example, in trying to
explain where our thoughts about cats get their meaning, they take
the causal sequence that begins with a cat and ends with a certain
specific brain state to have a significance that is not had by (say) the
causal chain that begins with some particular patch of fur on the cat
and ends with the photons present in the air six inches in front of
our eyes. In trying to explain how biological organs get their functions, they think it relevant to cite (for example) the fact that the
heart pumps blood and not the fact that it makes a certain sound

while doing so. In characterizing DNA, they think it important to note that having a certain kind of DNA causes bears to be furry and to grow to large size, but not important to note that it also thereby causes them to make good mascots for football teams. And so forth. Again, certain causal chains have a significance that others don't. But we've also seen that, unless we want to say that the significance of these causal chains owes entirely to human interests and the mind's projection of certain patterns onto nature – in which case these causal chains are not objective features of reality and therefore cannot provide us with a "scientific explanation" of anything – then we have to say that what we count as the "beginnings" of these causal chains *inherently* somehow *point to* or are *directed at* certain specific outcomes as their natural "end" state or culmination. That is to say, we have to recognize that they are teleological, and that certain efficient causes cannot even be identified as such without also identifying final causes.

But this applies to causal chains more generally. As the philosopher David Oderberg has noted, it is particularly evident in inorganic natural cycles like the water cycle and the rock cycle.[43] In the former, condensation leads to precipitation, which leads to collection, which leads to evaporation, which leads to condensation, and the cycle begins again. In the latter, igneous rock forms into sedimentary rock, which forms into metamorphic rock, which melts into magma, which hardens into igneous rock, and the cycle begins again. (In both cases I am of course leaving out many details.) Scientists who study these processes identify each of their stages as playing a certain specific role relative to the others. The role of condensation in the water cycle, for example, is to bring about precipitation; the role of pressure in the rock cycle is, in conjunction with heat, to contribute to generating magma, and in the absence of heat to contribute to generating sedimentary rock; and so forth. Each stage has the production of some particular outcome or range of outcomes as an "end" or "goal" toward which it points. Nor will it do to suggest that either cycle could be adequately described by speaking of each stage as being the efficient cause of certain others, with no reference to its playing a "role" of generating some effect as an "end" or "goal." For each stage has many other effects that are not part of the cycle. As Oderberg points out, sedimentation might (for example) happen to block the water flow to a certain region, the formation of magma might cause some local birds to migrate, or condensation in some area might for all we know cause someone to have arthritic pain in his big toe. But blocking water flow and causing birds to migrate are no part of the rock cycle, and causing arthritic pain is no part of the water cycle. Some causal chains are relevant to the cycles and some are not. Nor is it correct to say that the student of the rock or water cycles just happens to be interested in the way some rock generates other kinds and how water in one form brings about water in another form, and is not interested in bird migration patterns or arthritis, so that he pays attention to some elements in the overall causal situation rather than others. For the patterns described by scientists studying these cycles are *objective* patterns in nature, not mere projections of human interests. But the only way to account for this is to recognize that each stage in the process, while it might have various sorts of effects, has only the generation of certain *specific* effects among them as its "end" or "goal" and that this is what determines its role in the cycle. In short, it is to recognize such cycles as teleological.

C. *Basic laws of nature*: As we have seen, the founders of modern philosophy sought to eliminate "substantial forms," "essences," "natures," "powers," "final causes" and so forth from science, and to replace them with the idea of events related by "laws of nature." Hence, when a brick is thrown at a window and the window shatters, it's not (on this view) that the brick, by virtue of its nature or essence, has a power to break glass, etc. It's rather that events like the throwing of bricks just happen to be regularly followed by events like the shattering of windows.

Hume's radical empiricism provided the cover for this anti-Aristotelian program. Since we cannot observe essences, powers, final causes and the like, but only events succeeding one another, it "follows" on a Humean view that we can have no concepts of the former sort, and must couch our scientific picture of the world in terms of the latter alone. In fact this doesn't follow at all, and only seems to if we make the demonstrably false assumption that to have an idea or concept of something is to have a mental image of it, where mental images derive ultimately from sensation. As we saw when discussing of the problem of universals in Chapter 2, we have all sorts of concepts or ideas that cannot possibly be identified with mental images: Our concepts of men, triangles, trees, and countless other things are completely general, applying to these things universally; but any mental image we can form of a man, triangle, tree, etc., is always necessarily an image of some particular man, dog, or tree, and thus not universal. Mental images are vague and indistinct when their objects are complex or detailed, but the related concepts or ideas are clear and distinct regardless of their complexity; for example, the concept of a chiliagon, or 1000-sided figure, is clearly different from the concept of a 999-sided figure, even though a mental image of a chiliagon is no different from a mental image of a 999-sided figure. We have many concepts or ideas of things for which it is impossible to form any mental image at all: abstractions like economics, law, knowledge, etc.; the absence of something, or a specific point in time; logical notions like conjunction, disjunction, negation, and the like; and so on. The concept of a substantial form, essence, nature, power, or final cause is simply no more problematic than any of these other various concepts; if we accept the latter despite Hume's theory of ideas (and it would be insane not to), then we have no reason to consider that theory a serious challenge to the former.

Even if we bought the Humean story about the origins of our ideas, it would, as we have also seen, undermine the very possibility of science rather than provide an alternative to the Aristotelian account of science. For one thing, the notion of causation becomes notoriously problematic in a Humean account. For Hume, the idea of a necessary connection between events can have no objective validity, since (he says) we never observe such a connection, but at most only a constant conjunction between the events. The idea that events of type A *necessarily* bring about events of type B reflects in his view only the tendency of the human mind to expect B on the occurrence of A, rather than anything objectively true of A and B themselves. Hence if science is in the business of discovering objective necessary connections between events, there can be no science. Nor will it help to re-define science as concerned only with establishing law-like correlations between events, without claiming any necessary connections between them. For to be a consistent

Humean is to deny that any universals exist, since all we ever perceive are particulars. Yet to say that events of type A are regularly followed by events of type B is to appeal to universals, since A and B would be universals; indeed, the very notion of an "event" is itself a universal. Moreover, even if science were not concerned with discovering necessary connections, it definitely *is* concerned with predicting unobserved events on the basis of the observed ones. But this assumes that inductive reasoning is objectively valid, and as we saw in the previous chapter, given Hume's account of causation, our confidence in induction becomes rationally unjustifiable. All told, then, even on the deflated conception of science in question, science would be impossible if Hume's philosophy were true.

Contemporary advocates of the Humean view that science is in the business of discovering mere regularities between events rather than essences, powers, natures, final causes, or even necessary connections, wouldn't rest their case on Hume's preposterous theory of ideas. Though the *point* of advocating it isn't entirely clear if one doesn't buy the rest of Hume's philosophy – unless, that is, one simply wants to avoid Aristotelianism at all costs. In any event, as we have seen, this anti-Aristotelian ideological program – and an ideological program is all it is – does not fit the actual practice of biological science (even if it fits the *rhetoric* of some biologists when they are in public-relations mode). Yet neither, as it turns out, does it fit the practice even of physics or chemistry, those sciences which are supposed to provide the great success story of the mechanistic revolution.

As the philosopher of science Nancy Cartwright has emphasized, a serious problem with the Humean idea that science is merely in the business of establishing regularities on the basis of observation is that the sorts of regularities that the hard sciences tend to uncover are rarely observed, and in fact are in ordinary circumstances impossible to observe.[44] Beginning students of physics quickly become acquainted with idealizations like the notion of a frictionless surface, and with the fact that laws like Newton's law of gravitation strictly speaking describe the behavior of bodies only in the circumstance where no interfering forces are acting on them, a circumstance which never actually holds. Moreover, physicists do not in fact embrace a regularity as a law of nature only after many

trials, after the fashion of popular presentations of inductive reasoning. Rather, they draw their conclusions from a few highly spe-
cialized experiments conducted under artificial conditions. None of
this is consistent with the idea that science is concerned with cata-
loguing observed regularities. But it is consistent, in Cartwright's
view, with the Aristotelian picture of science as in the business of
uncovering the hidden natures or powers of things. Actual experimental practice indicates that what physicists are really looking for
are the inherent powers a thing will naturally manifest when interfering conditions are removed, and the fact that a few experiments,
or even a single controlled experiment, are taken to establish the
results in question indicates that these powers are taken to reflect a
nature that is universal to things of that type.

A Humean might insist that we can avoid this conclusion by
treating the laws of physics as nothing more than counterfactual
statements: If such-and-such conditions had not interfered, then so-
and-so would have happened; and that's it. One problem with this
is that it is an odd thing for an empiricist to say, given that the
antecedents of such counterfactuals (the circumstance where the
interfering conditions do not hold) are never actually observed.
Another is that we still want to know *why* such a counterfactual
statement is true, that is, what facts about the world make it the case
that so-and-so would have happened in the absence of the interfering conditions (and while a Humean might feign a lack of curiosity
on this point, scientists themselves do not do so). The deeper point,
however, is that it only makes sense to regard certain conditions as
"interfering" in the first place if we assume that it has certain natural tendencies or powers that are being interfered with. Indeed, we
cannot make sense of certain experimental conditions as "ideal"
unless we assume that the thing being studied has a nature or inherent powers that the conditions will allow to operate unimpeded.
Without the notion of a nature or inherent powers, we have no idea
what exactly an experiment in physics is testing *for*.

The idea of "regularities" or "laws of nature" is accordingly
misleading, in Cartwright's view, given that science actually
uncovers few laws or regularities outside highly artificial conditions. (Indeed, she argues that the very notion of a scientific "law"
is a relic of the days when Newton and Co. took themselves to be

discovering the blueprints by reference to which God directs the world, and cannot be made sense of apart from the idea of a divine legislator – an idea few contemporary Humeans would endorse.[45]) Strictly speaking, what science discovers are the universal natures and inherent powers of things, and talk of "laws of nature" can only be shorthand for this. As Cartwright says, "the empiricists of the scientific revolution wanted to oust Aristotle entirely from the new learning," but "they did no such thing."[46]

Cartwright's views are by no means idiosyncratic. They reflect a growing trend within the philosophy of science toward a neo-Aristotelian "new essentialism," as Brian Ellis, one of its proponents, has labeled it.[47] Nor is this tendency motivated by a desire to uphold the sort of moral and theological worldview I've been defending in this book (a worldview I expect most of these "new essentialists" would be horrified by), but rather by a sense that the standard mechanistic and empiricist interpretation of science simply doesn't hold up in light of the actual discoveries of modern science or the facts of scientific practice.

Nor is it just Aristotle's doctrine of natures, forms, or essences that finds an echo in the new essentialism. As many of these theorists have recognized, to affirm the existence in physical phenomena of inherent powers or capacities is to acknowledge phenomena that are directed at or point to states of affairs beyond themselves. For example, to be fragile is to point to or be directed at *breaking*, and a fragile thing of its nature points to or is directed at this particular state even if it is never in fact realized. To be soluble is to point to or be directed at *dissolving*, and a soluble thing of its nature points to or is directed at this particular state even if it is never in fact realized. And so forth. The late "new essentialist" philosopher George Molnar concluded that the powers inherent in physical objects exhibit a kind of "physical intentionality" insofar as, like thoughts and other mental states, they point to something beyond themselves, even though they are unlike thoughts in being unconscious.[48] But the notion of something which points beyond itself to a certain goal or end-state even though it is totally unconscious is, of course, *nothing other than the Aristotelian notion of final causality*. Indeed, it is amazing how closely the conclusions of the "new essentialist" philosophers of science often parallel (apparently unbeknown to them) those of writers in the Aristotelian Scholastic tradition, whose view was precisely that "every power, exercised or not, has an object toward which it is directed – its *intentio*" and that "what is a natural law, if not the expression of the *inner tendencies of the nature* of [physical] things?"[49] It is also amazing that the persistence of final causality within purportedly mechanistic modern physics is not more generally acknowledged, especially given that, as in biology, contemporary writers on physics are absolutely smitten with the language of "information," "software," "computation," etc., and seem to think these concepts genuinely describe objective features of even inorganic physical reality. For as we have seen, there is really no way to make sense of "information," "software," and the like existing in nature apart from human interests unless we think of such talk as expressing a commitment to something like Aristotelian teleology.

Despite the undeniable advances in empirical knowledge made during the last 300 plus years, then, the work of the scientists who made those advances simply does not support the philosophical interpretation of those advances put forward by the proponents of the "Mechanical Philosophy" and the contemporary materialists or naturalists who are their intellectual heirs (despite their largely successful confidence trick of falsely peddling the philosophical interpretation as if it were inseparable from the advances). In this sense, though contemporary physical science is still rhetorically committed to the myth that medieval Scholasticism was somehow "refuted" by the scientific revolution, in philosophical substance it has moved not one whit beyond Thomas Aquinas, who held that "every agent acts for an end, otherwise one thing would not follow from the action of the agent more than another."[50]

By "agent" Aquinas did not just mean thinking beings like us, but anything that brings about an effect. This "principle of finality" (as it is traditionally known) is understood within the Aristotelian tradition to be a necessary concomitant of the "principle of causality," according to which every beginning of existence must have a cause. If there weren't something in the nature of a cause that orders or directs it toward the production of some particular effect or range of effects rather than another, then there would just be *no reason* why it produces that effect or range of effects specifically, rather than some other effect or none at all. Causation would be utterly unintelligible. To deny the reality of final causes ultimately entails denying the existence of efficient causes as well, and this is precisely what happened as Descartes's and Locke's abandonment of final causality gave way to Hume's skepticism about efficient causality – and with it the now "traditional" philosophical "problem" of causality and the "traditional" "problem" of induction and the "problem" of justifying the very presuppositions of scientific inquiry. The mechanistic-cum-materialistic abandonment of Aristotle has made unintelligible the very science that the advocates of the "Mechanical Philosophy" and contemporary materialists regard as the paradigm of rationality. At the same time, the actual practice and results of that science have only reinforced a broadly Aristotelian philosophy. That Aristotle was wrong about *physics* simply does not entail that he was wrong about *metaphysics*; indeed, it in the absence of Aristotelian metaphysical presuppositions, none of the sciences can ultimately be made sense of at all.

It's the moon, stupid

Aquinas, as I noted in a previous chapter, regarded final causality as "the cause of causes," the *most fundamental* of the four causes. The reason should be clear from what we've seen in this chapter. Nothing can even be made sense of as an efficient cause – as that which brings something else into being – unless it at the same time possesses goal-directedness or finality. Moreover, for it to be directed toward a certain end entails its having a form or essence appropriate to the realization of that end, and thus a material structure capable of instantiating that form or essence; a hammer, for instance, if it is to fulfill its function, must have a particular structure and be made of some material capable of maintaining that structure.[51] Thus the existence of final causes determines that there are formal and material causes too. Note that it also entails that a thing that has a final cause possesses potentialities which may or may not be actualized, but that (since nothing can be purely potential, or else it would not exist at all) those potentialities must be grounded, even when not actualized, in yet other actualities. Hence to acknowledge final causality is also to acknowledge the

Aristotelian distinction between actuality and potentiality. Insofar as modern science is, at least implicitly, as beholden as its predecessor was to final causality, it is thus also implicitly committed to the whole Aristotelian apparatus.

Of course, all of these matters could be pursued at much greater depth, and even many readers willing to acknowledge that the purported deficiencies of Aristotelian metaphysics have been greatly overstated by its critics would resist any suggestion that modern science licenses nothing less than a full-scale return to it. But as this book has, I think, established, (a) when rightly understood, the traditional arguments for an Aristotelian metaphysical picture of the world are powerful, (b) the modern philosophers' criticisms of that picture are no good and their own attempted replacements of it are fraught with various paradoxes and incoherencies, and (c) modern science is not only not inconsistent with that metaphysical picture but at least to some extent tends to point in its direction. *At the very least*, then, there can be no doubt that a broadly Aristotelian philosophical worldview is still as rationally defensible today as it ever was, and must be admitted to be so even by those who do not think (as I do) that when one pursues these matters to the end one will see that it, or something very much like it, is rationally unavoidable.

But if Aristotle has, by virtue of developments in modern philosophy and science, had his revenge on those who sought to overthrow him at the dawn of the modern period, why is this fact not more widely recognized? One reason is the prevailing general ignorance about what the Aristotelian and Scholastic traditions really believed, what the actual intellectual and historical circumstances were that led to their replacement by modern philosophy in its various guises, and what the true relationship is between the latter and modern science. Apart from scholars who specialize in these matters, most academics and other intellectuals, and certainly most journalists and popular writers, simply cannot think about the Middle Ages, Scholasticism, the scientific revolution, and related topics except in terms of the crudest clichés and caricatures.

As we have seen, the rabid anti-Scholasticism of the early moderns was driven less by dispassionate intellectual considerations than by a political agenda: to reorient human life away from the

next world and toward this one, and to weaken the rational credentials of religion so as to make this project seem justifiable and
inevitable. That brings us to the main reason why Aristotle's
revenge is not more widely acknowledged. Even in Aristotle's own
work, we find a very conservative ethics grounded in human
nature, a doctrine of the immateriality of the human intellect, and
an Unmoved Mover of the universe contemplation of whom is the
highest end of human existence. By the time Aquinas and the other
Scholastics were done refining and drawing out the implications of
the Aristotelian system, it was evident that it entailed nothing less
than the entire conception of God enshrined in classical monotheism, the immortality of the soul, and the natural law system of
morality. To acknowledge the truth of the Aristotelian metaphysical
picture of the world is thus unavoidably to open the door to everything the Scholastics built on it. In short, *Aristotle's revenge is also
Aquinas's revenge*; and for that reason alone, contemporary secular
intellectuals cannot allow themselves to acknowledge it. For the
project of the early moderns is their project too.

But that project is built on a lie. To quote a famous Confucian
proverb, "When the finger points at the moon, the idiot looks at the
finger." The modern secularist is, as it were, positively fixated on
the finger – unsurprisingly given that, if (as he falsely assumes)
there really are no fixed natures and natural ends in the world, no
formal and final causes, then nothing could naturally point beyond
itself to anything else. In fact, the material world points beyond
itself to God; but the secularist sees only the material world. The
material side of human nature points beyond itself to an immaterial and immortal soul; the secularist sees only the brain and body.
The sexual act points beyond itself to marriage and family; the secularist sees only the sexual act. And so on, and on and on. What else
can one say? *It's the moon, stupid.*

Endnotes

Preface

1 260C, Jowett translation.
2 Translated by Robert P. Goodwin, in *Selected Writings of St. Thomas Aquinas* (Prentice-Hall, 1965), Preface.
3 *Seeing Through the Eye: Malcolm Muggeridge on Faith*, ed. Cecil Kuhne (Ignatius Press, 2005), p. 76.
4 Richard Dawkins, "Review of *Blueprints: Solving the Mystery of Evolution* by Maitland A. Edey and Donald C. Johanson," *New York Times* (April 9, 1989).

Chapter 1: Bad Religion

1 Quoted by James A. Beverley in "Thinking Straighter: Why the world's most famous atheist now believes in God," *Christianity Today* (April 2005). See also Gary Habermas's interview with Flew in the Winter 2005 issue of the journal *Philosophia Christi*. As this book was being completed, Flew published *There Is a God: How the World's Most Notorious Atheist Changed His Mind* (HarperOne, 2007), co-authored with Roy Abraham Varghese, wherein he sets out his current position in more detail.
2 Both quotes taken from Beverley's "Thinking Straighter."
3 Professor Brian Leiter, of the influential philosophy weblog *Leiter Reports*, in a postdated December 16, 2004.
4 *Secular Web* contributor Richard Carrier, quoted by Beverley in "Thinking Straighter."
5 Beverley's article notes that Flew "gives first place to Aristotle in having the most significant impact on him," and that his reconsideration of Aristotle was prompted by his having read David Conway's book *The Rediscovery of Wisdom: From Here to Antiquity in*

Quest of Sophia (St. Martin's Press, 2000), which defends Aristotle's arguments for the existence of God. This book is mentioned prominently in Flew's Introduction to the reissue of his *God and Philosophy* (Prometheus, 2005). Flew has also made reference several times to the possibility of reading St. Thomas Aquinas's famous Five Ways (which are largely Aristotelian in spirit) as arguments for a purely Aristotelian God rather than the God of Christianity. (See, for example, his interview with Habermas and the Introduction to *God and Philosophy*.) Yet Flew's critics have ignored all of this; in particular, they have said nothing in reply to Conway's arguments, despite their apparent direct influence on Flew's conversion.

6   Quoted by Stuart Wavell in "In the beginning there was something," *The Sunday Times* (December 19, 2004).

7   The "New Atheism" label seems to have originated with a cover story on Dawkins, Dennett, and Harris in the November 2006 issue of *Wired* magazine. Hitchens would join the club a few months later, after his own book appeared.

8   Daniel C. Dennett, "The Bright Stuff," *New York Times* (July 12, 2003).

9   Conway, *The Rediscovery of Wisdom*, p. 79. The rational demonstrability of theism is in Conway's view the core of what he calls the "classical conception" of philosophy, a conception he attributes to Plato, Aristotle, the Stoics, Plotinus and the other Neo-Platonists, Augustine, Boethius, Maimonides, Aquinas, Renaissance thinkers like Marsilio Ficino and Erasmus, and even (despite their rejection of certain key ancient and medieval philosophical ideas) modern thinkers like Descartes, Spinoza, Leibniz, Benjamin Whichcote and other Cambridge Platonists, Newton, Shaftesbury, and Hutcheson. To this list of philosophical theists could be added, of course, Anselm, Duns Scotus, and many other medieval Scholastic writers; Islamic philosophers like Avicenna, al-Ghazali, and Averroes; modern philosophers like Locke, Berkeley, Samuel Clarke, and William Paley; Suarez and other Late Scholastic philosophers; Garrigou-Lagrange, Maritain, Gilson, and other Neo-Scholastics and Neo-Thomists of the 19th and 20th centuries; A.E. Taylor, F.R. Tennant, and other 20th-century Anglican philosophers; and, among contemporary analytic philosophers, David Braine, William Lane Craig, Brian Davies, John Haldane, Robert Koons, Barry Miller, David Oderberg, Alvin Plantinga, Alexander Pruss, James Ross, Richard Swinburne, Charles Taliaferro, and William Vallicella – to name just a few.

10 I explain the relevant views of Frege (briefly) and Russell, Searle, and Nagel (at length) in my book *Philosophy of Mind: A Short Introduction* (Oneworld Publications, 2005). We will also have reason to consider some of these ideas in later chapters.

11 In the twentieth century this tradition was defended most prominently by: Mortimer Adler in his popular writings; Reginald Garrigou-Lagrange, Jacques Maritain, Etienne Gilson, Ralph McInerny, and many other Neo-Scholastics and Neo-Thomists in the context of Roman Catholic philosophy and theology; John Wild and Henry Veatch in the context of secular academic philosophy; and, within analytic philosophy in particular, by Peter Geach, Elizabeth Anscombe, John Haldane, and other philosophers sometimes classified as "analytical Thomists." Some representative works by these thinkers include: Adler's *Ten Philosophical Mistakes* (Collier Books, 1985); Garrigou-Lagrange's *Reality: A Synthesis of Thomistic Thought* (Herder, 1950; reprinted in 2006 by Ex Fontibus Co.); Maritain's *An Introduction to Philosophy* (Sheed and Ward, 1930; reprinted in 2005 by Rowman and Littlefield); Gilson's *God and Philosophy* (Yale University Press, 1941); McInerny's *Characters in Search of Their Author* (University of Notre Dame Press, 2001); Wild's *Introduction to Realistic Philosophy* (Harper, 1948); Veatch's *Swimming against the Current in Contemporary Philosophy* (Catholic University of America Press, 1990); Anscombe and Geach's *Three Philosophers: Aristotle, Aquinas, Frege* (Basil Blackwell, 1961); and Haldane's *Atheism and Theism*, Second edition (co-written with J.J.C. Smart) (Blackwell, 2003).

12 Quentin Smith, "The Metaphilosophy of Naturalism," *Philo: A Journal of Philosophy* (Fall-Winter 2001).

13 Jeremy Waldron, *God, Locke, and Equality: Christian Foundations in Locke's Political Thought* (Cambridge University Press, 2002), p. 20.

14 Thomas Nagel, *The Last Word* (Oxford University Press, 1997), pp. 130–31.

15 C.F.J. Martin, *Thomas Aquinas: God and Explanations* (Edinburgh University Press, 1997), pp. 98–99. It might be objected that many religious believers do not think that they are *themselves* in danger of Hell, but only that nonbelievers are. But this is certainly not true of e.g. Catholicism, which teaches that no one in this life can be assured of his salvation, and thus it is not true of those medieval religious believers whom secularists would presumably assume were most in thrall to wishful thinking. It might also be objected that modern theologically liberal versions of Christianity, Judaism, etc., do not feature belief in eternal damnation, preferring to hold

that everyone will be saved. But I readily concede that theological liberalism, like liberalism generally, *is* (in this respect as in so many others) based on little more than wishful thinking.

16 Ibid., p. 131.

17 See, for example, Edward Grant's *God and Reason in the Middle Ages* (Cambridge University Press, 2001); Régine Pernoud, *Those Terrible Middle Ages! Debunking the Myths* (Ignatius Press, 2000); and James J. Walsh, *The Thirteenth: Greatest of Centuries* (Fordham University Press, 1952).

18 From a piece in the *New York Review of Books* (January 9, 1997), quoted by J. Budziszewski in "The Second Tablet Project," *First Things* (June/July 2002).

19 Paul Davies, *The Fifth Miracle: The Search for the Origin and Meaning of Life* (Simon and Schuster, 1999), pp. 28 and 17–18, emphasis added.

20 Tyler Burge, "Mind-Body Causation and Explanatory Practice," in John Heil and Alfred Mele, eds., *Mental Causation* (Oxford University Press, 1995), p. 117.

21 John R. Searle, *Mind: A Brief Introduction* (Oxford University Press, 2004), p. 48.

22 William G. Lycan, "Giving Dualism Its Due," a paper presented at the 2007 Australasian Association of Philosophy conference at the University of New England. The draft is available on Lycan's website.

23 See Richard Dawkins, *The Selfish Gene*, New edition (Oxford University Press, 1989) and David Stove, *Darwinian Fairytales* (Encounter Books, 2006).

24 John R. Searle, *Mind, Language, and Society* (Basic Books, 1998), pp. 34–35.

25 Vincent Bugliosi, *Reclaiming History: The Assassination of President John F. Kennedy* (W. W. Norton, 2007), p. xxvi.

26 Ibid., p. xxix.

27 Ibid., pp. xxiv–xxv.

28 Ibid., p. xxvi.

29 Edward Feser, "We the Sheeple? Why Conspiracy Theories Persist," *TCS Daily* (September 20, 2006).

2. Greeks Bearing Gifts

1 Julia Annas says a little bit about all this in *Plato: A Very Short Introduction* (Oxford University Press, 2003), and it gave David

Stove the title for his very funny book *The Plato Cult and Other Philosophical Follies* (Basil Blackwell, 1991) (which is mostly not about Plato, incidentally).

2 Friedrich Nietzsche, *Beyond Good and Evil*, translated by Walter Kaufmann (Vintage, 1966), p. 3.

3 Alfred North Whitehead, *Process and Reality* , Corrected edition (The Free Press, 1978), p. 39.

4 Accessible introductions to Greek philosophy in general include Julia Annas, *Ancient Philosophy: A Very Short Introduction* (Oxford University Press, 2000) and Christopher Shields, *Classical Philosophy: A Contemporary Introduction* (Routledge, 2003). The standard work on the pre-Socratic philosophers is Jonathan Barnes, *The Presocratic Philosophers* (Routledge, 1982). A briefer and more accessible introduction can be found in Merrill Ring, *Beginning with the Pre-Socratics*, Second edition (McGraw-Hill, 1999).

5 A useful brief introduction to Socrates' life and thought can be found in C.C.W. Taylor, *Socrates* (Oxford University Press, 1998).

6 Among Plato's many dialogues, the ones most relevant to our discussion here are the *Phaedo*, *Republic*, and *Parmenides*. For a fine introduction to Plato's thought in general and his Theory of Forms in particular, see David Melling, *Understanding Plato* (Oxford University Press, 1987). A lucid introductory-level defense of a modern version of Platonism can be found in Chapter 3 of Michael Jubien, *Contemporary Metaphysics* (Blackwell, 1997).

7 Plato's theory is also sometimes called "the Theory of Ideas," but as we are about to see, he does *not* mean by "idea" what most people mean by it today, i.e. a subjective mental entity of some sort. Hence it is less misleading to use the term "Form."

8 One sometimes hears it suggested that if we decided to use the word "triangle" to mean "four-sided figure," then triangles *would* be four-sided; or that if we decided to write "5" whenever we would ordinarily write "4," then 2 and 2 would make 5; and so forth. Usually hapless undergraduates are the sources of such "arguments," but I have a heard a grown man with a Ph.D. say such things on at least one occasion. It is, in any event, an *extremely* stupid sort of argument. One might as well argue that we could change the planet Jupiter into a cheeseburger just by deciding to call it "Cheeseburger." The fallacy in both cases lies in assuming that to change the meaning we attach to the *words* we use to talk about things entails a change in the *things themselves*. It is easier to see the fallacy when the things in question are physical objects, but it is no less a fallacy when applied to other sorts of things.

CHAPTER 2

9 David Conway, in *The Rediscovery of Wisdom* (cited in Chapter 1), is a contemporary defender of the claim that Plato would identify the Form of the Good with God.

10 Here again one sometimes hears some very bad arguments to the contrary. For example, it is sometimes suggested that if the physical world were set up in such a way that whenever we put two objects together with two other objects, a fifth object magically appeared among them, this would be a case where 2 + 2 = 5. People who give such arguments really should listen to themselves more carefully. For by their own account, what they've described is *not* 2 and 2 *equaling* 5, but rather the act of placing 2 objects together with 2 other objects (which makes 4 objects total) suddenly and magically *causing* a new fifth object to appear. ("X causes Y" doesn't mean "X equals Y.")

11 See J.P. Moreland, *Universals* (McGill-Queen's University Press, 2001) for an introduction to the debate written from a point of view sympathetic to realism.

12 Richard M. Weaver, *Ideas Have Consequences* (University of Chicago Press, 1948). As noted above, Plato's Theory of Forms is also often called the Theory of Ideas. Weaver's title is a play on words.

13 The difficulties with identifying propositions with anything material or mental go well beyond this, and are well summarized by Alvin Plantinga in *Warrant and Proper Function* (Oxford University Press, 1993), Chapter 6.

14 D.M. Armstrong is a naturalist who endorses realism about universals on the basis of their role in science, and W.V.O. Quine is a naturalist who accepts the existence of some abstract objects (though of sets, actually, rather than numbers) on the basis of the role mathematics plays in science. Armstrong squares this with his naturalism by trying manfully (if unsuccessfully, as Moreland argues) to show that universals aren't abstract. (As we will see, Aristotle does something similar, but not in a way any naturalist could approve of.) Quine does it by shrugging his shoulders. (More seriously, he does it by defining "naturalism" expansively enough that anything science leads us to postulate is consistent with it.)

15 It is possible to be a nominalist about only one sort of purportedly abstract object, or several sorts, without being a nominalist about all of them. That is to say, one might deny that one sort of abstract object exists while accepting that another sort does. But those attracted to nominalism usually seek to press it as far as it can go, and understandably so. For if one's nominalism is motivated by a desire to defend materialism or naturalism, there isn't much point

to being selective about it, since to admit that at least some sorts of abstract (hence non-material and non-natural) objects exist seriously weakens the plausibility of materialism or naturalism as a general position.

16 Bertrand Russell, *The Problems of Philosophy* (Prometheus Books, 1988), Chapter 9.

17 See for instance Frege's essay "Thought," in Michael Beaney, ed., *The Frege Reader* (Blackwell, 1997).

18 For a recent lengthier defense of this sort of argument, see Crawford L. Elder, *Real Natures and Familiar Objects* (MIT Press, 2004), pp. 11–17.

19 Stove, *The Plato Cult*, p. 62.

20 The question of the difference between "analytic" and "continental" philosophy is a complicated one. The standard oversimplified story goes like this: Analytic philosophy tends to emphasize clarity of expression, explicit and rigorous argumentation, and heavy use of the tools of modern symbolic logic. Its originators tended to think that the solution of traditional philosophical problems would be facilitated by a careful analysis of the language in which they were expressed, and they also often looked to empirical science as the paradigm of rational inquiry. It is the predominant school of thought in the English-speaking world, and its heroes are thinkers like Frege, Russell, Wittgenstein, Carnap, and Quine. Continental philosophy, by contrast, tends to be more literary and humanistic in character. Its approach derives from the idealism of Kant and Hegel, and more immediately from the "phenomenological" method of analyzing human experience from the inside, seeking thereby to formulate an accurate description of the way the world seems to the human subject while bracketing off the question of objective truth. It tends to predominate on the European continent, and its modern heroes are thinkers like Husserl, Heidegger, Sartre, Gadamer, and Foucault. The typical analytic complaint about continental philosophy is that it is unrigorous, muddleheaded, subjectivist, inattentive to science, and written in impenetrable prose. The typical continental complaint about analytic philosophy is that it is superficial, reductionistic, anal retentive, inattentive to human concerns, and boring.

21 Quoted in Shields, *Aristotle*, pp. 419–20.

22 See Michael Ruse, *Homosexuality: A Philosophical Inquiry* (Blackwell, 1988), Chapter 8, for discussion of the attitudes of Greek (and other) philosophers toward homosexuality.

23 The works of Aristotle most relevant to our discussion here are the

Physics, Metaphysics, and *De Anima.* Useful brief introductions to Aristotle's thought include Jonathan Barnes, *Aristotle: A Very Short Introduction* (Oxford University Press, 2000) and Timothy A. Robinson, *Aristotle in Outline* (Hackett, 1995). Two excellent in-depth introductions are Jonathan Lear, *Aristotle: The Desire to Understand* (Cambridge University Press, 1988) and Christopher Shields, *Aristotle* (Routledge, 2007). David Oderberg's *Real Essentialism* (Routledge, 2007) is an important contemporary defense of Aristotelian metaphysics.

24 The Twenty-Four Thomistic Theses are a list of defining principles of Thomism proposed by the Vatican's Congregation of Sacred Studies in 1914 under Pope St. Pius X after consultation with various Thomistic professors. For discussion, see Garrigou-Lagrange, *Reality: A Synthesis of Thomistic Thought,* cited in the previous chapter.

25 Incidentally, this distinction between the essence of a thing and the properties that flow from its essence is one mark of the difference between Aristotle's version of essentialism (the doctrine that things have essences) and contemporary versions associated with philosophers like Saul Kripke. See Shields, *Aristotle,* pp. 99–105 and Oderberg, *Real Essentialism,* Chapter 1, for discussion of this and other differences.

26 Note that to say that a ball can be analyzed into its form and matter is not to say that it can be "reduced" to them, for the form and matter themselves can in turn be understood only in terms of the entire ball of which they are constituents. The Aristotelian conception of substance is in this regard holistic rather than reductionist.

27 The key difference between Plato and Aristotle is that Plato thinks there can be uninstantiated universals existing outside any mind and Aristotle does not. The sort of forms-without-matter described here are *instantiated* universals.

28 For a useful comparison of Aristotelian and empiricist accounts of causality, see pp. lix–lxxiii of Alfred Freddoso's "Introduction" to his translation of Francisco Suarez, *On Creation, Conservation, and Concurrence: Metaphysical Disputations 20–22* (St. Augustine's Press, 2002).

29 Dawkins, citing Dennett, makes a related claim on p. 117 of *The God Delusion.*

30 Paul Davies, *The Fifth Miracle: The Search for the Origin and Meaning of Life* (Simon and Schuster, 1999), Chapter 2.

31 For discussion of the various interpretive issues surrounding Aristotle's notion of final causation, see Allan Gotthelf,

"Understanding Aristotle's Teleology," in Richard F. Hassing, ed., *Final Causality in Nature and Human Affairs* (Catholic University of America Press, 1997) and Monte Ransome Johnson, *Aristotle on Teleology* (Oxford University Press, 2005). Useful surveys of the Scholastic understanding of Aristotelian final causality can be found e.g. in Celestine Bittle, *The Domain of Being* (Bruce Publishing Company, 1939), Chapter 23; Reginald Garrigou-Lagrange, *God: His Existence and His Nature, Volume 1* (Herder, 1939), pp. 199–205; D.Q. McInerny, *Metaphysics* (Priestly Fraternity of St. Peter, 2004), Chapter 14; and R.P. Phillips, *Modern Thomistic Philosophy, Volume 2* (Newman Press, 1950), part 2, Chapter 10.

32 A.W. Sparkes, *Talking Philosophy: A Wordbook* (Routledge, 1991), p. 218.

3. Getting Medieval

1 G.E.M. Anscombe and P.T. Geach, *Three Philosophers: Aristotle, Aquinas, Frege* (Basil Blackwell, 1961), p. 68.

2 The edition of the *Summa contra Gentiles* I am referring to is published by the University of Notre Dame Press, and includes *Book One: God, Book Two: Creation, Book Three: Providence (Part I), Book Three: Providence (Part II)*, and *Book Four: Salvation*. The *Summa Theologiae*, under the traditional title *Summa Theologica*, is available in a five-volume edition from the Christian Classics imprint of Ave Maria Press.

3 The most recent major biography of Aquinas is Jean-Pierre Torrell, O.P., *Saint Thomas Aquinas, Volume 1: The Person and His Work* (Catholic University of America Press, 2005).

4 See pp. 77–80 of Dawkins, *The God Delusion* (Houghton Mifflin, 2006) for the howlers alluded to, and the rest of the book for many others.

5 Daniel Dennett, *Breaking the Spell*, p. 242.

6 Tadeusz Zawidzki, *Dennett* (Oneworld Publications, 2007), p. ix.

7 The exchange was published with Ruse's permission by William Dembski on the blog *Uncommon Descent*, in a postdated February 21, 2006.

8 Cf. J.P. Moreland and William Lane Craig, *Philosophical Foundations for a Christian Worldview* (InterVarsity Press, 2003), Chapter 17.

9 E.A. Burtt, *The Metaphysical Foundations of Modern Physical Science* (Humanities Press, 1952), pp. 228–29.

10 See Plantinga's unpublished but widely read set of lecture notes

"Two Dozen (Or So) Theistic Arguments," which can be easily found online. Some of these are, shall we say, underdeveloped as Plantinga states them (though he doesn't claim to provide more than a quick summary in some cases), but most have been developed at length by other writers.

11 Plantinga briefly puts forward this argument in his article "Arguments for the existence of God" in the *Routledge Encyclopedia of Philosophy* (Routledge, 1998). It is also defended by R. P. Phillips in his *Modern Thomistic Philosophy, Volume 2: Metaphysics* (Newman Press, 1950), pp. 298–99. He calls it "the argument from the eternal truths." On the other hand, some modern Scholastic writers who would accept the idea that eternal truths exist in the mind of God are doubtful that this notion can form the basis of an independent proof of God's existence. See e.g. P. Coffey, *Ontology* (Longmans, 1938), pp. 89–95, and Cardinal Mercier et al., *A Manual of Modern Scholastic Philosophy, Volume 2* (B. Herder, 1933), pp. 32–35.

12 For a contemporary defense, see John Peterson, *Introduction to Scholastic Realism* (Peter Lang, 1999).

13 See my book *Aquinas* (Oneworld Publications, forthcoming) for a more detailed discussion of the arguments to follow, as well as discussion of all of the Five Ways and of some of Aquinas's other arguments. For good general introductions to Aquinas's thought which include useful brief treatments of his arguments for God's existence, see F.C. Copleston, *Aquinas* (Penguin Books, 1991) and Brian Davies, *The Thought of Thomas Aquinas* (Oxford University Press, 1992). Important detailed treatments of the Five Ways can be found in: Reginald Garrigou-Lagrange, *The One God: A Commentary on the First Part of St. Thomas's Theological Summa* (B. Herder, 1943); Reginald Garrigou-Lagrange, *God: His Existence and His Nature, Volume 1* (B. Herder, 1934); Maurice Holloway, *An Introduction to Natural Theology* (Appleton-Century-Crofts, 1959); Christopher Martin, *Thomas Aquinas: God and Explanations*, cited in Chapter 1; D.Q. McInerny, *Natural Theology* (Priestly Fraternity of St. Peter, 2005); Henri Renard, *Philosophy of God* (Bruce Publishing Co., 1951); and John F. Wippel, *The Metaphysical Thought of Thomas Aquinas* (Catholic University of America Press, 2000).

14 In addition to the sources cited in the previous note, important discussions of the argument from motion can be found in: Celestine Bittle, *God and His Creatures* (Bruce Publishing Co., 1953); William Lane Craig, *The Cosmological Argument from Plato to Leibniz* (Harper and Row, 1980); John Haldane's contribution to Smart and Haldane, *Atheism and Theism*, cited in Chapter 1; G.H. Joyce,

Principles of Natural Theology (Longman's, 1924); Norman Kretzmann, *The Metaphysics of Theism* (Oxford University Press, 1997); Scott MacDonald, "Aquinas's Parasitic Cosmological Argument," *Medieval Philosophy and Theology, Volume 1* (University of Notre Dame Press, 1991); and Phillips, *Modern Thomistic Philosophy, Volume 2: Metaphysics,* cited above.

15 There are arguments for God's existence that try to prove this, most importantly the *kalam* cosmological argument (as it is known), which has been skillfully defended in recent years by William Lane Craig among others. See William Lane Craig and Quentin Smith, *Theism, Atheism, and Big Bang Cosmology* (Oxford University Press, 1993) for a debate between a theist and a serious atheist over this argument. But Aquinas rejects this approach – rather famously, though Dawkins does not seem to have heard the news.

16 MacDonald, cited above, suggests that such a move from focusing on the motion of things to focusing on the existence of the things doing the moving makes the argument from motion "parasitic" on another kind of argument from God's existence (such as a First Cause argument of the sort I'll be stating next). As MacDonald realizes, even if this were true, it wouldn't mean that the argument from motion fails, but only that it isn't really as distinctive an argument as it might seem at first glance. But I don't think what MacDonald says is quite right. As Kretzmann and McInerny (also cited above) have noted, if the point of the argument from motion is to explain motion, and to explain motion requires explaining the existence of the things doing the moving and the way in which factors outside them contribute to their ability to move, then a focus on the existence of moving things is quite naturally going to be a part of any argument from motion. Furthermore, from an Aristotelian point of view the explanation of motion or change is fundamentally about explaining the transition from potentiality to actuality, and even at those stages in which it is the existence of moving things rather than their motion that the argument focuses on, explaining this transition is always what is in view.

17 That is not a good objection in any case, since any being who caused the entire world of time and space to come into being at some point in the past would have to be outside time and space, and thus eternal, in which case He would still be around now. See Craig's contribution to Craig and Smith, *Theism, Atheism, and Big Bang Cosmology,* cited above.

18 Dawkins, *The God Delusion,* pp. 77–78.

19 I am not saying that the theist should concede that any of these

theories is true, or even that any one of them is even plausible. Craig and other defenders of the *kalam* cosmological argument are, I think, probably right to hold that it can be demonstrated on purely metaphysical grounds that the universe is not infinitely old, and that Aquinas here conceded too much to his opponents. The point is just that none of this matters for assessing Aquinas's own arguments.

20 The argument that follows is perhaps most clearly stated in Aquinas's *On Being and Essence*, and is defended in Renard's *Philosophy of God* (pp. 26–29), cited above, and most recently by Brian Davies in Chapter 2 of his *The Reality of God and the Problem of Evil* (Continuum, 2006). It is also related to the Second and Third Ways of the *Summa Theologiae*.

21 See David Oderberg, *Real Essentialism* (Routledge, 2007), Chapter 6, for a recent discussion and defense of the distinction between essence and existence.

22 One must be careful in using this expression. There are many principles going by the name "principle of sufficient reason" (or PSR), and not all of them are equally plausible. In particular, formulations of the principle deriving from the modern rationalist tradition in philosophy and associated with thinkers like Leibniz make much stronger claims than the principle of causality, and have been criticized on grounds that do not apply to the latter principle. In general, it is always dangerous to read modern philosophical ideas and assumptions, whether rationalist, empiricist, Kantian, or whatever, back into Aquinas and other Scholastic thinkers. For a very detailed study of PSR, its various possible formulations, and the debate surrounding it, see Alexander R. Pruss, *The Principle of Sufficient Reason: A Reassessment* (Cambridge University Press, 2006).

23 See G.E.M. Anscombe, "'Whatever has a beginning of existence must have a cause': Hume's argument exposed," in her *Collected Philosophical Papers, Volume 1* (Basil Blackwell, 1981).

24 See G.E.M. Anscombe, "Times, beginnings and causes," in her *Collected Philosophical Papers, Volume 2* (Basil Blackwell, 1981).

25 Again, see the work of Craig and other defenders of the *kalam* cosmological argument.

26 No, this does not conflict with the doctrine of the Trinity, since that doctrine does not say – indeed, it denies – that there are three Gods; rather, it says that there are three *Persons* in *one* God. But this is an issue that goes well beyond what there is space for in this book.

27 C.F.J. Martin, *Thomas Aquinas: God and Explanations*, p. 204, note 6.

28 If like some "modern" philosophers one adopts a "Cartesian dualist" conception of the mind, some of this would have to be qualified, but the overall picture of the physical world remains the same either way. More on this later.

29 There are other aspects of human nature, such as our capacity for self-sacrifice and aesthetic appreciation among others, that even many irreligious or atheistic thinkers doubt can be explained by natural selection. See e.g. David Stove, *Darwinian Fairytales*, cited in Chapter 1; Anthony O'Hear, *Beyond Evolution* (Oxford University Press, 1997); and John Dupre, *Human Nature and the Limits of Science* (Oxford University Press, 2001). There are also very grave conceptual and empirical difficulties with the notion that the origins of life and of sexual reproduction can be explained in Darwinian terms. See John Haldane's contribution to Smart and Haldane, *Atheism and Theism* (cited earlier), at pp. 90–96. There can be no question that whatever its admitted strengths, Darwinism is not without serious problems as a completely general theory of the biological realm, and in trying to silence and discredit its critics the theory's most vocal proponents have been guilty of the same sort of intellectual dishonesty and dogmatism of which they accuse their opponents.

30 See Harris's *Letter to a Christian Nation* (Knopf, 2006), p. 73.

4. Scholastic Aptitude

1 For some important recent discussions see Mortimer Adler, *Intellect: Mind over Matter* (Collier Books, 1990); David Braine, *The Human Person: Animal and Spirit* (University of Notre Dame Press, 1992); Ric Machuga, *In Defense of the Soul* (Brazos Press, 2002); Herbert McCabe, "The Immortality of the Soul," reprinted in Brian Davies, ed., *Aquinas's Summa Theologiae: Critical Essays* (Rowman and Littlefield, 2006); J.P. Moreland and Scott B. Rae, *Body and Soul* (InterVarsity Press, 2000); David Oderberg, "Hylemorphic Dualism," in Ellen Frankel Paul, Fred D. Miller, Jr., and Jeffrey Paul, eds., *Personal Identity* (Cambridge University Press, 2005); and James Ross, "Immaterial Aspects of Thought," *The Journal of Philosophy* 89 (1992). See also Chapters 7 and 8 of my book *Philosophy of Mind*, cited earlier.

2 For detailed discussion of this issue, see John Haldane and Patrick Lee, "Aquinas on Human Ensoulment, Abortion and the Value of Life," *Philosophy* 78 (2003). It is sometimes suggested that the fact

that twinning occasionally occurs within the first few days after conception indicates that what existed prior to twinning was not really a distinct human individual. But as Haldane and Lee point out, this is like saying that since a divided flatworm will develop into two new flatworms, a distinct individual flatworm didn't really exist prior to the division.

3 Harris, *Letter to a Christian Nation*, p. 30.

4 Dawkins, *The God Delusion*, p. 264. Since I wouldn't want Dawkins to accuse me of leaving out one jot or tittle of his blasphemous new law, let me note that this "commandment" continues as follows: ". . . and leave others to enjoy theirs in private whatever their inclinations, which are none of your business."

5 Ibid., p. 316.

6 For a general introduction to Aquinas's natural law theory, see Ralph McInerny, *Ethica Thomistica*, Second edition (Catholic University of America Press, 1997). For an excellent set of books on contemporary moral problems written from a traditional natural law point of view, see David S. Oderberg's *Moral Theory* (Blackwell, 2000) and *Applied Ethics* (Blackwell, 2000). (Also important is Oderberg's recent essay "The Metaphysical Foundations of Natural Law," in H. Zaborowski, ed., *Natural Law and Contemporary Society* [Catholic University of America Press, 2008].) Some of the best modern books on traditional natural law theory were written in the mid-20th century. Three good general introductions of this sort are Celestine Bittle, *Man and Morals* (Bruce Publishing Company, 1950), Austin Fagothey, *Right and Reason*, Second edition (C.V. Mosby Co., 1959), and Thomas J. Higgins, *Man as Man: The Science and Art of Ethics*, Revised edition (Bruce Publishing Company, 1959). For an excellent in-depth treatment, see (if you can find them) the two thick volumes of Michael Cronin's *The Science of Ethics*, Second edition (M.H. Gill and Son, 1920). These books are all refreshingly clear-headed and unfashionable, free of cant and free of Kant; Fagothey and Higgins have recently been reprinted. A recently developed view that goes by the name of the "New Natural Law Theory" attempts to reformulate traditional natural law theory in a way that makes no reference to the classical, and especially Aristotelian, metaphysical ideas that natural law has always rested on. As with Paley's attempt to replace the older teleological argument with a non-Aristotelian alternative, the result is a position that (in my estimation) concedes all the crucial metaphysical ground to its opponents and opens itself up to all sorts of objections that do not apply to the older theory.

7 Relativize to Euclidean space if you're worried about Riemannian triangles. Riemannian triangles will, in any case, have their own fixed natures, and thus could be equally well used to make the point.

8 For detailed criticism of the so-called "fact/value distinction," see Oderberg, *Moral Theory*, pp. 9–15, and Christopher Martin, "The Fact/Value Distinction," in David S. Oderberg and Timothy Chappell, eds., *Human Values: New Essays on Ethics and Natural Law* (Palgrave, 2004).

9 That one human being can literally own another as his property, or can kidnap another and make him a slave, or that some races are naturally suited to being enslaved by others, are notions condemned by natural law theory as intrinsically immoral. It is true that natural law theory has traditionally allowed that *lesser* forms of "slavery" could in principle be justified. But what this would involve is a prolonged period of servitude as a way of paying off a significant debt, say, or as punishment for a crime (as criminals today are enjoined to work and to give up their freedom). Even so, natural law theorists have tended to see the practice as too fraught with moral hazards to be defensible in practice; and the suggestion that the legitimacy of racial chattel slavery as it was known in early American history follows from natural law theory is, as I say, a slander.

10 Andrew Sullivan, *The Conservative Soul* (HarperCollins, 2006), pp. 82–84.

11 Sigmund Freud, *A General Introduction to Psycho-Analysis*, trans. Joan Riviere (Liverwright, 1935), p. 277, quoted by John F. Kippley, *Sex and the Marriage Covenant*, Second edition (Ignatius, 2005), p. 38.

12 The reference is to a *Washington Post* editorial of March 22, 1931, cited in John F. Kippley, "'Casti Connubii': 60 Years Later, More Relevant Than Ever," *Homiletic and Pastoral Review* (June 1991).

13 Laura Sheahen, "Religion: For Dummies," *Beliefnet.com* (no date).

14 I Corinthians 15:14, Revised Standard Version.

15 The philosopher William Lane Craig is one of the most prominent and capable defenders of the historicity of the resurrection. For a useful brief survey of his case, see Chapters 7 and 8 of his *Reasonable Faith* (Crossway Books, 1994). For more detailed treatments, see Craig's *The Son Rises: The Historical Evidence for the Resurrection of Jesus* (Moody Press, 1981) and *Assessing the New Testament Evidence for the Historicity of the Resurrection of Jesus* (Edwin Mellen Press, 2002). See also Richard Swinburne, *The Resurrection of God Incarnate* (Oxford University Press, 2003).

CHAPTER 5

16 Stove, *The Plato Cult*, p. 5.
17 Hitchens, *God Is Not Great*, p. 81.
18 See Brian Davies, *The Reality of God and the Problem of Evil* (Continuum, 2006) for an excellent recent full-length treatment.
19 *Summa Theologiae*, I, q. 2, a. 3, ad 1, emphasis mine.
20 Romans 8:18, Revised Standard Version.

5. Descent of the Modernists

1 See Stephen Gaukroger, *Descartes: An Intellectual Biography* (Oxford University Press, 1995), pp. 1–2
2 For discussion of the decline of the medieval Scholastic tradition, see Arthur F. Holmes, *Fact, Value, and God* (Eerdmans, 1997), Chapter 7; C.F.J. Martin, *An Introduction to Medieval Philosophy* (Edinburgh University Press, 1996), Chapter 7; Josef Pieper, *Scholasticism* (St. Augustine's Press, 2001), Chapter 11; Joseph Rickaby, *Scholasticism* (Dodge Publishing, 1908), Chapters 4 and 5; Maurice de Wulf, *An Introduction to Scholastic Philosophy* (M.H. Gill and Son, 1907), pp. 145–54; and John S. Zybura, "Scholasticism and the Period of Transition – The Neo-Scholastic View," in John S. Zybura, ed., *Present-Day Thinkers and the New Scholasticism*, Second edition (Herder, 1927).
3 Christopher Hitchens, *God Is Not Great* (Twelve, 2007), pp. 68–71.
4 Aquinas's formulation was "that which can be achieved by a smaller number of originating principles is not brought about by a larger number" (*Summa Theologiae*, I, q. 2, a. 3, second objection). See William Thorburn, "The Myth of Ockham's Razor," *Mind* 27 (1918), 345–53 for discussion of the antecedents of "Ockham's" principle, and of how it came to be associated with Ockham.
5 See *Physics*, 259a12.
6 Paul Tillich, *A History of Christian Thought* (Touchstone, 1968), pp. 198–201.
7 An indispensible classic study of the relationship between early modern philosophy and modern science, and of both to Aristotelian Scholasticism, is E.A. Burtt, *The Metaphysical Foundations of Modern Physical Science* (Humanities Press, 1980). An important recent treatment is Dennis Des Chene, *Physiologia: Natural Philosophy in Late Aristotelian and Cartesian Thought* (Cornell University Press, 1996). For a useful brief introduction to the subject, see the essays by Donald Rutherford, Stephen Gaukroger, and Dennis Des Chene in Donald Rutherford, ed., *The Cambridge*

Companion to Early Modern Philosophy (Cambridge University Press, 2006). Holmes, *Fact, Value, and God*, Chapter 8 and Montague Brown, *Restoration of Reason* (Baker Academic, 2006) provide useful brief discussions of some of the cultural and historical factors that underlay the early modern philosophers' and scientists' abandonment of Aristotelianism.

8 See *Lib.* ii. *de Coelo* lect. 17, and *Summa Theologiae* I, q. 32, a. 1, ad 2. Incidentally, Hitchens dishonestly asserts that Aquinas "half believed in astrology" (*God Is Not Great*, p. 63). In fact Aquinas did not believe in astrology at all. What he did believe were rather certain astronomical theories that some other people used to try to support astrology. (Hitchens believes in Darwinism, and the Nazis appealed to Darwinism in support of their crackpot racial theories. Does this entail that Hitchens "half believes in" Nazi racial theories?)

9 For a recent treatment of the Galileo incident that avoids the popular caricatures, see William R. Shea and Mariano Artigas, *Galileo in Rome: The Rise and Fall of a Troublesome Genius* (Oxford University Press, 2004).

10 See Bacon's *The Great Instauration*, in *The New Organon and Related Writings*, edited by Fulton H. Anderson (Liberal Arts Press, 1960), pp. 8 and 16, and Descartes's *Discourse on Method*, translated by Donald A. Cress (Hackett, 1980), p. 33.

11 Pierre Manent, *An Intellectual History of Liberalism* (Princeton University Press, 1995), pp. 114 and 116.

12 Pierre Manent, *The City of Man* (Princeton University Press, 1998), p. 113.

13 Mark Lilla, *The Stillborn God: Religion, Politics, and the Modern West* (Alfred A. Knopf, 2007), pp. 75 and 87.

14 Gilbert Ryle, "John Locke," in Jean S. Yolton, ed., *A Locke Miscellany* (Thoemmes, 1990), p. 318.

15 Burtt, *Metaphysical Foundations*, pp. 305–6.

16 William Hasker, *The Emergent Self* (Cornell University Press, 1999), p. 64. Hasker cites philosopher of science David Hull as having made a similar point.

17 See e.g. William Wallace, "Quantification in Sixteenth-Century Natural Philosophy," in John P. O'Callaghan and Thomas S. Hibbs, eds., *Recovering Nature* (University of Notre Dame Press, 1999) and William Wallace, *Galileo and His Sources* (Princeton University Press, 1984).

18 Recent interpretations of the findings of modern science written from a broadly Aristotelian point of view include Anthony Rizzi,

The Science Before Science (IAP Press, 2004) and William A. Wallace, *The Modeling of Nature: Philosophy of Science and Philosophy of Nature in Synthesis* (Catholic University of America Press, 1996). See also some of the references to be given in the next chapter.

19 This point is developed in C.F.J. Martin, *Thomas Aquinas: God and Explanations*, pp. 188–90. Cf. Stephen Mumford, *Dispositions* (Oxford University Press, 1998), pp. 136–41.

20 Cf. R.S. Woolhouse, *Locke* (University of Minnesota Press, 1983), p. 112. and Des Chene, *Physiologia*, p. 24, n. 5.

21 For a survey of the recent debate over the "qualia problem," see Chapters 4 and 5 of my book *Philosophy of Mind* (Oneworld Publications, 2005).

22 See Nagel's influential article "What Is It Like to Be a Bat?" in his collection *Mortal Questions* (Cambridge University Press, 1979).

23 Accordingly, Locke was what is today called a "property dualist" rather than a "substance dualist" à la Descartes. See pp. 79–87 of my book *Locke*. (Oneworld Publications, 2007). For Cudworth's influence on Locke's views on this issue, see Michael Ayers, *Locke, Volume 2: Ontology* (Routledge, 1991), pp. 170–76.

24 Peter Geach, *The Virtues* (Cambridge University Press, 1977), p. 52.

25 See Jerry Fodor, *Psychosemantics* (MIT Press, 1987), p. 97, and Joseph Levine, *Purple Haze: The Puzzle of Consciousness* (Oxford University Press, 2001), pp. 17–21.

26 For a recent study of the differences between the Aristotelian-Thomistic account of knowledge and the modern one, see John P. O'Callaghan, *Thomist Realism and the Linguistic Turn* (University of Notre Dame Press, 2003).

27 Some contemporary philosophers have begun to consider the idea that an appeal to the "proper functioning" of our sensory and cognitive capacities might help to solve the problem, and they are right to think this. But as we will see in the next chapter, we cannot make sense of the idea of proper functioning unless we acknowledge that there are such things as final causes.

28 See Derek Parfit, *Reasons and Persons* (Oxford University Press, 1984).

29 For a useful recent discussion see pp. 96–101 and 144–47 of J.J.C. Smart and J.J. Haldane's *Atheism and Theism*, Second edition (Blackwell, 2003).

30 But see Fred D. Miller, Jr.'s *Nature, Justice, and Rights in Aristotle's Politics* (Oxford University Press, 1995) for the case for Aristotle's having an implicit doctrine of rights.

31 Jeremy Waldron, *God, Locke, and Equality* (Cambridge University Press, 2002).

32 Daniel Dennett, *Darwin's Dangerous Idea* (Simon and Schuster, 1995), Chapter 3.

33 W.T. Stace, "Man against Darkness," *The Atlantic* (September 1948), pp. 53–55, quoted in Leo Sweeney, S.J. (with William J. Carroll and John J. Furlong), *Authentic Metaphysics in an Age of Unreality*, Second edition (Peter Lang, 1996), pp. 268–70. Emphasis mine.

6. Aristotle's Revenge

1 Quoted from Larissa MacFarquhar, "Two Heads: A Marriage Devoted to the Mind-Body Problem," *The New Yorker* (February 12, 2007), p. 69.

2 Paul M. Churchland, *Scientific Realism and the Plasticity of Mind* (Cambridge University Press, 1979), p. 30.

3 Ibid., p. 119.

4 Ibid.

5 MacFarquhar, "Two Heads," p. 61.

6 David Stove, *The Plato Cult and Other Philosophical Follies* (Basil Blackwell, 1991), p. 108.

7 Any casual perusal of their writings will reveal such locutions. Geoffrey Hunter usefully gathers and lists some of them in his article "The Churchlands' Eliminative Materialism, or The Result of Impatience," *Philosophical Investigations* (January 1995), though as the date of this article indicates, it does not take account of their more recent works.

8 Hilary Putnam, *Representation and Reality* (MIT Press, 1988), pp. 59–60.

9 M.R. Bennett and P.M.S. Hacker, *Philosophical Foundations of Neuroscience* (Blackwell, 2003), p. 377. The objection that eliminative materialism is self-undermining is developed at length in Lynne Rudder Baker, *Saving Belief: A Critique of Physicalism* (Princeton University Press, 1987), Chapter 7; William Hasker, *The Emergent Self* (Cornell University Press, 1999), Chapter 1; and Angus Menuge, *Agents under Fire* (Rowman and Littlefield, 2004), Chapter 2.

10 Putnam cites a personal conversation with Churchland to this effect at p. 60 of *Representation and Reality*, and refers the reader to an exchange between them published in Zenon Pylyshyn and William Demopoulos, eds., *Meaning and Cognitive Structure* (Ablex Publishing Corporation, 1986), pp. 244 and 252.

11 See Hasker's discussion at pp. 24–26 of *The Emergent Self*. In a foot-note, he credits Reppert for having suggested this diagnosis to him.
12 John R. Searle, *The Rediscovery of the Mind* (MIT Press, 1992), Chapter 2.
13 Some, not all. Again, see my book *Philosophy of Mind* for a more complete account, and also for references to other relevant litera-ture.
14 See *The Rediscovery of the Mind*, Chapter 9. This line of argument is not to be confused with Searle's earlier and better known "Chinese Room" argument, which is also important but less fundamental as a criticism of the computer model of the mind.
15 See Karl Popper, "Language and the Body-Mind Problem," in *Conjectures and Refutations* (Routledge, 1962) and Hilary Putnam, *Renewing Philosophy* (Harvard University Press, 1992), Chapter 3. A similar line of argument can be found in Josep E. Corbi and Josep L. Prades, *Minds, Causes, and Mechanisms* (Blackwell, 2000), Chapter 5.
16 See C.S. Lewis, *Miracles* (Macmillan, 1978), Karl Popper, *Objective Knowledge*, revised edition (Oxford University Press, 1979), Chapter 6; Alvin Plantinga, *Warrant and Proper Function* (Oxford University Press, 1993), Chapter 12; and William Hasker, *The Emergent Self*, Chapter 3. Victor Reppert provides a useful book-length treatment in *C. S. Lewis's Dangerous Idea: In Defense of the Argument from Reason* (InterVarsity Press, 2003). I discuss the argument at slightly greater length in (where else?) my book *Philosophy of Mind*.
17 It might be suggested that true beliefs have greater survival value, so that natural selection would favor them and thus ensure that our thought processes are reliable. But there are two problems with this reply. First, there is no reason to think that true beliefs always have greater survival value; there might be some truths that it would be dangerous for us to know, so that natural selection shapes our minds in such a way that we are kept from believing them. Secondly, even if true beliefs did always have greater sur-vival value, there is still no way that natural selection could favor them. For a belief's truth or falsity is tied up with its meaning, and as we have seen, on the materialist's account meaning plays no causal role whatsoever in any of our thought processes. Hence truth or falsity can play no causal role either. That entails in turn that when our behavior is caused by our beliefs, the truth or falsi-ty of the beliefs plays no role in causing it. And since natural selec-tion could weed out false beliefs only by weeding out the behavior caused by them, it follows that it cannot weed out false beliefs.

18 D.M. Armstrong, *The Mind-Body Problem: An Opinionated Introduction* (Westview, 1999), pp. 138–40.

19 G.F. Schueler, *Reasons and Purposes: Human Rationality and the Teleological Explanation of Action* (Oxford University Press, 2003) and Scott Sehon, *Teleological Realism: Mind, Agency, and Explanation* (MIT Press, 2005).

20 Of course, even the second description still contains a reference to Bob's "intention," and this, as an instance of intentionality, is something that we have seen cannot possibly be either reduced to some material feature of Bob or coherently eliminated. But the point for now is just that even if the materialist had a way out of this difficulty, his proposed elimination of any teleological element from explanations of human action would (as we will see) still fail.

21 See Sehon, *Teleological Realism*, Chapter 7, for a detailed analysis of the example in question and refutation of various attempts to get around these problems.

22 Alfred North Whitehead, *The Function of Reason* (Princeton University Press, 1929), p. 12.

23 More precisely, this is the only way to avoid these alternatives if one believes that there is a material world in the first place. Another option is idealism, the view that matter is an illusion and that only mind is real. But naturalists or secularists are unlikely to find this view any more attractive than Descartes's dualism or Aristotelianism. For a discussion of some problems with contemporary versions of idealism, see Chapter 5 of my book *Philosophy of Mind*.

24 Etienne Gilson, *From Aristotle to Darwin and Back Again: A Journey in Final Causality, Species, and Evolution* (University of Notre Dame Press, 1984) and David Stove, *Darwinian Fairytales* (Encounter Books, 2006), especially Essay 10, "Paley's Revenge, or Purpose Regained." See also Stanley L. Jaki, *The Purpose of It All* (Scottish Academic Press, 1990).

25 In a letter to A. de Candolle, quoted in Michael Ghiselin, *Metaphysics and the Origin of Species* (SUNY Press, 1997), p. 63.

26 Stove, *Darwinian Fairytales*, p. 279.

27 Two useful anthologies of work on this problem are Colin Allen, Marc Bekoff, and George Lauder, eds., *Nature's Purposes: Analyses of Function and Design in Biology* (MIT Press, 1998); and David J. Buller, ed., *Function, Selection, and Design* (SUNY Press, 1999).

28 Quoted by J.O. Wisdom in a review of L. Susan Stebbing's *Philosophy and the Physicists*, in *The International Journal of Psycho-Analysis* 20: 204–11 (1939).

29 See e.g. Millikan's *Language, Thought, and Other Biological Categories* (MIT Press, 1987) and Dennett's *Darwin's Dangerous Idea* (Simon and Schuster, 1995), especially Chapter 14.

30 Jerry Fodor, *In Critical Condition: Polemical Essays on Cognitive Science and the Philosophy of Mind* (MIT Press, 1998), p. 210.

31 Jerry Fodor, *The Mind Doesn't Work That Way* (MIT Press, 2000), p. 85.

32 The widely discussed "swampman" thought experiment was presented by Donald Davidson in his article "Knowing one's own mind," reprinted in Quassim Cassam, ed., *Self-Knowledge* (Oxford University Press, 1994).

33 Searle, *The Rediscovery of the Mind*, pp. 51–52.

34 Ibid., p. 52.

35 Ibid.

36 Similar criticisms of Dennett can be found in Fodor, *In Critical Condition*, Chapter 15, and Menuge, *Agents Under Fire*, Chapter 3, though Fodor and Menuge fail to note that another way to make Dennett's position intelligible (even if it is not a way he would endorse) would be to read him as committed to something like Aristotelian final causes.

37 See Daniel C. Dennett, *The Intentional Stance* (MIT Press, 1987).

38 G.E.M. Anscombe, "Modern Moral Philosophy," in her *Collected Philosophical Papers, Volume III: Ethics, Religion, and Politics* (Basil Blackwell, 1981), at p. 28.

39 For discussion of some of these limits, see Stove's *Darwinian Fairytales* and Anthony O'Hear, *Beyond Evolution* (Oxford University Press, 1997).

40 Paul Davies, *The Fifth Miracle: The Search for the Origin and Meaning of Life* (Simon and Schuster, 1999), pp. 121–22.

41 Max Delbrück, "Aristotle-totle-totle," in Jacques Monod and Ernest Borek, eds., *Of Microbes and Life* (Columbia University Press, 1971), p. 55.

42 That teleology is real suffices to show this, but it should be emphasized that there is more to the Aristotelian understanding of biological phenomena than merely regarding them as teleological. As I have said, a match is "directed toward" the production of fire, but a match is neither a living thing nor part of a living thing. What is characteristic of the causal processes existing within an organism is not merely that they are directed toward some end or other, but that they are directed specifically toward the flourishing of the whole of which they are a part. For a recent defense of the

Aristotelian conception of living things, see David Oderberg, *Real Essentialism* (Routledge, 2007), Chapter 8.

43 David Oderberg, "Teleology: Inorganic and Organic," in A.M. González, ed., *Contemporary Perspectives on Natural Law* (Ashgate, 2008).

44 Nancy Cartwright, "Aristotelian Natures and the Modern Experimental Method," in John Earman, ed., *Inference, Explanation, and Other Frustrations: Essays in the Philosophy of Science* (University of California Press, 1992), and *Nature's Capacities and Their Measurement* (Oxford University Press, 1989).

45 Nancy Cartwright, "No God, No Laws," unpublished paper available on her website at: http://personal.lse.ac.uk/cartwrig/Papers.htm

46 Cartwright, "Aristotelian Natures," p. 70.

47 See Brian Ellis, *The Philosophy of Nature: A Guide to the New Essentialism* (Acumen, 2002) and *Scientific Essentialism* (Cambridge University Press, 2001). For another recent book-length treatment, see Alexander Bird, *Nature's Metaphysics: Laws and Properties* (Oxford University Press, 2007). For defense of a position that is even more consistently Aristotelian than the "new essentialism," see Oderberg, *Real Essentialism*, especially Chapter 6.

48 George Molnar, *Powers: A Study in Metaphysics* (Oxford University Press, 2003).

49 The first quote is Dennis Des Chene's summary of the Scholastic understanding of causation in his essay "From Natural Philosophy to Natural Science," in Donald Rutherford, ed., *The Cambridge Companion to Early Modern Philosophy* (Cambridge University Press, 2006), p. 84, and the second is from Celestine Bittle's *The Domain of Being: Ontology* (Bruce Publishing Company, 1939), p. 364. As anyone familiar with Scholastic philosophy manuals knows, such quotes could easily be multiplied.

50 *Summa Theologiae*, Ia, q. 44, a. 4.

51 The example comes from Christopher Shields, *Aristotle* (Routledge, 2007), p. 93.

Index